Phaidon Press Limited
Regent's Wharf, All Saints Street
London N1 9PA

Phaidon Press Inc
180 Varick Street
New York, NY 10014

www.phaidon.com

First published 2002
©2002 Phaidon Press Limited
ISBN 0 7148 4174 9

Text ©2002 Michael Johnson

A CIP catalogue record for this book is
available from the British Library

Designed by johnson banks
Printed in China

Author's Acknowledgements

Thanks to Jeremy Myerson for
persuading me to change from
vanity to value

Thanks to my principal researcher,
Alice Beard, for a long summer's
digging for detail

Thanks to johnson banks people
past and present for their input:
Anna for tireless research, fact-
checking and proof-reading; Sarah for
her signs; Alexis for his knowledge of
Nazis; Luke for his work on the
original roughs; Harriet for finding the
interrobang for the cover; Kath and
Julia for their dividers (and Kenneth
for his original thoughts); Yin for
researching famous designers; David
(Palazon) for his help with the scans;
David (Jones) for lending his book to
be shot and Betty and Stanley for their
entertainment value

Thanks to the team at Phaidon: to
Vivian for seeing the book's potential;
to Iona for seeing it through (and
putting up with a first-time author);
to Mari, Sian and Rosie for tireless
picture research and to Alan and
Amanda for their encouragement

Thanks to my long-suffering children,
Joe and Molly who spent too many
holidays with dad hunched over a
portable rather than playing

Thanks to Lizzie for her remarkable
understanding and support thoughout

Thanks to you, for buying it, looking
at it (and maybe even reading it)

Michael Johnson
johnson banks
June 2002

The symbol used opposite and
on the cover of this book is called
an *interrobang*

It is derived from a printer's mark
which used a question mark
superimposed onto an exclamation
point – a simultaneous question
and exclamation

Problem Solved

*A primer in
design and communication
by* Michael Johnson

Φ

Contents

Problem: Where's the best place to start a book?
Solved: At the beginning, of course.

Ask a 'creative' within design and advertising what it is that they do, and many will explain to you that they are a 'problem-solver'. It's the closest thing there is to a central tenet of most creative professionals' lives.

But what is problem-solving, exactly? Some weird kind of masonic practice they only teach at art college to the privileged few? 'Hey, I learned how to problem-solve today, Dad – I would tell you about it but I'm sworn to secrecy'. I don't think so.

We all know what problem-solving is, surely? We problem-solve constantly. Wake up, problem – bath or shower? Then another problem – cornflakes or muesli? Then another: bus or train to work? Problem: latte or cappuccino? Problem: take the lift or walk up the stairs?

In many respects problem-solving is our whole lives and maybe the ability to problem-solve is innate; it doesn't need teaching. But in a profession that depends on clients walking through the door with significant problems to be solved, you can see why some teaching might be needed. There's money at stake. And whilst (to paraphrase a friend's quote) a fine-art student can get away with creating his or her own problems to solve, a communications student is usually handed someone else's, with a looming deadline thrown in.[1]

When I began this project I was startled to find that there was no book called Problem Solved. So this book sets out to remedy that. I also wanted to distil two decades of working, reading and writing in design and art direction into one single book rather than a big and expensive bookshelf. (You'll find a selected list of further reading on page 284 which might help if you want to find out more).

This book is aimed fairly and squarely at those who may be new to, or training in, the communications business. Or those mildly interested, or the many who are practising but who never read much. And creative types are notorious for never really reading anything. Look – ufsoi hbsoi kpogj bnpo sdjd sgbpj bpod jpob fgposj gbposj bgpoj? See? (None of you actually read that bit did you; you were just busy looking for the next picture).

The book was inspired in its style by a wonderful book by John Berger, called *Ways of Seeing*, which I strongly urge you to read, if you haven't already.

For some reason (maybe because of its origins as a TV script), *Ways of Seeing* is designed in quite an odd way where the words and the pictures are almost

BELOW
Ways of Seeing, John Berger

ABOVE
WH Smith Chalk packaging
IAN LOGAN DESIGN COMPANY
UK 1995

intertwined – Berger talks a bit, then there's a picture. Bit more chat, another picture. And so on. And eighteen editions (and counting) later it continues to educate the world's art students as to his particular way of looking at the world.

So this book, as you will notice, has pretty strict rules as well. If we discuss a project there's a picture right next to the text. Here, I'll show you. Problem: Cheap pack for white chalk please. Solved: Cartoon of alligator and hole in the pack, chalk makes teeth. Round of applause for the designers, please.

This book has its roots in graphic design. But as its reach broadened, it became apparent that keeping 'design' and 'advertising' separate was a fairly petty exercise since the boundaries between the two disciplines continue to blur on an almost daily basis. My apologies if you don't agree, but my advice to you if you think you only need to know about design and not advertising, or vice versa, is to wake up and smell the coffee. The communications business has become one big blender with someone pouring all the stuff in the top, while jabbing away at the 'pulse' button on the side.

Since more and more colleges don't ask their students to specialize until later and later into their courses (and sometimes never), that seemed another reason to keep the reach of the book as wide as possible. And then of course there's the best reason of all – it's much more interesting this way. The communications business is a fascinating one: in what other world can you be expected to name a company one minute, write an ad the next, re-design a logo tomorrow and design an exhibition the day after?

I'll admit that my own personal love of the poster has affected the selection of a lot of the examples illustrated here. But I'm not losing too much sleep about that either. All graphic designers would probably quite happily bash out posters all day, and the truth is that within advertising, it still remains the quickest way to assess an idea. If the thought doesn't work as a quick picture and a scribbled headline, well, it's probably never going to work.

Then there's the tricky subject of my own work. Having been persuaded early on that the last thing I should do was a showcase of my own work, I then deliberated extensively as to whether to include any at all.

In the end I fudged it. There are twelve and a half of my own projects in this book (three of which were abject failures) out of over 600 projects in total (and more than 1,000 images). So forgive me for that paltry 2 per cent. I just needed them occasionally to make a point.

Anyway, back to solving problems. To a certain age and experience of designer 'problem-solving' had become associated with particular style and

approach of a particular brand of designer. It probably all started with the
'New York School' of graphic designers (see 'the *funny boo-hoo* problem', page
106) whose disciples spread out on both sides of the Atlantic in the 1960s.

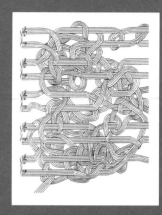

One of them, Bob Gill, wrote a famous book, *Forget all the rules you ever
learned about graphic design. Including the ones in this book*, which succinctly
illustrated his particular way of solving problems, often by turning the questions
upside-down to reveal a new starting place entirely. Gill's re-interpretation of the
brief to make a graphic representation of jazz ran thus: 'Since jazz is improvised
music, make an improvised musical graphic image'.

Inspiration for this new way of seeing could come from anywhere. American
illustrator Saul Steinberg used thumbprints to illustrate his passage to
America in the 1940s and 1950s, immediately handing the language of the
thumbprint to an up-and-coming new generation who then merrily recycled it
in their layouts.

In fact, for a while there, problem
solving seemed pretty simple. One British company told anyone that would
listen that there was always one, irrefutable solution to a client's problem and
they would, of course, find it first. A famous visual encyclopedia, first printed in
1980, made it clear that if you were searching for ways to solve a problem about,
say, listening, that ears were the way forward. And if that weren't enough, they
happily printed nine ear layouts for you, just in case you felt like indulging in a
spot of appropriation.

The message had become obvious – there
are clearly defined solutions to the problems
we face – use them and your life will then become
a lot simpler.

Some firms simply peddled the same solution
with minor tweaks for

TOP RIGHT
'Last word on jazz' illustration
BOB GILL USA 1960

ABOVE LEFT
'The Passport' illustration
SAUL STEINBERG USA 1954

ABOVE
Save the Alps poster
PER ARNOLDI DENMARK 1993

LEFT
The Dictionary of Visual Language
PHILIP THOMPSON
& PETER DAVENPORT
UK 1980

each completely different problem. Surely all of the companies that walked through their doors had different problems at first, but when they had passed though the Saul Bass & Associates design factory, they all left with a curved-edge symbol centred and hovering in white space above a piece of quasi-modernist, sans-serif type.

Once Canadian Railways had established the default setting, the railways of the world seemingly flocked to symbolize themselves with sinuous continuous lines echoing the sinuous continuous rails of their services.

Little wonder that a generation of designers training in the 1980s came to deride what they saw as a formulaic approach to design. Big ideas went out of fashion. 'Style' became the new idea, soon to be replaced by another, 'self-expression', as design and communications veered closer and closer to art, especially that of the conceptual variety.

But this reaction to problem solving in its original guise as expressed by the newer generation wasn't with the principle of *solving a problem*, it was with the idea that there could ever be a *set of generic solutions*.

When British design company Why Not Associates produced this poster for an art show entitled 'Apocalypse', they turned their backs on their previously style-based way of working to produce a disturbing piece that jars with itself – and its subtitle –'beauty and horror in contemporary art'.

By placing a crudely adapted piece of type across a stock idyllic scene they had suggested more horror than any of the exhibits were ever going to – a genuine 'stopper' that no amount of layered type would ever have surpassed.

Not only had they stepped away from their conventional way of working, they had also solved the communication problem in a manner that suggested that 'problem-solving' as an approach was far from dead.

The point of this book is not to identify generic solutions. I'm not preaching for a return to the old received order. Far from it. All that this book concerns itself with is grouping together eighteen recognizable generic problems, and then showing you, the reader, how various communicators have dealt with them.

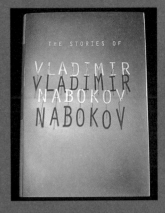

For example, communicators long ago learned that to make their customers sit up and notice their messages, a degree of astonishment was going to help (see the chapter on page 20). So this book of stories by Vladimir Nabokov (keen collector of butterflies in his spare time) suspends the letters of the author's name like trapped insects in the 'frame' of the book cover.

This information poster shows us how simple life becomes (union difficulties apart) when using underground railways. It takes out everything on a map of London apart from the viewer's home, the river Thames and their final destination, the middle of town. Some images are plainly impossible (like this set

(see the chapter on page 20)

ABOVE
Vladimir Nabokov book jacket
DRENTTEL DOYLE PARTNERS USA 1995

LEFT
Making London Simple poster
BMP DDB UK 1997

BELOW LEFT
Barcelona Olympics posters
ADDISON UK 1991

BELOW
Image from Paul Smith
ad campaign
ABOUD SODANO UK 1998

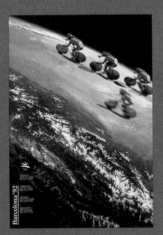

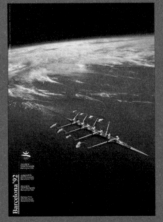
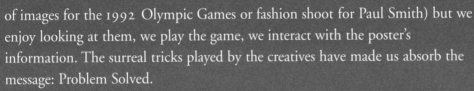

of images for the 1992 Olympic Games or fashion shoot for Paul Smith) but we enjoy looking at them, we play the game, we interact with the poster's information. The surreal tricks played by the creatives have made us absorb the message: Problem Solved.

Sometimes creatives are given the opportunity to re-assess an entire area of design or advertising. The problem of communicating the strategic sense of the merger of Time Warner in the late 1980s fell to American design group Frankfurt Gips Balkind with their 1989 annual report. But rather than solve this particular problem within the tedious and stuffy vernacular that report design

RIGHT
Time Warner Annual Report
FRANKFURT GIPS BALKIND USA 1989

BELOW
Rémy Martin cognac re-design
LEWIS MOBERLY UK 1998

BELOW MIDDLE
Yes logo and image from
'Tales from Topographic Oceans'
ROGER DEAN 1973, 1974

BELOW BOTTOM
Yes 'Big Generator' album sleeve
MOUAT/AI UK 1987

had then acquired, the company managed to completely turn a particularly sedentary business sector upside-down with an astonishing paradigm shift that simply asked 'why' on the front in huge black letters. They then bombarded the reader with fluorescent inks, amazing imagery and attention-grabbing layouts inside.

If the designers had begun the project intending to move the goalposts of report design, they certainly succeeded. But also, and probably just as importantly, they showed the world that hugely expensive and serious documents such as this could have style, wit and panache, and could still communicate that year's message.

Sometimes the problem faced is whether a company or product should undergo radical or evolutionary change. When world-famous cognac producer Rémy Martin approached Lewis Moberly to look at their highly prestigious champagne cocktail, the designers simply put them on an evolutionary road, putting the bottle on a kind of diet and making it just a little taller and slimmer. A good example of evolving, rather than revolutionizing, an historic brand.

But sometimes other factors come into play. When British supergroup once known as Yes reformed themselves after a lengthy hiatus, they faced significant problems. Firstly, it was by no means certain that they could 'trade' under the 'Yes' moniker since important members of the original band were no longer present. Secondly, the graphic style of the band was umbilically linked to that of world-famous artist Roger Dean.

At the last minute, permission was granted to use the original name, but the decision had been taken to radically change the graphic style of the band's output, which was dragged kicking and screaming into the 1980s with some computer-generated, squashed pink and yellow type. Never has an identity change been more marked.

But whilst the graphic revolution signalled the shift in musical style that the new version of the band had taken (a sort of glossier 'stadium rock' take on their original 'progressive' roots), it didn't fit with the fans' image of their heroes.

Since merchandizing now plays such a significant role in touring income, when the new style didn't 'sell', it came as no surprise when the next incarnation of the band happily returned to their airbrushed homeland in search of some floating fish, foggy scenes and Tolkienesque landscapes.

Sometimes the problem isn't so much with the brief, it's with the person doing the briefing. I've called this the 'fear and loathing' problem (see page 250)

and it's beautifully visualized in this image developed for the cover of an awards annual where the creative (we presume sporting the obligatory bow-tie) shakes hands with the client (decked out in innocuous grey suit) but each hides an instrument of death or torture behind their backs.

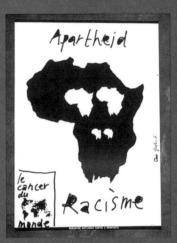

Some creatives channel their anger with perceived problems of the world through their work. These two images by European poster masters Pierre Bernard of Grapus and Gunter Rambow are very personal solutions to different problems. One concerns apartheid, the other a play about an ex-concentration camp doctor reliving his past on an archeological dig. Both communicate with enormous economy of means, proving that it can sometimes take very few elements to solve a communication problem.

ABOVE
Art Directors Club of New York
Annual cover
BOB GILL USA 1986

LEFT
Anti-apartheid poster
GRAPUS FRANCE 1989

BELOW
KambeK poster
GUNTER RAMBOW
GERMANY 1987

A more traditional way of solving the problems of the world (and perhaps legitimizing a creative's other, less than ethical, paying clients) is the time-honoured route of 'the charity client'. These powerful and dramatic press ads for War on Want are a classic of their genre; probably briefed to be hard hitting and

uncompromising, they definitely succeed.

But as you will see in the chapter on page 76, there is more to the charity client (and the agencies pursuing them) than meets the eye. Suffice it to say, creatives who give their all to producing subversive

LEFT
War on Want press ads
BOASE MASSIMI POLLITT UK 1986

communication (such as this poster from American agitators The Guerilla Girls or the 'No-shop' project shown left) without falling prey to the lure of mega-bucks from megalopolis are pretty rare. The 'McShit' student project shown left rails against the power of the multinational, but will she stay true to her beliefs when, and if, she sees the colour of their money?

Bizarrely, the new and welcome obsession with ethical responsibility takes us down some strange paths. Some of them seem to suggest severe repercussions for the communication arts; the project below shows copies of a British newspaper from succeeding days with broadly similar editorial content.

The significant difference is that a financial institution paid, on the second day, for all the ad-space, resulting in a newspaper with no ads, on less paper which used less trees and simply let you read the paper's contents, unimpeded by any advertising interruptions.

What this has got to do with a fairly staid building society isn't entirely clear. What is apparent, however, is that such as this has significant implications for the way many of us will approach the future.

And in the end, that's all I'm trying to do with this book. Simply grouping the world's communication problems into eighteen types may sound unlikely, but it at least allows me to show you the massive variety of solutions that can come from a similar starting place. Problem-solving is not a restrictive art but a liberating one.

If you get as much out of this book by reading it as I did by writing it, then I've succeeded and the problem – that there are no books on problem-solving – has been solved. (I hope so, because that was a confusing sentence to write).

Anyway, back to the real problem: how to end the introduction?

Solution: use an unexpected ending.

The RE-APPRAISE OR DIE *problem*

Often older brands, companies or even countries become so caught up in their past that it overtakes them. Only when faced with extinction do they realize that they need to challenge people's perceptions head-on. Sometimes they are ripe for re-appraisal and a designer is given the chance to question perceived wisdom. It's probably the most interesting brief there is, but it's an obstacle course for the uninitiated.

It is always difficult to pinpoint why something goes into decline – maybe a product's original target market grows up and moves on (like the teenage fans of pop groups), or maybe a company simply becomes increasingly out-of-step with its audience. In a later chapter, we will see how some older brands deal with this by re-naming themselves, shedding one skin and growing another in an attempt to revitalize themselves.

But for some, simply starting again with something new is not an option. They cannot change what they do, they just have to find a way to market themselves more effectively.

A classic example is the ever-changing market for jeans. By the mid-1970s, Levi's had found themselves diversifying too far. They were into polyester, they weren't cool, they were too far away from their core product which they had been making for over a hundred years – simple, straightforward denim jeans. And they had themselves become a fashion victim – their 1960s market of hippies had grown up and moved on and they had struggled to persuade the glitter, glam and disco generation to wear jeans like the generation before them.

BELOW
Stills from Levi's commercials
(Airport, Launderette,
Swimmer, Creek)
BARTLE BOGLE HEGARTY
UK 1985-93

By the 1980s, market conditions were becoming dire, sales were radically down and some drastic action was needed. It arrived in the shape of a series of ads that transformed the sector. While a dramatic film concerning a young man smuggling jeans into Stalinist Russia gathered accolades, the ad that really changed everything showed a young man stripping down to his boxer shorts in a launderette whilst washing his jeans. Whether it was the jeans, the looks on the faces of the other launderette inhabitants or the fact that the film's hero was drop-dead gorgeous, who knows, but what is definite is that demand for Levi's immediately increased eightfold, as well as bringing boxer shorts back into fashion overnight.[1]

A new benchmark had been set and there ensued fifteen years of award-winning advertising that made its agency, Bartle Bogle Hegarty, world-famous. Almost never featuring the same actor or actress twice, always making great use of music soundtracks that often went high in the singles charts, the release of a new ad

began to be met with the same amount of attention and column inches as would the release of a major new pop album.

BBH's skills at selling their sepia-tinted view back to the world became so successful, senior executives from the British company regularly made new business trips to the States clutching a presentation on 'The American Dream', searching for more brands looking to re-invent themselves in the eyes of a gullible European market.

But now the jeans marketers face a new and insidious threat to their empires – how can they pretend their clothes are cool when world leaders like Bill Clinton and Tony Blair are regularly spotted wearing their favourite pairs? Some drastic thinking will be needed to persuade the world's youth that it's OK to wear the same clothes as their presidents, not just their parents.

Sometimes organizations have become so set in their ways and so out-of-step with reality that drastic measures are needed. *Rolling Stone* magazine, once the standard-bearer of flower power, patchouli oil and Jimi Hendrix, realized that by the 1980s their precious advertising revenue was in danger.

They knew that their baby-booming readers had swapped their patchouli for Porsches, but did their advertisers? The answer was to run a good old-fashioned set of trade ads, cleverly targeted to make potential advertisers realize how drastically their readership had changed from their original incarnation.

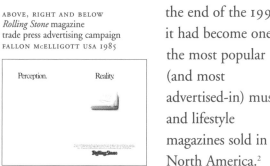

With the simplest of 'before and after' layouts comparing perception and reality, they were able to revitalize advertiser perceptions about the magazine.

Rolling Stone never looked back and by the end of the 1990s it had become one of the most popular (and most advertised-in) music and lifestyle magazines sold in North America.[2]

Previously considered a taboo area, the changing European political landscape in the 1990s allowed a British identity consultancy to apply branding principles at the highest level. Approached by a British TV channel, branding specialists Wolff Olins were asked to undertake a theoretical exercise in re-branding the nation.

This was at a time when the then British Prime Minister John Major happily described the nation he led as best summed up by 'warm beer and cricket'.[3]

Unsurprisingly, Wolff Olins returned with thoughts that were deliberately modern and mould-breaking, removed the anachronistic accent on royalty and applied their solution as they would for one of their blue-chip identity proposals.

The proposals proved to be ahead of their time. After eighteen years of right-wing government, 1997 saw a more centre-left Labour government elected, which immediately set off on a period of re-branding the country in the eyes of the world through government-related think-tanks and agencies.

A year later, the same firm was given an opportunity to apply their thinking to the newly unified East and West Germany. They side-stepped negative historical issues and re-presented the German identity as DE, short for Deutschland Europa. While both schemes attracted substantial attention and some criticism, they showed that, at a theoretical level at least, even a government could begin to think about re-presenting themselves.

At the same time as these 're-branding of Britain' experiments,

ABOVE LEFT AND RIGHT
Britain re-branding project
WOLFF OLINS UK 1997

BELOW LEFT AND RIGHT
Germany re-branding project
WOLFF OLINS UK 1998

the British Council was embarking on a *real* and ambitious poster project for the walls of its hundreds of offices and classrooms worldwide.

With thousands of young people moving through the Council's offices every day, here was a perfect opportunity to tell the world's next generation that Britain really was changing.

Global research had revealed that while the world's teenagers were now much more likely to associate Britain with comedians, football and pop music, many were still aware (and respectful)

of the country's historical traditions. So a campaign was developed which balanced previous and current icons of a nation that has managed to swap roast beef and Yorkshire pudding for a slightly more appetizing meal of art, comedy and genuinely multi-racial culture.

IF THE WELDING ISN'T STRONG ENOUGH, THE CAR WILL FALL ON THE WRITER.

Sometimes attempts at the re-appraisal of brands have debatable effects, especially in the automotive sector where historical images are notoriously difficult to shake off.

For years, the Swedish car manufacturer Volvo had promoted their cars on their safety-first features. They advertised the size of their turning circle, wrapped children in cotton wool and compared their cars to that. Volvo filmed slow-motion ads about the quality of their side-impact protection. The agency's creative director even wrote an ad which suspended a car above him, the copywriter. But then Volvo decided they wanted to shake off and update their old 'warhorse' image.

Suddenly, the newer cars were re-positioned with the thought that 'you can't have safety without danger'. Overnight Volvo turned from being safe, comfortable cars for all the family to precision machines engineered for tracking down and battling tornadoes, traversing ravines on flimsy train tracks or chasing

aeroplanes up runways, as our heroine photojournalist gets the perfect shot. Quite a switch from the school run and the weekly shop.

Whilst creating a lot of attention within the creative industry, it came as little surprise that the brand soon returned to more natural territory. More recent TV ads show the car parked outside in all weathers, the ever-present family car waiting for its owners to actually start it (going right back to the original 'safe family car' positioning). We are left to conclude that twister-chasing and ravine-jumping was a re-appraisal too far for the Volvo brand.

OR BUY A VOLVO.

ABOVE AND ABOVE LEFT
Volvo press and TV still
ABBOTT MEAD VICKERS UK
1983–7

BELOW
Volvo TV stills
AMV BBDO UK 1994–8

VOLVO   NOW ALL YOU NEED ARE SOME KIDS

The British Royal Automobile Club, RAC for short, was one of the great old British car brands. Their badge was always enshrined in chrome on the front of Jaguars and Aston Martins, their image one of between-the-wars pottering in Austin Healeys on the way to windy picnics on Devon cliff-tops. Some distance from the nitty-gritty of car recovery – breaking down on a remote stretch of wet motorway miles from any kind of help.

The arrival of a revitalized marketing team in the mid-1990s sparked off an initial period of work looking at the organization's identity, and 'modernized' RAC crests were investigated, which probably seemed like the appropriate way to develop and evolve the brand.

But the RAC had begun to think that they needed a more drastic change. A new generation of younger motorists associated the organization with their grandfathers, not themselves (and grandfather's car was always breaking down, wasn't it?). After rejecting the initial set of tweaked crests they set off in a far more radical direction. Their new positioning was to be all about mobility and they were going to reflect that in their identity and advertising.

A few months later, the new identity was revealed. Using an ultra-modern piece of type more akin to a nightclub than car breakdown, and a fiercely modernist palette, the RAC had catapulted themselves firmly into the twenty-first century. The van (probably the most visible element of the whole change) became bright orange, sporting vertically biased white chevrons which made it look more like a European police car than the snuggly old RAC. The new advertising for the brand tried various different routes before admitting defeat

and finally used the van as the hero on its advertising, which shows how simple and strong a good piece of design, rather than a series of overblown advertising statements, can be.

Sometimes organizations in the arts are also in need of radical change. From 1967, New York's Public Theater became associated with great productions, and a particular style of poster by the designer and illustrator Paul Davis. Lush, hand-crafted, these posters became the public face of the organization and presented a coherent, illustrated style for all its events.

But the death of the theatre's original producer led to decline. When revived by a new director in search of a younger audience for his new version of the project, a new identity was developed that centred on muscular typography, simple screen-printed images and a fresh, lively

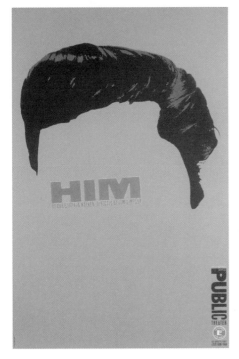

attitude that immediately put it back in the vanguard of pioneering East Village theatre. By continuing to use the same designer for their communications, the theatre has once again created its own uniquely recognizable and different style, fifteen years after the original.

Even the church isn't immune to a complete facelift every now and again. When the Episcopal Church of Minneapolis commissioned the local advertising agency to devise some ads to draw in the crowds, they received and approved religious advertising that put the church and its agency on the map in world terms. We're all used to those huge fluorescent posters outside our local church pronouncing the imminent arrival of the Son of God, but to see a church's wares advertized so brazenly (and cleverly) was just about as shocking as it gets.

Just as arresting in its own way was the British publisher Canongate's decision to break the Bible down into bite-sized pieces. With introductions by contemporary authors, gritty photographic illustrations of everything from nuclear explosions (for Revelation) to long and winding roads (for Exodus), the re-design signalled that here was a Bible that was intended for contemporary reading, handily packaged in its simple slip-case.

So, from jeans to countries, from theatre to God, in the hands of capable creatives most subjects can be radically re-appraised – assuming, of course, that there is something worth re-appraising in the first place.

CENTRE & LEFT
Pocket Bible, Canongate books
PENTAGRAM UK 1999

TOP LEFT AND OPPOSITE PAGE
Episcopal Church ad campaign
FALLON McELLIGOTT USA 1983

**He didn't rise
from the dead to
hunt Easter eggs.**

✠ The Episcopal Church

Whose birthday
is it, anyway?

The Episcopal Church believes the important news at Christmas is not
who comes down the chimney, but who came down from heaven. We invite you to come and join
us as we celebrate the birth of Jesus Christ.
The Episcopal Church

**If you think
being a Christian is
inconvenient today,
just look back 1500 years.**

If you're ready to make the hour and inconvenience that being a Christian sometimes requires,
the Episcopal Church invites you to come and join us as we worship and fellowship of Jesus Christ.
The Episcopal Church

**You can't meet
God's gift to women
in a singles' bar.**

If the singles life sometimes leaves you feeling alone and empty, remember that God's gift to all
women and men is Jesus Christ. Come join us to worship this Sunday in the Episcopal Church.
The Episcopal Church

Problem: French Connection is just another of those high street brands.

Solved: Stop selling cotton trousers, start selling sex.

The turning of French Connection, a simple high-street retailer of the kind of cotton T-shirts, skirts and trousers you used to buy for your beach holiday in August, into a brand synonymous with sex and style has to be one of the most dramatic and controversial advertising campaigns in recent memory.

The entire campaign has revolved around one central idea: that the acronym for French Connection United Kingdom, FCUK, is remarkably similar to a famous Anglo-Saxon swear-word that doesn't have a lot to do with clothes, more to do with what you might do after removing them.

The company and its agency have run rings around the UK courts – at one point, putting a simple full stop between the capitals was enough to escape censure (F.C.U.K.) – regularly running ads that get banned almost as soon as they come out (hence gaining the pre-requisite column inches of outraged tabloid coverage).

ABOVE
FCUK shop design
DIN ASSOCIATES UK 2000

THIS SPREAD
AND FOLLOWING SPREAD
FCUK advertising campaign
TBWA\LONDON UK 1997–2001

fcuk fashion

© FRENCH CONNECTION UNITED KINGDOM

f.c.u.k.   advertising

fcuk is a trademark of French Connection UK

french connection yourself

fcuk'

But whilst the campaign has been heavily criticized (perhaps by those who fear its power the most) there is no doubt that this is 'selling' at its most powerful, showing us what communication teetering right on the edge of outrage can really achieve.

Whilst it's easy to dwell on the controversy created by the work, that obscures the fact that this is fashion advertising building a rebellious brand

yes, both

 subliminal
advertising
experiment

fcuk

with recognizable attitude, often without showing any actual clothes at all – brand building in the purest sense, often without referring to the product.

The business figures behind the campaign are remarkable too – the company's share price has jumped by nearly 300 per cent since the campaign began and the company's profits have trebled.

That's an almost obscene amount of clothing to sell.

 fancy
conquering
uncharted
kingdom?

www.frenchconnection.com

fcuk®

doing the sea.
They're
it in

fcuk

The ASTONISH ME *problem*

Sometimes plain old flat, straight and normal just doesn't get people to sit up and take notice. But since most ads or designs appear on flat surfaces, whether they be poster sites or TV screens, how can you create the illusion of something that isn't really there?

Who knows where it comes from, perhaps would-be creatives spend too much of their teenage years studying Salvador Dalí, musing over Magritte or hallucinating at Bridget Riley prints. For designers and advertisers, visual effects and the surreal have long been a favourite standby.

Early poster artists such as AM Cassandre channelled art movements such as Futurism into astonishing posters like this piece for Nicolas wines as early as the 1930s.

But as the discipline of advertising design begins to mature, the ability to astonish people visually

becomes progressively more difficult. Ideas get picked up and appropriated into the mainstream at an ever-increasing pace. A thought that once seemed powerful, such as this idea using a blown-off head by Kurt Haimann now seems a little tame – we have absorbed it as a cliché into our visual language and now we want to move on to the next fifteen minutes of graphic fame.

But nothing will stop the advance of *trompe l'œil* (the trick of the eye) because it remains a useful tool in the communicator's armoury, and to some an indispensable one.

A set of innocuous-looking aeroplane stamps

ABOVE
Nicolas poster
AM CASSANDRE FRANCE 1935

LEFT
'Don't blow it with drugs' poster
KURT HAIMANN USA 1970

BELOW
'Architects of the Air' stamp
TURNER DUCKWORTH UK 1997

appeared in post offices throughout Britain in 1997 and seemed, at first glance, to be simple photographic celebrations of famous aeroplanes.

But then came the idea, creeping up on the unsuspecting philatelist, of having the aeroplane designer's face appearing in the clouds behind.

Is it too subtle? Maybe. Will some people never have seen the twist? Perhaps. But all those small boys and grannies out there tending to their stamp albums will remember them as one of the cleverest twists ever seen on a one-inch-square piece of gummed perforated paper.

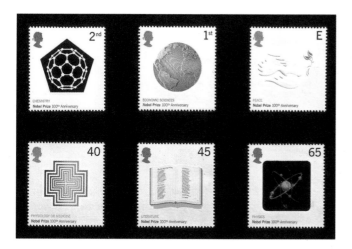

Possibly buoyed by the success of these, Royal Mail then commissioned another set, purporting to celebrate the Nobel prize but in reality providing a golden opportunity to apply all types of printing techniques at a previously unexplored size. So a stamp celebrating the discovery of the Buckminsterfullerene (the Carbon 60 molecule) is overprinted with heat-sensitive ink, which when pressed by suitably hot hands reveals the molecular ion trapped inside (dull old scientific theory brought dramatically to life).

Another stamp, celebrating physiology and medicine, is printed with scented ink so the stamp will smell of eucalyptus and hospitals, not the local sorting office. The celebration of literature shows a TS Eliot poem of which only the title can be understood – the remainder requires micro-printing to produce and a magnifying glass to read.

In the world of publishing, many are strangely reticent about ideas which elevate their product above the competition.

This must give the commissioners and designers of book jackets such as these great satisfaction – designs with apparently 3D qualities using printing onto silk, creating false depth or utilizing overlaid book jackets raises them above their hum-drum bookshelf companions without resorting to multiple-embossed, gold-foiled folly.

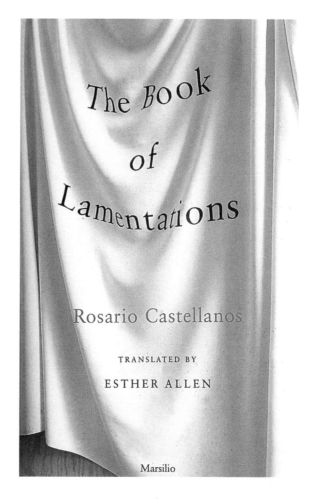

Sometimes designers employ the effect of superimposition to such good effect that viewers might even be seen scratching at the surface to check if it is real or not.

For this poster for a film about Stalin, designers Howard Brown and John Gorham created the illusion of the squashed tomato on the now clown-like tyrant's nose, criticizing and ridiculing in one deft photographic sleight-of-hand.

For a poster about posters, shown left, Dutch designer Rene Knip used the language of the multiple layers of pasted billboard messages to reveal the exhibition information as though it belonged to previously run posters.

Although posters normally depend simply on their power, sometimes the visual jarring of the extraordinary image or the impossible die-cut brings a new dimension to what is a simple piece of paper.

Graphic master Milton Glaser has regularly shaped his posters to trick the viewer into examining them in more detail.

For the poster shown right, the separate items were assembled then re-photographed with a folded corner, then re-printed. It is not 'real' but was so well done the deception was perfect; many recipients could be seen trying to lift the edge with their fingers.

For another poster, its gently curved edges were not the sign of a warped transparency, but the actual physical cropping of the poster whose image had been intentionally curved and photographed, taking what on paper was a simple list of lectures into a separate dimension entirely.

ABOVE
Red Monarch film poster
JOHN GORHAM/HOWARD BROWN
UK 1983

LEFT
Poster for a BNO exhibition
at the Stedelijk Museum
RENÉ KNIP THE NETHERLANDS 1989

BELOW
Art Directors Club of New York
Call for Entries poster
MILTON GLASER USA 1987

ABOVE
Artifort posters
STUDIO DUMBAR THE NETHERLANDS
1985

BELOW RIGHT
Annie Kuan business card
SAGMEISTER INC USA 1998

BOTTOM RIGHT
HP Zinker CD sleeve
SAGMEISTER INC USA 1994

RIGHT & BELOW
American Photography 15
SAGMEISTER INC USA 1999

These posters for Dutch furniture manufacturer Artifort are cut out into these bizarre, amoeba-like shapes, immediately helping to give the impression that this is innovative, avant-garde furniture, not run-of-the-mill also-rans.

Some designs are derived entirely from that of optical art – this photography book features a quintissential American landscape on the last few millimetres of each page, only viewable by splaying the pages in a certain way.

The solutions shown below for a business card and CD cover are really meant only to grab attention (and perhaps demonstrate the designer's knowledge of optical trickery). In that sense, one could argue that they only add to the communication exercise by being clever, rather than particularly legitimate, but then if they get attention in the first place, perhaps they are justified.

In the designer's own words, at least they 'made you look'.

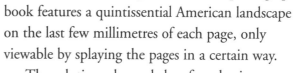

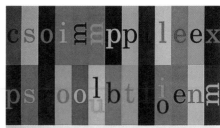

It seems appropriate, however, that a book on optical art such as one by publisher Lars Müller should make the most of the opportunity to have an optical cover. And the device of lenticular folding, whilst a little tokenistic in this self-promotional poster for Cahan & Associates, comes into its own when used on a grand scale for this hoarding. This massive building-wide display can be viewed in either direction, reading visually one way and verbally in the reverse direction.

Sometimes designers produce objects that require genuine physical intervention from the user or reader (rather than merely turning the pages).

In a radical convergence of children's flick books, magazines and editorial design, this piece for a designer of film titles seems relatively straightforward until you realize that it has two grooves cut all the way through the document. This allows the reader either to read the magazine in a conventional way, or to flick through the piece in many different directions as though it were a flick book to study a sequence of film in concurrent frames.

Asking viewers and readers to move or manipulate a piece of work is a relatively common device. The most often-used notion is the forwards/backwards idea, sometimes used by advertisers to 'claim' the back few pages of a magazine as their own.

ABOVE LEFT
See Saw book cover
HANS KNUCHEL/JÜRG NÄNNI/
LARS MÜLLER SWITZERLAND 1994

TOP RIGHT
Complex solutions poster
CAHAN & ASSOCIATES USA 1996

ABOVE
The British Land Company
STUDIO MYERSCOUGH/
ALLFORD HALL MONAGHAN
MORRIS ARCHITECTS UK 1995

BELOW
Cut mailer
ATELIER WORKS UK 2001

A twist on this is the 'upside-downside' treatment, once memorably used on this anti-apartheid poster then emulated by this small postcard mailer designed for two events at the International Design Center in New York.

Looking for a cost-effective way to explain two events in one small mailer, the designer realized that a rocket and a vase consisted of similar elements depending on which way up you looked at them.

He simply signalled this with the print of the mandatory type in two directions, and saved on print bills in the process.

The notion of completely interfering with the physical structure of a piece of design can be used to the most dramatic effect. Cahan & Associates' report for Heartport seems like a straightforward piece of print design until you realize that those black dots appearing at identical points on every spread aren't printed dots or a problem with the transparency.

They are real, one-inch diameter holes drilled throughout the document. A dramatic idea, and thankfully a perfect visual explanation of the dramatic nature of the client's core business, supplying minimally invasive products for heart surgery that avoid the wholesale and traumatic open-heart approach.

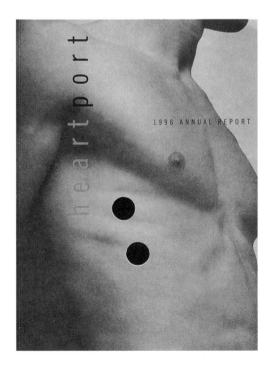

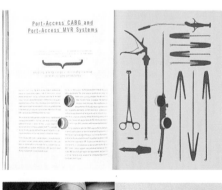

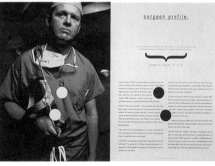

ABOVE
International Design Center, New York, mailer
PENTAGRAM USA 1984

ABOVE RIGHT
'Black Power, White Power' poster
TOMI UNGERER USA 1967

RIGHT
Heartport annual report
CAHAN & ASSOCIATES USA 1996

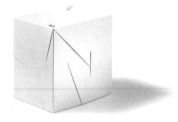

Many of these ideas have attempted, with varying types of optical and technical trickery, to raise themselves out of their flat, two-dimensional origins and into something better.

But sometimes embracing three dimensions becomes the only way to explain something especially complex. Every attempt to show the form of a controversial proposed extension to London's Victoria & Albert Museum in London in a 2D brochure form simply failed to do the 24-plane continuous spiral structure justice. So the museum happened on an ideal (albeit expensive) solution – the 'brochure' was placed on the inside of a white box which theatrically deconstructed to reveal a paper model of the building, to be studied

at the recipient's leisure (and hopefully encourage a donation from them).

Although many of the world's packaging designers still tend to take flat ideas and wrap them around boxes, these designs for Hovis bread and Wildbrew flavoured alcoholic beer show how the physical surface of the pack (whether glass or plastic) can become a fantastic opportunity for *trompe l'œil* of the highest order (and also successful trickery – Wildbrew's sales increased by 30 per cent after the re-design).

ABOVE
Victoria & Albert Museum
Spiral mailer
JOHNSON BANKS UK 1998

LEFT
Wildbrew alcoholic beer
WILLIAMS MURRAY HAMM UK 2000

BELOW LEFT
Hovis packaging
WILLIAMS MURRAY HAMM UK 2001

OPPOSITE MIDDLE
Greenpeace ambient advert
SAATCHI & SAATCHI
NEW ZEALAND 1998

OPPOSITE BOTTOM LEFT
Samaritans bus ad
SAATCHI & SAATCHI
NEW ZEALAND 1996

OPPOSITE BOTTOM RIGHT
Gun vending machine
THE JUPITER DRAWING ROOM
SOUTH AFRICA 1999

Heineken refreshes the bars other beers cannot reach.

Once the creative takes his or her ideas outside, the strictures of two dimensions often become forgotten altogether. Billboards have been stuck-on, tacked-on, added, burnt, taken away, you name it. The glue manufacturer Araldite fixed cars onto poster sites in a dramatic three-part stunt to gain attention. It didn't take long for creative teams to make the three states of the turning billboard (called a tri-wonder) come to life, as in this three-way poster for Heineken.

In South Africa, an agency co-opted the seemingly innocuous vehicle of the food dispenser to make a telling point about the availability of handguns in the country, whilst the examples below from New Zealand show how to use the possibilities of outdoor media to make powerful points against nuclear testing, or the critical role (at a critical time) of the Samaritans. In Britain a campaign for

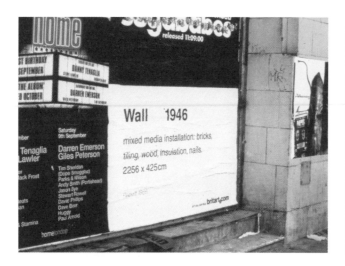

an art website side-stepped all obvious routes and veered off into the area of conceptual art. The campaign brought home the fact that everything is in a way a piece of art by plastering London with 'art-alisers' (actually fly posters) that proclaimed the media they were affixed to as art itself.

All of a sudden, in a Duchampian[1] twist, walls and lamp-posts turned from poster sites into art and a junction box became a limited edition.

THIS PAGE
Britart.com advertising campaign
MOTHER UK 1999

OPPOSITE TOP LEFT
Massive Attack poster
TOM HINGSTON STUDIO UK 1999

OPPOSITE TOP RIGHT
Massive Attack boxed set
TOM HINGSTON STUDIO UK 1999

OPPOSITE BELOW
Friends of the Earth poster campaign
McCANN-ERICKSON UK 1990

Britart.com is a fantastic re-use of the elements around us and essentially makes the point of this chapter, which is that sometimes we all get too used to the everyday. Sometimes we need to be jogged out of the expected and into the unexpected. Not only is it a radical re-think of

much that we take for granted, it also really worked as well, generating tens of thousands of inquiries and multiplying sales twenty-fold.

But consider this campaign for trip-hop band

Taxi receipt   / /

paper, ink, fingerprints.
7.8 x 11cm

Homage to the faceless urban nomad.

£ _____

art you can buy **britart.com**

Massive Attack: the poster shown left astonishes the viewer with its complex mixture of images. The CD box shown right is alluring in its use of heat-sensitive materials and for a while at least the purchaser can 'play' with the package and discover hidden drawings underneath the surface.

But we're left wondering what the design actually has to do with the band or their music – it's a conjuring trick that doesn't really take us anywhere once we've played with it for a while.

Devices and illusions only really work when their use is entirely justified and supports the central premise of a campaign.

To give you an example, Friends of the Earth wanted to make a powerful statement about acid rain. By using specially treated paper, the poster literally faded away in front of passers-by's eyes over a series of weeks as the chemical contents of London literally dissolved the original message. I'd say that was legitimate use of a trick, wouldn't you?

Problem: How to gain the maximum effect with the minimum means.

Solved: Go on optical manoeuvres with Shigeo Fukuda.

In a career spanning many decades, Shigeo Fukuda's ability to create simple graphic shapes that twist and turn in front of our eyes make him one of the world's finest exponents of optical graphic design.

Despite intentionally restricting his colour palette, many of his designs still work effectively in one or two colours. Many could work just as easily in just one colour because he communicates his messages so strongly and simply.

Often using the world or a globe as his starting point, we can only marvel at how he manages to twist his solutions in front of our eyes, time and time again, and seems happy and willing to return to previous themes and work on them more, sometimes decades later.

His motto, 'play is the essence of work', is borne out in his posters, some highlights of which are shown here and overleaf.

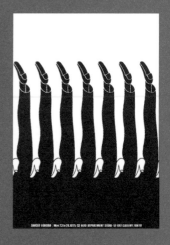

ALL WORK BY SHIGEO FUKUDA

ABOVE
Poster for exhibition
of work by Shigeo Fukuda
JAPAN 1975

LEFT
Poster for exhibition
of work by Shigeo Fukuda
JAPAN 1982

BELOW MIDDLE
'Les Droits de l'Homme'
Artis 1989
FRANCE 1989

BELOW RIGHT
'Graphic Design Today'
The Museum of Modern Art, Tokyo
JAPAN 1990

OPPOSITE
Poster for 2nd
United Nations Conference
Rio de Janeiro
JAPAN 1992

Rio 92

THE 2ND
UNITED NATIONS
CONFERENCE
ON ENVIRONMENT
AND DEVELOPMENT.
RIO DE JANEIRO.
BRAZIL. 1992

Design by Shigeo Fukuda.
Printed by Dai Nippon Printing Co., Ltd. 1992

ALL WORK BY SHIGEO FUKUDA

LEFT
'Urban Frontier – Tokyo '96'
JAPAN 1996

BELOW
'Think Japan', Japan exhibition
JAPAN 1987

OPPOSITE TOP LEFT
'Water is Life, Life on Earth'
Water exhibition
JAPAN 1989

OPPOSITE RIGHT
'Remembering for the Future'
Holocaust Conference
JAPAN 1988

OPPOSITE BOTTOM LEFT
'Shigeo Fukuda Illustrick' exhibition
JAPAN 1990

WATER IS LIFE

LIFE ON EARTH

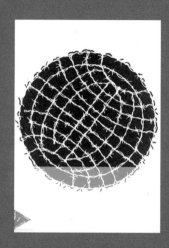

THE IMPACT OF THE HOLOCAUST AND GENOCIDE ON JEWS & CHRISTIANS

Remembering for the Future

An International Scholars' Conference,
Oxford, 10–13 July 1988
Public Conference,
London, 15 July 1988

The SOAP POWDER *problem*

With the way products and services are marketed becoming increasingly similar (like detergents on a supermarket shelf, their boxes almost identical) the onus falls more and more upon designers and advertisers to create believable brands, often out of thin air. But does this work? Do customers still fall for it? And if so, for how long?

Competitive advantage doesn't last for long in any market. Imagine for a minute that you have invented something completely new that people really want. Well, selling this idea to people will be easy, won't it, as long as no-one else muscles in on your act? The old adage about people beating a path to the door of the inventor of a better moustrap is famous[1] because we all know that it isn't true – even if there really was a better mousetrap it wouldn't stay better for long. Because products and services are rarely unique, designers and marketing executives are brought in to provide that missing link, the 'x' factor.

Don't believe me? Most commodity products are just that – the same as something else. When Bill Bernbach had worked out that he might as well sell the Beetle on its ugliness, he had found what a lot of products simply don't have – something different, something unique. He called it a Unique Selling Proposition, now ingrained into communicators' heads as the 'USP'.

But if your product seems the same as everyone else's, you have a problem. At advertising college, students are often made to work on commodity products like matches, the theory being that if they can do a good ad for something generic, they will be outstanding with something exciting to go on.

Let's take an example; a colourless alcohol like vodka. This classic campaign from the advertising archives began by pointing out the whole premise of this chapter, that in this instance all vodkas seem, on appearance at least, the same. The idea then developed into an early example of creating 'characters' for their advertising, hence enlivening a product similar to its competitors. But it's not much more than a couple of ads, really, and could be any type of alcohol.

ABOVE
'Lemon' Beetle ad
DOYLE DANE BERNBACH USA 1960

BELOW
Wolfschmidt Vodka ads
PAPERT KOENING LOIS USA 1962

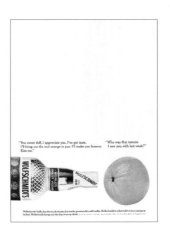

What happens if we want to do some ads that will last for years, that consumers will think about every time they drink your particular brand of colourless stuff in preference to a competitor's?

At one time Smirnoff developed a classic series of ads based on the proposition that the effect of drinking it was shattering; enough to end your accountancy career and turn you to liquor and cigars, for example. Then turned to a long-running campaign that implied that the drink helped you discover your 'other' (often somewhat more hedonistic) side.

Meanwhile, Absolut side-stepped the problem of finding a central proposition by making their bottle and its shape their entire campaign idea; a limited idea, perhaps, but a global campaign that has managed to run for seventeen years, and counting.

Strangely, consumers lap it all up and never seem to question it. Ordering Smirnoff rather than Absolut says something about them – perhaps they really do think that the Smirnoff drinker is a closet hedonist, the Absolut drinker a true appreciator of a classier, more knowing type of colourless liquid.

In many respects consumers like to pretend they are canny, that they have an ingrained sense of cynicism and can spot when they are being duped, but when they see an ad or a design they like they trade with it, empathize with it and they're hooked. The soap powder problem solved.

ABOVE
Smirnoff ad
YOUNG & RUBICAM UK 1971

RIGHT
Smirnoff ad
LOWE HOWARD-SPINK UK 1997

BELOW LEFT & RIGHT
Absolut Vodka ads
TBWA WORLDWIDE 1999–2000

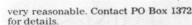

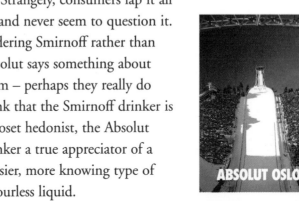

In the glory years of British advertising a particular skill was developed by one man at one agency. When faced with the soap powder problem, he would create memorable devices, figures, cartoons, anything that would plant itself in the customers' minds rather than allow them to dwell for too long on the product itself. The instant potato, Smash, that was developed by Cadbury's in the 1970s wasn't even the best on the market, but with the aid of tin Martians driven to helpless fits of giggles by the Earthlings' penchant for time-consuming potato preparation, it stayed the best-selling product of its kind for many years.[2]

The same creative, John Webster, dreamt up a polar bear wearing shades with a memorable line ('It's frothy, man') for a sticky sweet soft drink; he also persuaded us that if we didn't drink our milk the Humphreys would get it and that the best way to sell German beer was to have a cuddly bear as a spokesman.

What Webster had discovered was that the British public (perhaps less sophisticated then than now) had begun to enjoy ads, to see them as entertainment in themselves, and wanted characters to recognize and begin a relationship with. Who cares if Cresta was actually a sickly sweet liquid eventually withdrawn from the shops?

Now the public likes its heroes real – the Virgin brand is associated entirely with its very real, woolly jumper-sporting chairman, Richard Branson. What

Branson has discovered is that the consumer is willing to let Virgin badge a whole variety of different products and services, from records to wine, from air travel to financial services.[3] Brands like this which stretch over many sectors are envied – the public trusts them and is willing to be pulled by them into new product areas.

So it helps that Virgin's chairman has made a name for himself flying balloons, wearing

TOP LEFT
Smash advertising image
BMP UK 1974

TOP RIGHT
The Hofmeister bear
BMP UK 1983

TOP MIDDLE
John Smiths TV advertising still
BMP UK 1981

ABOVE
The Cresta bear
BMP UK 1972

IMMEDIATELY ABOVE
Virgin record sleeve symbol
ROGER DEAN UK 1970S

LEFT
Virgin logo
UK 1970S

jumpers, not suits, and acting the clown at parties. He is the living, breathing embodiment of a brand whose whole *raison d'être* is to be the people's champion, the brand that dares to break up long-held cartels or make phone tariffs understandable.

The Virgin way of working is to continually challenge the establishment; it enables them to crash into new markets, set up their stall as 'the ones who are going to give you, the consumer, a fair deal' and upset the received wisdom of whichever sector they enter. Some argue that, like rubber bands, brands can only stretch so far before they break, and it remains to be seen if the undeniable magic surrounding the Virgin brand can survive problem areas like trains and cosmetics and a global decline in the fortunes of the air industry.

But to make things worse for their design critics, most of the Virgin branding seems to have been done in seconds. The logo? Reputedly scribbled in a meeting. Each new product name? Seemingly dreamt up in the bath. Even more annoying for those who would turn them into a rigid, monolithic organisation, the public seems to forgive Virgin its slightly incoherent identity and the occasional product gaffe. Perhaps they know that it wouldn't be Virgin if everything was perfect – if Virgin is like a person, well people make the occasional mistake, don't they?

Virgin's managers have been able to make the most of this happy positioning and build one of the world's most flexible brands in the process.

In the States, Nike long ago discovered the power of the personality endorsement when it co-opted a series of sporting superstars to promote its products, beginning with Michael Jordan and continuing, most controversially, with the Brazilian football team. Early Nike trainers designed by Bill Bowerman solved genuine problems – no-one made comfortable long-distance running shoes – but did Bowerman realise as he poured rubber into his waffle-maker (as he experimented with spongy soles) that he would help create one of the world's biggest and most controversial brands?

Probably not. But as the world caught up in terms of product, Nike realized that they had to keep ahead of the pack with the best marketing they could buy.

ABOVE
Virgin sub-brands
UK 1980s, 1990s

RIGHT
Nike billboard poster
SIMONS PALMER CLEMMOW JOHNSON
UK 1992

EVER HEARD THE ALGERIAN NATIONAL ANTHEM? YOU WILL.

LEFT
Nike billboard poster
SIMONS PALMER CLEMMOW JOHNSON
UK 1992

BELOW LEFT
Nike Euro 2000 football tournament
newspaper ad
SIMONS PALMER CLEMMOW JOHNSON
UK 1996

Of course, the company has successfully kept re-inventing their product, creating desire in their audience for every new item. But it is the use of the world's finest ad agencies which has kept Nike at the forefront of their target market's mind for twenty-five years. The soap powder problem is solved by creating an edgy, distinctive brand that, in the consumer's mind at least, will help to win the race (even though most of the sportswear never goes anywhere near a track).

Rack theirs and everyone else's trainers up, take the logos off and what have you got? Similar products, effectively, but a confused customer forced to choose one designer trainer from another. Put the logos back on and now in the consumer's eyes it is easy – this is the trainer that will help them jump like Jordan or bend footballs like Beckham (for Adidas).

The rise of celebrity athletes and their priceless endorsements have created a bizarre worldwide marketing environment where the actual shoes themselves

ITALY'S GOALKEEPER: EASIEST JOB IN EUROPE.

VENABLES, QUIT NOW.

NIKE WOULD LIKE TO WISH GERMANY GOOD LUCK. (THAT SHOULD DO IT.)

have been long forgotten (save for the occasional product-based ad).

The headlong pursuit of the sporting celebrity can have its problems, of course. Nike's agencies and their 'win at all costs' attitude can sometimes unseat them from their ivory towers – their long-held strategy of choosing winners for ads came unstuck with a series developed to coincide with a major European football tournament. The footballers started doing the unthinkable, namely losing matches. Paolo Maldini (Italy) and Patrick Kluivert (The Netherlands) had starred in portentous posters that were ridiculed when their teams performed badly. Nike eventually

OPPOSITE TOP LEFT
Nike Suzy Hamilton TV stills
WEIDEN + KENNEDY USA 2000

OPPOSITE TOP RIGHT
Nike 'Dri-Goat' ad
WEIDEN + KENNEDY USA 2000

OPPOSITE BOTTOM LEFT
Nike protest poster, Untitled:
subvertising session in the streets of
Riga, Latvia, September 2001
ART BUREAU OPEN LATVIA 2001

OPPOSITE BOTTOM RIGHT
Cartoon of Peretti story
DAN McHALE USA 2001

why sport?

you'll live longer.

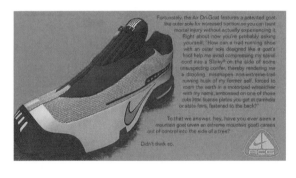

ran an ad seeking to reverse the 'curse' that the poster series had seemingly created. In the USA, they began to push their brand regularly into difficult and controversial areas. Women's groups reacted in horror when a TV ad featuring runner Suzy Hamilton seemed to suggest that being fit and wearing Nike shoes would get you out of a jam with chainsaw-wielding cannibals.

The endline 'why sport? you'll live longer' was clearly meant to be ironic but seemed to be slightly misunderstood by some customers.[4]

An ad for a trail-running shoe (Nike Dri-Goat) was pilloried for suggesting that if you lost your footing you could be left disabled (leaving you 'drooling and misshapen', to quote the ad).[5] A product innovation that allowed customers to brand their shoes personally led to some difficulties when an anti-brand Massachusetts Institute of Technology graduate, Jonah Peretti, claimed that his request for a pair of trainers named 'sweatshop' was mysteriously blocked by the machinery at Nike. The reason given by the company was that 'sweatshop' was slang and hence not allowed.[6]

The speed at which the world's email systems transferred the Jonah Peretti story around the globe has shown the big brands that there is a new force in the minds of their target audience.

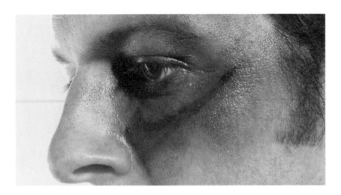

The anti-brand, anti-capitalist movement has left an undeniable question-mark in the heads of the world's students, and for the first time since the 1960s a generation seems to be growing up questioning whether the headlong pursuit of designer labels is actually such a smart thing to do, especially as more truths come out concerning the worrying practices of the major players in their production methods.

Squeaky clean, preppy dancers are all very well as Gap sells the world a chino-wearing vision of a perfect America. But as more and more people learn of the 36-hour shifts of the Asian workers toiling over boxer-shorts for less than a dollar a day, though, a point may be reached where the world sits up, takes notice and finally says no.[7]

Whilst once design students' main concern was the size of their first pay packet and when they might get a company car, today's are starting to use their skills to examine their relationship with their former heroes. Addled by Adidas? Scrape the stripes into a foot to make a point. Think Nike is naff? Turn the tick into a bruising thump. Recently, one design student ploughed through her collection of designer trainers, carefully cutting them in half or echoing her 1960s bra-rejecting predecessors by ceremonially burning them.

ABOVE, LEFT, BELOW LEFT
Images from student project
JADE STRACHAN
GLASGOW SCHOOL OF ART UK 2001

BELOW RIGHT
Image from student project
JODIE FOWLER
GLASGOW SCHOOL OF ART UK 2001

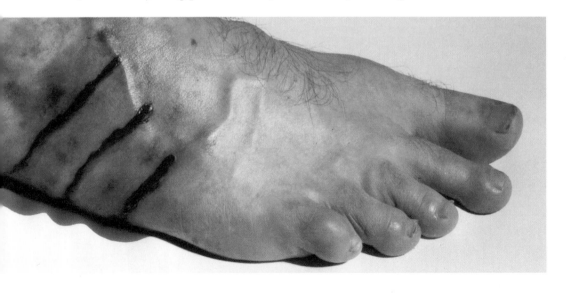

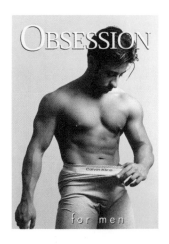

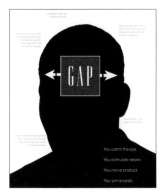

And a whole generation of students has grown up reading *Adbusters*, the satirical magazine that aims to take a side-swipe at the advertising and design industry. Interestingly, the magazine receives the most support and spoof ads from practising professionals working anonymously, eager to criticize but not wanting to bite the hand that feeds them.

Theoretically, a world turning against branding has significant implications for the creative industries (and presumably you, the reader). The cynics among us would say that the arrival of Seattle chic clothing in the world's shops is indicative of how long it takes the mainstream to absorb the radical. Our fashion-loving trainer-burner eventually admitted that she couldn't burn her seventh and favourite pair (i.e. protest had a cut-off point, and she reached it).

But we can see interesting trends such as the success of Muji (which literally translates as 'no-brand' in Japanese), the fiercely minimalist Japanese retailer who defiantly un-brands their products (leaving the brand-obsessed to keep price-stickers on the goods in order to obtain their brand points).

ABOVE & ABOVE RIGHT
Adbusters 'ads', 'Obsession',
'Tommy' & 'Gap'
ADBUSTERS.ORG CANADA 1994–2001

RIGHT
Muji pencils + olive oil
MUJI JAPAN 1990S

The Californian skate brand Alien Workshop carefully maintained an identity that was always changing and modulating, never the same twice.

'Do', was a anti-branders brand created by advertising guerrillas KesselsKramer, which calls upon 'lame-duck couch potatoes' and asks them to enter their own concepts and project ideas for a brand that 'doesn't have any products or services, just a dream'.

But whilst the world's companies continue to produce things that look and sound the same, communicators will be called upon to differentiate one soap powder from another, by shape, by feeling, by brand. Not until the message of the anti-branders sinks in will the problem begin to go away. When a British newspaper decided to test the public's appetite for branding, they opted for a non-existent company called 'Joy', featuring a naked hairy man in a rubber ring supported with the line 'Sing, laugh, drive, sleep, eat, breathe, cry – but do it with Joy'.

They ran a few ads, a single web-page, and toured London with a billboard, canvassing public opinion on what was being presented to them. Whilst few were certain what the deliberately obscure piece represented, 19 per cent had decided that Joy was about travel (only 2 per cent felt it had anything to do with donating or giving). If an entirely fictitious idea can still receive thousands of enquiries, it would seem that the public still want and need new brands in their lives. And let's face it, what the public wants, they will probably get.[8]

ABOVE RIGHT
Alien Workshop logo variants
IN-HOUSE DESIGN USA 1990S

ABOVE LEFT
Do branding campaign
KESSELSKRAMER THE NETHERLANDS
2000

OPPOSITE
Image from Joy campaign
KARMARAMA UK 2001

Problem: You own a 500-bed budget hotel in the centre of Amsterdam. Your hotel has few facilities, it's dirty, it's smelly. What do you do?

Solved: Hire an agency like KesselsKramer.

ALL ADS/DESIGNS BY KESSELSKRAMER
THE NETHERLANDS

THIS PAGE
Hans Brinker 'Now' campaign
1996

OPPOSITE TOP AND LEFT
'Not included' ad campaign
1998

OPPOSITE BOTTOM RIGHT
'Check in, Check out' campaign
1999

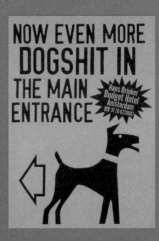

In a little under five years, Amsterdam-based KesselsKramer has turned most of the received wisdom of branding upside-down by doing the unthinkable – telling the honest truth.

If the hotel has no facilities – run an ad campaign which shows exactly what isn't included in the room (nearly everything). If most rooms don't have windows, they're noisy and you could step in dog faeces in the hall – sounds like a perfect poster campaign, doesn't it?

If your typical visitor often leaves the Brinker somewhat the worse for wear after sampling Amsterdam's seedier pleasures? - print pictures of them before and after in a brochure. The disarming truth of the most recent campaign (shown overleaf) celebrates the dubious fact that the smelly beds are often stained by previous inhabitants with the line 'just like home'.

It may be little more than an exercise in truth-vending that could never apply to the big-budget corporations. But the willingness of a hotel to accept reality so passionately, and for it to be communicated in such a way, really makes you wish for a major company to do it too, doesn't it?

The HansBrinker Budget Hotel Amsterdam (31) 20-6220687

* *not included*

The HansBrinker Budget Hotel Amsterdam (31) 20-6220687

* *not included*

Check in

Check out

THIS SPREAD
'Just like home' ad campaign
KESSELSKRAMER
THE NETHERLANDS 2001

THIS BED BELONGS TO: Dayaa Sanders
HOME: North Carolina, USA
HANS BRINKER HOTEL VISIT: 20 - 27 December 2000
ROOM NUMBER: 124
GUEST BOOK COMMENT: There's nothing here except a bed, four walls,
and screaming, banging neighbours. I slept as if I was home in my
own bed. I also like that I can sometimes find other people's mess
in or under the bed - some of them are still warm and wet.
It makes every stay at the Hans Brinker Budget Hotel a surprise.

THIS BED BELONGS TO: Samantha Bishop
HOME: Birmingham, England
HANS BRINKER HOTEL VISIT: 10 - 15 May 2001
ROOM NUMBER: 145
GUEST BOOK COMMENT: There's nothing like waking up with the familiar smell that I'm used to back home - that's the comforting feeling I get at your hotel.

THIS BED BELONGS TO: Massimo di Pietro
HOME: Bassano del Grappa, Italy
HANS BRINKER HOTEL VISIT: 27 February - 4 March 2001
ROOM NUMBER: 09
GUEST BOOK COMMENT: I know some of my friends complain about the stains, but I say to them - hey, all our own beds back home have big stains too - what's the problem!

The MESSAGE IS THE PRICE *problem*

The brief that most professionals dread is one that focuses on price or value-for-money. Dealing with a cheap 'n' cheerful message is one of the toughest assignments there is, and one of the least loved in the creative department. Conversely, the opposite message, communicating 'expensive' and 'exclusive', has just as many pitfalls.

It's not often that someone walks into a agency and says 'make it look as cheap as you can, guys'. In a world in headlong pursuit of the next dollar, there isn't often a case for making things look cheap and nasty, given that cheap and nasty rarely makes much money.

Of course there are a few historical precedents: many supermarkets have experimented with economy ranges within their master range which are targeted towards the price-conscious consumer and are necessarily designed to look as 'budget' as possible. A famous example is the British Fine Fare yellow label series in the 1970s which used the simple coding of 'yellow = cheap'. In the jargon of packaging and branding, the products certainly achieved 'shelf stand-out' but, like the supermarket itself, soon ended up in the bargain bucket.

More recently, enlightened supermarket chains have discovered that they are able to offer both discount and luxury products within their ranges – the consumers appreciate the choice and the chance to buy to what suits their budget, or to splash out on a luxury purchase.

The pricing problem gets trickier when we come to a market sector that has traded for years on elitism and snob appeal, the marketing of airlines. The advent

BELOW LEFT
EasyJet identity
STELIOS HAJI-IOANNOU
UK 1995

BELOW
Freddie Laker

BELOW MIDDLE
Buzz identity
THE PARTNERS UK 1999

BOTTOM RIGHT
Go livery
WOLFF OLINS UK 1998

OPPOSITE TOP LEFT
Go logo
WOLFF OLINS UK 1998

OPPOSITE TOP RIGHT
EasyJet 'anti-Go' livery
EASYJET DESIGN DEPARTMENT
UK 1998

OPPOSITE MIDDLE, BOTTOM RIGHT
Porsche press ads
FALLON McELLIGOTT USA 1985

of cheap transatlantic flights with Laker airlines in the 1970s simply announced that air flight, like bus, coach and train travel before it, was about to be commodified.

In the mid-1990s in Europe a budget brand called EasyJet emerged, offering no-frills flights at coach-like prices. Gleefully throwing the rules of corporate identity design out of the window, the earliest planes simply sported, right down the side, the company name and phone number in a massive, bulbous orange typeface more redolent of 1960s psychedelic posters than 'corporate branding'.

Stirred (and probably scared) into action, British Airways created its own low-cost carrier, Go, and KLM followed suit with Buzz. Each tried to capitalize on the informal feeling that EasyJet, following Laker's lead, had established.

go

The rules of the game had been broken – no longer did air flight have to look or even be expensive. It was OK to be cheap 'n' cheerful, to 'Go-go', as the British Airways offshoot promised.

Established identity design firms found themselves presented with the challenge of presenting cheapness and affordability on their biggest palette yet, the side of a plane. Of course neither competitor could bring itself to sink quite as low as EasyJet, a design that looks as though it has never been near a professional graphic designer (and is probably all the better for it).

There are leaders and there are followers. Life is really quite simple, isn't it?

Then there's the challenge of making the expensive *look* expensive. It sounds easy, doesn't it? – here's an expensive product, make it look just that.

These famous US ads for Porsche seemingly tapped into the ideal mindset of the potential buyer, almost challenging them to think of the car as the ultimate experience. The kind of car only affordable by a chosen few, seemingly balancing their huge bank accounts with finding time to be with the kids, all the time dealing with their mid-life crisis (hence the need for the new Porsche).

But within packaged goods it's amazing how often the clients and agencies fall back on a bit of gold type and some embossed card to establish a 'pricey' feel, not realizing that they have crossed the invisible line between classy and crummy. Whereas, once, department

It's like children. You can't understand until you've had one.

stores such as Harrods could provide witty packaging such as the oil bottles shown here, in the present day luxury retailers seem to be devoid of original thought when it comes to expensive goods.

When Michael Nash Associates competed – without any substantial packaging portfolio – to create the packs for the proposed food hall for Harvey Nichols in London, they won the contract not by the quality of their strategic presentation or the thickness of their leave-behind document,

but by making a simple promise at the meeting. 'We will package your food as if it were a silk scarf' they proposed. Having been added at the last minute to the end of a long list of packaging 'experts', it was astonishing that they should win the project.

And then followed one of the finest breakthroughs in contemporary packaging design. From oils, to bread, to spices, they brought an aesthetic honed on record sleeves to high-end packaging. They packaged bread in sky bags, Christmas puddings in foil sixpences, spices with photographs of arid deserts.

TOP RIGHT
Harrods Oils packaging
MINALE TATTERSFIELD UK 1969

THIS PAGE AND OPPOSITE
Harvey Nichols food packaging
MICHAEL·NASH UK 1992–3

OPPOSITE BELOW LEFT
Eau de parfum
COMME DES GARÇONS/
MARC ATLAN FRANCE 1994

OPPOSITE BELOW RIGHT
'2EDT' CDG2 packaging
COMME DES GARÇONS/
MARC ATLAN FRANCE 1998

By using sumptuous photography and minimal containers, they cracked the problem of how to make something look expensive (relatively simple) but also cool (much more difficult). If the implicit problem was 'let's do prestige packaging with style and panache, not crammed with over-the-top clichés', they certainly solved that one, producing a range of work more akin to perfume packaging than food and turning the world of packaging design upside-down in the process.

Genuine 'luxury' brands such as Comme des Garçons perfume also seem to adhere to the mantra of 'less is more', but this could apply to most of the luxury perfume market, populated as it is almost entirely by bottles of coloured liquids with

screen-printed brand-names. At least the Comme packs attempted to break the mould by arriving shrink-wrapped or bubble-wrapped like commodity goods, hanging like supermarket packs from bent metal stands.

Does everyone want everything to look more expensive? Not always. Retailer of some of the world's finest (and most expensive) watches, the Watch Gallery had been experimenting with bizarre catalogues for some time. One catalogue showed their finest pieces on faux-luxury marble backgrounds at life-size, printed on to adhesive background paper so the recipient could select their favourite watch,

peel it off and try it on their wrist for size.

But for their next catalogue they turned all the clichés for expensive goods upside-down. They knew that their clientèle probably didn't aspire to the traditional images of 'richness' (yachts, tropical beaches, girls in skimpy bikinis, etc.) on account of their being phenomenally rich already. They thought that Hell's Angels and roadside labourers would make funnier, unexpected models. The models of course had no idea that they could probably retire early if they had run away from the shoot clutching their diamond-encrusted Audemars Piguet or suchlike, but that's what gives the project its twist.

Of course stick-on watches and greasy bikers as models make great ironic, post-modern references, but many marketing budgets are spent trying to justify the sheer expense of the products on offer.

Belgian-brewed beer Stella Artois is not considered a premium beer in Europe but is marketed in the UK as 'reassuringly expensive'. By creating this 'positioning' and backing it up through a series of clever ad campaigns, they say to their drinkers that they are people of taste, of discernment, and of course that they are that little bit richer. Some might say that this is an entirely fatuous idea for a gold liquid that tastes similar to many of its competitors, but nonetheless, it's an approach that made Stella the third largest-selling UK beer by 1999.

In a twist of their own long-running campaign, a recent set of press ads featured scratched and despoiled rare designer objects that had been used to prise off the top of a bottle of the beer (in the absence of a bottle opener) – ie. 'Can't find the bottle opener? Just use the edge of your collector's item Eames chair instead.'

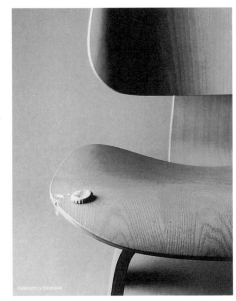

RIGHT
BMW TV stills
WCRS UK 1983

BELOW
Mercedes press ad
LEO BURNETT UK 1996

The impression of luxury and the expensive cachet has long been a critical factor in the marketing of cars. The BMW may be relatively middle-of-the-road in its German home market (with a strapline that translates as 'a pleasure to drive'), but abroad it is sold a little more ambitiously – 'the ultimate driving machine' in the UK and the USA.

In the UK the ads show the cars driving through car graveyards, the only cars 'still alive' when others have died, the only cars you can create a still Martini on (whilst others are stirred), and so on.

(Meanwhile, over in Belgium, BMW take a more pragmatic approach and use the line 'If you like to drive', which hardly sets the pulse racing, does it?)[1]

Mercedes have picked up on the 'ultimate' positioning and taken it even further – this press ad simply featured an overhead shot of its newest model surrounded by copious skid marks (summoning up a powerful image of over-braking petrol-heads gawking at the latest addition to the luxury car range). Another just showed the side view of one of their most desirable cars, with a set of lottery balls underneath (ie. 'you'll need a bit of help to afford this').

Even a faltering product in its home market, such as Rover, has demonstrated that by selling carefully through its 'heritage' and adding the MG marque to selected products, it can achieve decent sales abroad whilst its home market remains resolutely distrustful and still more inclined to save for a more glamorous foreign option.

The strength of the 'luxury' car brands can often be gauged by the tactics of their competitors. Having decided that they wanted to enter the super-luxury sector of the market, Toyota concluded that they could not move the image of their core brand, firmly entrenched in value-for-money mid-range motoring, into the 'hand-written cards at airport arrivals' brigade. How did they solve this particular pricing problem? They simply created a different marque. Enduring the inevitable early criticisms, the Lexus brand, complete with its swooshy logo and walnut-finish-fetish advertising (and a good product), has become a genuine competitor to the major German luxury brands.

But some car manufacturers have used their 'cheap' positioning to their advantage. In the 1980s, Citroën ran a series of charming ads that managed to compare its cars (in a knowing, self-deprecatory way, of course) to Ferraris and Rolls Royces by declaring that they had as many wheels, for example (and more room than the Porsche).

Having been the joke of European car manufacturing for decades, Skoda and its London agency have managed to turn the joke on its head with a campaign that shows users refusing to believe that it really is a Skoda (now that they have managed to produce quite decent-looking cars). One poster advertises a logo helpline at the bottom, assuming that the public will not believe that it is in fact a Skoda and will immediately need to check up. In another they repeat the logo purely because they don't think people will believe it first time.

ABOVE
Lexus SC430 and Lexus logo
TOYOTA MOTOR CORPORATION
JAPAN 2002, 1989

LEFT
Citroën press ad
COLMAN RSCG & PARTNERS UK 1984

OPPOSITE PAGE
Skoda posters
FALLON UK 2000

no really,

WRONG LOGO HOTLINE 08450 565 565

We are left to conclude (a little depressingly) that with a good agency, significant long-term ad spend and a suitably gullible target market you can create any image you like for your product, especially abroad and 'away' from the truth, as it were. So desperate are middle managers for the 'prestige' of driving a BMW that they will accept the lowest specification car available, foregoing the power and extras on offer from the competitors, making sure that it arrives 'debadged'. This means that an average, non-car-magazine-reading passer-by or possible date will be suitably impressed by the BMW marque but unable to tell whether it is the budget entry model or a car costing twice as much. The desire for that luxury tag will even stretch to deception, so powerful is the brand image.

Whilst there is a willingness within certain consumers to fall for these 'created' identities, there will always be that niche for a luxury product, whether the apparent luxury is real or simply created for them and priced accordingly.

Problem: How can 'cheaper than you think' be made into a unique campaign?

Solved: Make affordability surprising.

The 1960s ads for the VW Beetle have been quite rightly lauded since their inception as they heralded the advent of modern advertising as we know it (ie. knowing, witty, self-deprecatory and disarmingly honest). Once the New York team of Doyle Dane Bernbach (DDB) had recognized the fact that the Beetle's ugliness and lack of size might just be its saving grace (rather than the 1950s streamlined attempts that had preceded it), they were off and running.

Thirty years later, their European descendents have been working for some time with a set of cars much less original in thought and style than the Beetle, with a straightforward price/affordability/reliability promise.

On paper, a frustrating proposition (especially considering the historical precedents).

But the London office of BMP DDB pulled off a series of startling ideas that tap into the shock value of seeing such a big brand at apparently reasonable prices.

For example, one TV ad simply shows a woman reading the paper. But at the beginning she has hiccups, at the end she doesn't (having passed a VW 'price'). The 'shock' of the price of the car has cured her.

One passer-by in a shopping centre has to sit down in apparent distress after passing a poster telling her the price of 'a new Polo'. In the *pièce de resistance*, we see a long and convoluted set-up of men wrapping a lamp-post in padding (we don't understand why) until we see a man approaching who turns to see the ad and we anticipate the collision without ever seeing it.

The poster applications took the idea on again when the wedding photographer's focus is drawn by the price on a passing bus, rather than the happy couple.

Heralded in some quarters as a return to 'real' advertising, all that the agency had really done was to make an honest and witty campaign with apparently mediocre initial material.

BELOW
'Think small' Beetle press ad
DOYLE DANE BERNBACH USA 1960

BOTTOM AND OPPOSITE
VW Polo press and poster ads
BMP DDB UK 1998

Think small.

Surprisingly ordinary prices

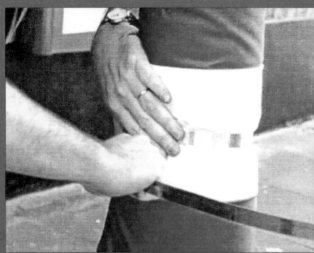

Polo L, only £8145.

Surprisingly ordinary prices.

www.volkswagen.co.uk

Polo,
from only
£7,990.

Polo L

THIS SPREAD
VW Polo TV ad stills
BMP DDB UK 1998

Surprisingly ordinary prices.

www.volkswagen.co.uk

The CHARITY BEGINS AT WORK *problem*

Blue-chip clients with generous budgets may buy the respect of their creative consultants, but they can't buy their love. And love is what the creative always craves. So how do you solve this particular problem? Enter the charity clients – seemingly grateful for your time and expertise, initially respectful of your understanding and infinite patience. But make the most of it – it may not last for ever.

In the field of charitable or institutional work there is often an inverse relationship between the creative freedom on a project and the level of the fees. There's an implicit rule: the charity client gives a degree of freedom that corporations often cannot, in return for work for a lower fee. This is a deal that can be fraught with danger – it needs an extraordinary bond between the creative and the client to survive years of calls to do something else for a handful of pennies, often at a day's notice or less.

Most charity clients have become adept at dangling the carrot of creativity in front of the designer or advertiser. Here is a chance to 'put something back', a chance to leave those big-buck blue-chips alone for a few days and do something that really matters, that might even change people's lives for the better. Whatever the reason, most creatives want to turn their skills to something that will do us all some good, or at least enhance our cultural milieu.

Probably because of the emotional involvement with the subject matter (sometimes difficult to maintain with a bottom-line-obsessed client), most design and advertising agencies will cite their charity clients and

institutional work as the work they are most proud of.

Opera companies, theatre companies and museums worldwide have all become adept at playing the charity card. And great work is often the result.

The design style developed by the Brooklyn Academy of Music is a great example of this. The simple combination of bars and cut-out images is deliberately designed to be flexible enough to work on anything from plastic cups to newspaper ads, and the designer has enjoyed the restrictions of budget and space while somehow using them to enhance the project.

ABOVE, LEFT AND BELOW
Brooklyn Academy of Music identity
PENTAGRAM USA 1995

The release of a series of beautiful CD covers for the London Chamber Orchestra prompted the English National Opera, London's second most famous opera house, to ask the same designers to take on the immediate transformation of their public image. The new, and immediately classic, identity cleverly represented the open face of the opera singer (without overstating it) and portrayed it in a clear, logical house-style. At one point the agency concerned was regularly producing posters for a fraction

TOP LEFT
London Chamber Orchestra
Minimalist music CD
CDT UK 1990

ABOVE, RIGHT & BELOW
English National Opera identity
and applications
CDT UK 1991 ONWARDS

of their true cost, purely in the interest of maintaining and developing an idea that had won instant worldwide acclaim for its single-minded clarity and its

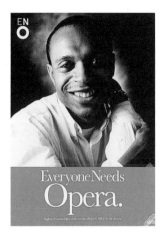

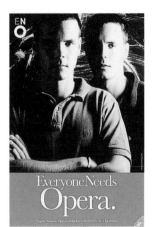

strikingly modern portrayal of opera. One set of posters was produced, photographed, designed and artworked single-handedly by the creative director who simply asked visitors to the foyer of the opera house if they would like to star in the campaign (doubtless with his miniature budget in mind all the while).

Because charities offer such low fees, it becomes part of the brief to the designer to find a way around the restrictions. Studio Dumbar was able to produce four months' worth of posters for the Zeebelt festival

in the Netherlands by printing one four-colour example then overprinting each month's information (hence avoiding the expensive production of four separate posters). For years, everyone from circuses to rock bands has overprinted the dates of their next gig onto 'blank' posters; here the Dutch studio took that simple idea to its logical conclusion and made the money last four times as long.

This set of posters produced for the Seattle-based Bathhouse Theatre was part of a series by the acclaimed American designer Art Chantry, who regularly used his theatrical commissions to allow him to experiment with new stylistic twists and turns that his other more moneyed projects did not.

London agency The Partners turned the yearly request for a poster from a photographers' association into a kind of endurance game. Since 1987 they have produced the posters for the organization's yearly show, and have collated a fascinating case study of work for just one client in the process, working 'at cost' (making no real profit) and often using the association's photographers to photograph the poster ideas themselves.

TOP LEFT & ABOVE
Zeebelt Theatre poster campaign
STUDIO DUMBAR
THE NETHERLANDS 1993

LEFT
Bathhouse Theatre posters
ART CHANTRY USA 1994

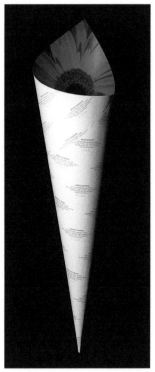

THIS PAGE
Association of Photographers
exhibition posters
THE PARTNERS UK 1989–99

Occasionally the arrival of a charity client and a greater degree of freedom allow a studio to spread its wings and change the emphasis of its work.

British agency Radley Yeldar had gained a solid reputation as a respected producer of annual reports. The arrival of a new client, Comic Relief, which features plastic red noses as the key identifier of the bi-annual charity days, allowed them to produce some great examples of unbridled creativity, previously a little stifled by their 'stiffer' clients in the City.

Using children's colouring-book vernacular and enclosing red pencils with the document, or by making covers entirely of sticky-back red nose stickers (which could be placed on to the noses of the celebrities within the document), they successfully transported the idea of the charity day

into what is often the most unforgiving of mediums, the annual report.

In advertising, agencies vie for the opportunity to represent institutions. One ad for the Victoria and Albert Museum's new café generated yards of free column inches of commentary when it wryly proclaimed that the V&A was 'an ace caff with quite a nice museum attached' – a perfect example of an institution (at that time) happy to jolt the public's perception of themselves with deliberately shocking tactics from their agency.

The same agency also routinely turns their attention to niche charities such as The Tinnitus Association and The National Society for the

There's nothing wrong with modern art that a good cup of tea won't cure.

V&A An ace caff with quite a nice museum attached.

"Let's go down the pub, if they wake up they wake up."

Supported by *Microsoft*

Cruelty to children must stop. FULL STOP ● NSPCC™

Some of the things we've removed from people's heads.

Prevention of Cruelty to Children (NSPCC), often working for low or non-existent fees. There are, of course, significant ethical issues to be asked here (such as how do some of these creatives square the demands of their blue-chips on one hand and the pleading of their charities on the other?), but the agencies will be happy with the arrangement as long as they have the finest of ads to show for their labours.

Some agencies even offer their skills without insisting on a huge creative change from the initial, existing concept. North American identity specialist Landor used its implementation skills to complete a worldwide review of the World Wildlife Fund's 40-year-old panda symbol. But this was not a radical re-design of the Panda, just an exercise in rationalizing the many versions of the mark in existence, and applying it consistently across the globe. Of course, at their next credentials presentation, the agency will have been able to show the Panda mark, discuss the project and bask in a little reflected glory.

Like their advertising colleagues, designers are often equally willing to leave the 'real' client alone for a few

WWF

days in order to produce work that, whilst in reality not moving many hearts and minds, at least makes the creators themselves feel better. These posters campaigning worldwide against violence, and the plight of children-at-arms are designed to attack the viewer right at the emotional jugular, and they succeed admirably.

German poster designer Uwe Loesche has carved a unique niche in the field of campaigning, protest posters, some of which are shown

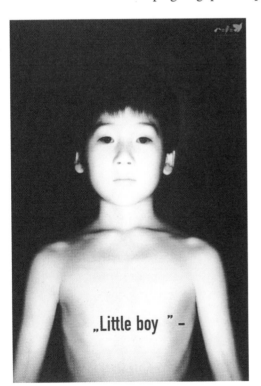

here. With the simplest and fewest elements, he makes his points without labouring them. Sometimes the meaning is hidden slightly, such as this peace poster that simply places the name of the atomic bomb dropped on Hiroshima (Little Boy) over an image of a Japanese child. But once discovered, the meaning is not easily forgotten.

However, a client might sometimes try to play the charity card without justifiable reason.

For several years Kodak's professional film division ran a series of three-page ads themed around the famous instruction

ABOVE LEFT
Against Violence poster
PENTAGRAM UK 1994

ABOVE
Infantry poster
LIPPA PEARCE UK 2000

LEFT
'Little boy' peace poster
UWE LOESCHE GERMANY 1995

BELOW
News – Child of the Century poster
UWE LOESCHE GERMANY 1997

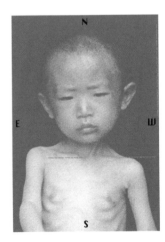

Help take the edge off the daily reductions of

HUMAN RIGHTS

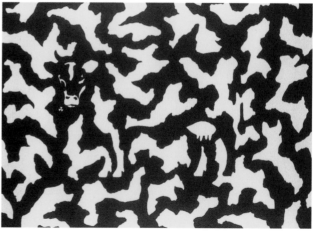

from art director Alexey Brodovitch to his photographers to 'astonish me'. The photos were commissioned from photographers around the world in return for a very low fee, a credit and, if they were lucky, some free film. For a couple of years the campaign ran quite successfully on this basis, sometimes producing genuinely astonishing imagery. Eventually it ran out of steam, however, as the photographers refused to believe that this moneyed global multinational actually had no money to pay reasonable rates for the images.

Offers of free film were found wanting – Kodak had tried to play the poverty card, but were finally exposed because the appeal simply wasn't genuine.

ABOVE
Human Rights poster, anniversary
of the French Revolution
UWE LOESCHE GERMANY 1989

ABOVE RIGHT
IQ poster against radioactive
pollution in Chernobyl
UWE LOESCHE GERMANY 1986

RIGHT
Kodak 'Astonish Me' campaign
MATRIX MARKETING/
JOHNSON BANKS UK 1993

astonish me.

The charity appeal can only work if the message is as simple as possible. This multi-part campaign for Voluntary Services Overseas (VSO) even makes an attribute of the fact that its ads are poorly designed – the point being that the real professionals who normally pasted up the posters or typeset the ad, or even the prostitute advertised in the telephone box, were off doing something genuinely useful with their lives, like decorating a Nigerian hospital, setting up a magazine in China or running safe-sex workshops in Ghana. And whilst the relationships between creatives and their charities are often under intense strain as the need for fee-paying projects inevitably vies with the demands of their favourite causes, it's that chance to help, that chance to change views, that makes it all worthwhile.

ABOVE, LEFT, BELOW LEFT & OPPOSITE
Voluntary Services Overseas ambient ad campaign
LEONARDO UK 2001

These student ads to raise awareness of depression say it all: whilst the future would ideally lie with charities and institutions paying more for better services, and with relationships being on a far more professional footing, the lure of the chance to change people's hearts and minds with a scratched headline into a piece of enamel will probably always prove irresistible.

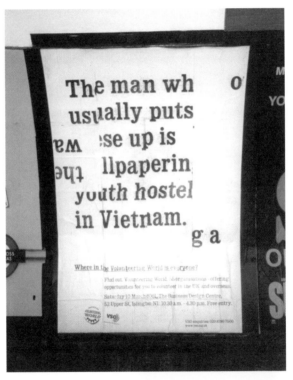

BELOW
'Depression' advertising concepts
SHAHEED PEERA AND SELDA ENVER
CENTRAL ST MARTINS
SCHOOL OF ART UK 2002
Responding to a student brief asking respondents to choose and explain misunderstood illnesses, this student team chose to show how sufferers of depression often keep their problem secret

Problem: You're disillusioned with your unethical corporate clients.

Solved: Lose the blue-chips, live frugally, rest your conscience.

Increasingly unhappy with the constraints imposed by his corporate clients, New York-based designer James Victore began to change his way of working to a much rawer and looser style. This initially polarized his client base and led to a few sticky years eking out an existence as a book jacket designer.

But gradually he began to find his voice as one of the angriest poster polemicists for a generation. By searching out like-minded potential clients, or simply publishing ideas himself he began to find a way of working that satisfied his desire to make a genuine mark with his graphics.

At the same time as his wholesale rejection of what most of the US design community stood for, Victore's charitable renaissance coincided with a back-to-basics way of designing that rejected the slick and polished aesthetic of much

of the computer-driven work around him. In returning to crude forms, clumsy cropping and hand-drawn elements he was able to develop his own unique style.

He began with a searing criticism of Columbus's discovery of America, turned his attention to racism and the death penalty, then railed against the worldwide march of Disney with a set of posters remarkable for their frankness in a world ever-afraid of the power of the multi-nationals' legal departments.

As his fame has grown, offers of exhibitions of his work have come in, accompanied by the opportunity to produce the

ABOVE
'Racism and the Death Penalty'
poster 1993

LEFT
'Celebrate Columbus' poster,
a comment on US treatment
of native Americans
1992

BELOW
'Traditional Family Values'
poster 1992

OPPOSITE
'The Death penalty mocks justice'
educational poster 1995

ALL PROJECTS JAMES VICTORE USA

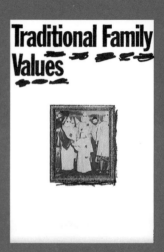

The Death Penalty Mocks Justice

The United States remains the only Western industrialized nation to retain the death penalty and carry out executions. While the rest of the world turns its back on state sanctioned killing, the death penalty in the U.S. continues to be applied in a racist and arbitrary manner. Capital punishment has never been implemented in a fair and non-discriminatory way. It has never been proven to be a deterrent, yet our nations death row, and executions continue to escalate. The death penalty is a mockery of justice. In the pursuit of equality before the law it must be abolished.

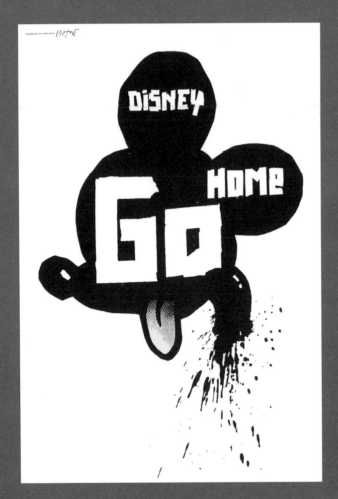

obligatory promotional poster. But rather than bask in the reflected glory of re-printing a previous idea, he has often used the funds to produce yet more vicious critiques. In his set for the DDD gallery in Japan, promoting Aids awareness, he used copulating flies and rabbits to illustrate the perils of the disease.

Victore has set a new precedent; a graphic designer can still do work he cares about, and become world famous (but probably at the expense of his bank account).

ABOVE
'Images of an Ideal Nation' poster for an exhibition of US social and political imagery
1998

LEFT
Images, Politics and Cross-Pollination
'Disney Go Home' poster
1998

BELOW LEFT
'RaCism' poster 1993

BELOW
'Choose or lose' voting poster
2000

OPPOSITE
'Use a condom' exhibition posters for the DDD gallery Japan
1998

ALL PROJECTS JAMES VICTORE USA

Victor09 F

The PARADIGM SHIFT *problem*

It's the holy grail for the designer or communicator – an opportunity arrives in a marketplace flooded with products that look the same, where a big idea can really make a difference. But breaking out of the mould can be a difficult and frustrating process.

You would think that a revolutionary breakthrough would be a relatively simple business in communications.

Every day, somewhere in the world, someone sits down and briefs a creative saying something like 'we want something truly revolutionary' or 'this is our opportunity to really shake things up'. The plain truth, however, is that genuine changes in the received way of doing things (or breaks in the paradigm) are much harder to achieve than they seem. Often the creative has to wage a battle of various sorts against the forces of evil around him or her – new and revolutionary ideas will polarize people and attract as many detractors as defenders. To zag when everyone else is zigging is difficult to do.

Genuinely new ideas tend to fail in research because consumers cannot relate the concepts to anything they attach to the idea or service – they fall outside their frame of reference and this confuses them completely. New ideas scare people, who are much happier with the devil they know than the devil they don't, but the benefits of genuine breakthroughs are immense. They can make the creator's name, triple sales of a product, even create world-famous brands.

Famous early attempts to shift paradigms sometimes met with disaster: for Strand cigarettes the line 'You're never alone with a Strand' may have made a lot of sense. It tapped into the disaffected psyche of the young man finding solace in his evening walk, puffing away at his cigarette.

While an interesting positioning to be explored (then probably discarded) in a contemporary advertising setting, 'you're never alone' became a fully fledged campaign. It failed miserably as the advertisers discovered that the ads simply encapsulated loneliness rather than rugged independence. And no target market likes to be summed up as 'lonely' or 'without friends'.

So the precedents for the 1960s campaign for American car rental giant Avis weren't good when their agency decided that the 'humility' approach that was working so well on their Beetle campaign could be transferred to their car rental client, Avis. Given that their client was basically the second most popular rental firm, their logic was simple – we'll tell everyone we're number two, and that's why we try harder.

ABOVE
Levi's ad
BARTLE BOGLE HEGARTY
UK 1982

BELOW & OPPOSITE TOP LEFT
Avis 'NO.2' ad campaign
DOYLE DANE BERNBACH
USA 1963, 1964

Avis is only No.2 in rent a cars. So why go with us?

We try harder.
(When you're not the biggest, you have to.)
We just can't afford dirty ash-trays. Or half-empty gas tanks. Or worn wipers. Or unwashed cars. Or low tires. Or anything less than seat-adjusters that adjust. Heaters that heat. Defrost-ers that defrost.
Obviously, the thing we try hardest for is just to be nice. To start you out right with a new car, like a lively, super-torque Ford, and a pleasant smile. To know, say, where you get a good pastrami sandwich in Duluth. Why?
Because we can't afford to take you for granted.
Go with us next time.
The line at our counter is shorter.

If you have a complaint,
call the president of Avis.
His number is CH 8-9150.

There isn't a single secretary to
protect him. He answers the phone
himself.
He's a nut about keeping in touch.
He has us working like crazy to keep our
vantages of a small company.
You know who is responsible for
what. There's nobody to pass the buck to.
One of the frustrations of complaining to a big company is finding someone to blame.
Well, our president feels responsible for the whole kit
and caboodle. He has us working like crazy to keep our
super-torque Fords super. But he knows there will be an
occasional dirty ashtray or temperamental wiper.
If you find one, call our president collect.
He won't be thrilled to hear from you, but he'll get
you some action.

INTERCITY SLEEPERS
NOW AVAILABLE WITH SAVER FARES

Even cheaper with a Railcard. Sleepers run nightly from Scotland to London
and Bristol. For full details pick up a leaflet at BR stations and Rail appointed travel agents.

We're getting there

But defying received wisdom, the campaign was a huge success, even forcing Hertz to justify why they were the true number one at one point. They had managed to shift the paradigm that says 'never admit you are second best'.

To illustrate how sensitively these ideas must be handled, when the notoriously inefficient British Rail tried to say 'we're getting there' in the 1970s, it met with a muted reaction. Probably a perfectly justifiable position, and a legitimate one for an advertising campaign (rather than corporate chest-beating), it was regarded with disdain by a public unable to treat its hated rail supplier with sympathy after years of strikes and industrial unrest.

In the world of corporate identity and branding, the pressures to keep to the agreed script are huge. It's simple – companies have a logotype, maybe a symbol that helps us work out what they do, they have recognizable typefaces and they present their wares in a consistent way. But as everyone adopted similar symbols, even similar typefaces (such as the ubiquitous Helvetica), differentiation became that much more difficult.

Identity firm Wolff Olins first began to test out a new way of expressing their clients' personalities with a scheme produced for a paint manufacturer, Hadfields, in the 1960s. Although this was short-lived as a scheme, Hadfields stood out a mile, partly because of some product innovations they had developed (such as domestic water-based paints) but mainly because of their innovative design scheme, featuring their very own quick brown fox. This was an innovative client, but also one happy to play a clever game with its key competitor, and attempt to jump over Dulux's lazy dog (the Old English Sheepdog that has featured in Dulux campaigns for decades).

No.2 says he
tries harder.
Than who?

Hertz

Hadfields
'Heolin'
Gloss Paint

Hadfields

Hadfields
Emulsion
Paint

When the construction firm, Bovis, approached them in the early 1970s, here was another opportunity. Construction was then, as now, an area dominated by billboards of men pulling ropes, or a thousand variations on the 'building blocks as logo' idea. Essentially, very predictable.

Rumour has it that they were first presented with a goldfish as a symbol (the rationale being that what would truly set them apart was a symbol that was completely different from the norm). The goldfish returned to its bowl but

reincarnated itself as another orange idea, a hummingbird.

Apparently chosen because it was 'nimble' and represented the 'antithesis of a heavy construction company', this remarkable conceptual leap was soon to be seen merrily hovering across construction sites throughout the United Kingdom.

In the 1990s the same consultants returned with another ground-breaking piece of work for Hutchison Telecom. The Hong Kong-based telecoms giant, seeking to establish the company in Europe but aware of the shortcomings (and lack of any profile) of their own name, appointed the agency to find a name and create a company that would stand out in the mobile telephone marketplace.

This was at a time when mobile phones seemed synonymous with used-car salesmen. The technology was young, full of confusing tariffs, and perceived by the public as a rip-off. The creation of the Orange brand with its 'transparent' image of helpfulness and calm was a revelation, an instant hit with the public and it became the first iconic brand of the sector. From a standing start, the company was worth £26 billion when sold to France Telecom a decade after the launch. And as the hummingbird had seemed a perfect fit twenty years

earlier, now an Orange square containing a word apparently irrelevant to the product now seemed to sum up perfectly the requirements of a brand trying to shift the paradigm of its sector.

In TV advertising massive breakthroughs have been harder to spot, perhaps because their

ABOVE TOP, LEFT AND RIGHT
Bovis identity,
before and after
WOLFF OLINS UK 1974

ABOVE
Orange logo
WOLFF OLINS UK 1994

LEFT
Orange ad
WCRS UK 1994

impact has been dulled by the passage of time or the appropriation of new ideas into mainstream television and cinema production.

Often credited with a huge shift in expectations of a simple TV ad (for Benson and Hedges cigarettes in this case, when still allowed in cinemas), Hugh Hudson's cinematic sweep of swimming pools, lizards, divers and helicopters looks a little pompous now but stood out dramatically in the mid-1970s.

Twenty years later the way we view thirty seconds of screen time was about to change again. film director Tony Kaye had gained a reputation as 'difficult' until he secured his breakthrough project for Dunlop tyres in 1994. From the starting proposition of 'tested for the unexpected', we see a black, unidentified car move through the most bizarre of obstacles, past gold-painted

fat men (uncannily similar to the Michelin man), sub-fetishist images of rubber-and-nail-helmeted women, demonic ball-bearing-spilling children, dodging grand pianos falling from the sky, all to the droning backbeat of 'Venus in Furs' by the 1960s cult favourites, The Velvet Underground.

What this ad did for the sales of Dunlop tyres or indeed the image of Dunlop itself is difficult to ascertain, but what is irrefutable is that Kaye was projected into the stratosphere of TV directors.

After Kaye had done the groundwork, the scene was set for another breakthrough.

By 1999 beer advertising had reached a particularly low point, dominated by the sector cliché of men cracking bad jokes in pubs, expressing

AUSTRALIANS WOULDN'T GIVE A XXXX FOR ANYTHING ELSE.

what Australians would call 'mateship'. Which is of course logical, given that beer is often drunk in pubs, by men, with their friends. Yet within that basic framework, nothing really new was being developed.

The manufacturers of the Irish stout, Guinness, had dipped their toes into experimental advertising a few times previously and had themselves established an avant-garde reputation with ads as diverse as Rutger Hauer strolling through the passage of time to a Louis Armstrong soundtrack, or a fish pedalling along the seafront (courtesy of the aforementioned Mr Kaye).

But while the script for their 1999 ad seemed almost ambient on paper (man waits for eternity for a big wave, sees one, catches it, we see shots of surf action intermingled with white horses, we hear strange beat poetry narration throughout, the surfer celebrates the journey on the wave with fellow surfers), when filmed on a budget-busting shoot in Hawaii and post-produced by the finest computer animators, the 'beer' paradigm wasn't just shifted, it was rocketed into orbit.

Although we do end the film with the obligatory mateship, everything else, from the eight-second pause at the beginning, to the horses, to the distorted drum-and-bass soundtrack, suggests that beer ads may never be the same again.

ABOVE
Guinness 'Surfer' TV still
AMV BBDO UK 1999

LEFT
The Man with the Golden Arm poster
SAUL BASS & ASSOCIATES USA 1955

BELOW
Se7en film titles
IMAGINARY FORCES USA 1995

In moving graphics, many of the fundamental developments have originated in America. Saul Bass's original (and still startling) work for the Frank Sinatra vehicle *The Man with the Golden Arm* which introduced the cut-paper, Matisse-like graphics to the general public; Robert Brownjohn's seminal Bond titles featuring projected type; Kyle Cooper's nervous and jittery introduction to the dramatic shocker *se7en*. They occurred in different decades but completely transcended anything that had preceded them.

But the actual selling of some of these breakthroughs sometimes requires some dramatic techniques.

In order to persuade the producers of the James Bond films of the validity of his idea of type appearing on a human body, Brownjohn's strategy was to strip to the waist in front of his client in a darkened room whilst clicking through a carousel of typographic slides aimed at his then rather ample belly.

Strangely, for all the time, effort and money spent on graphic design, true seismic shifts in the work produced for this medium are more difficult to identify. Peter Blake's sleeve for The Beatles' *Sergeant Pepper's Lonely Hearts Club Band*, was a huge step forward for the cause of 'record sleeve as art', and was almost matched for impact by Andy Warhol's 'Sticky fingers' sleeve for The Rolling Stones in the 1970s which came complete with zipped fly and bulging underwear beneath.

The metal tin packaging for The Small Faces' 'Ogden's Nut Gone' was an early attempt to break out of the strictures of the twelve-inch-square format but record sleeve art was glorying in the excesses of gatefold extravaganzas. When CDs arrived the 1980s, heroes of album design viewed them as too small a canvas for their art and turned their attentions elsewhere.

It took proper understanding of the opportunities afforded by the new technology (such as the ability to split a CD into mini CD singles) before another giant step was taken when Farrow Design appropriated the language of drug packaging for the Spiritualized album 'Ladies and Gentlemen, we are Floating in Space'. The designs investigated the language of blistered foil packaging, in both single and multi-CD formats, that meticulously echoed the album's pharmaceutical vernacular and drops substantial hints at the other things to 'drop' when listening to the music.

Apparently not content with the breakthough he had acheived with the foil packages, Farrow and his team repeated his innovations four years later for the same band when he utilized a sculpture by Don Brown blind embossed into a rounded cornered plastic box. This created an extraordinary optical effect as the face appears to modulate between concave and convex forms.

Most of the recent shifts within design have come as a result of the changing role of technology. The advent of computerization heralded by the invention of the Macintosh computer in the 1980s saw a huge cultural chasm develop between the users and the disabusers of the new technology.

With the tools to apparently shift paradigms in place, and available to everyone, the established order within design refused to recognize the early pioneers in the new industry. But we can see now that the early work of the digital pioneers changed our perception of graphic design.

April Greiman became so obsessed with the possibilities of the computer that

ABOVE
Let it come down
Spiritualized CD packaging
FARROW DESIGN UK 2001

BELOW LEFT
Vitra workspirit brochure
APRIL GREIMAN
USA LATE 1980S

BELOW
'Bastard' type experiments
JONATHAN BARNBROOK
UK 1990

the low-resolution image of a robot on a brochure for Vitra became preferable to the actual photo – the pixels were literally preferred to the reality. Jonathon Barnbrook's type experiments that began at college established him as an early pioneer in the use of computer-based, hand-crafted fonts, whilst in California the team of Rudy VanderLans and Susannna Licko were channelling their radical design ideas through the mouthpiece of their publication, *Emigre*, where, like Greiman, they embraced the pixel-based shortcomings of the computer and

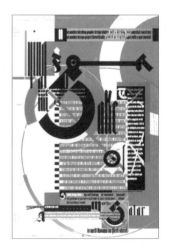

OAKLAND 6
OAKLAND 8
OAKLAND 10
OAKLAND 15

ABOVE
Oakland typefaces, *Emigre* fonts
EMIGRE USA 1985

RIGHT
Emigre cover, issue 19 using
the Keedy sans typeface
EMIGRE USA 1991

BELOW
Harvey Nichols 'Autumn Intrusion'
store front installation
THOMAS HEATHERWICK STUDIO
UK 1997

BOTTOM
Identity Crisis exhibition
THOMAS HEATHERWICK STUDIO
UK 1999

turned them into an advantage. When designer Jeffrey Keedy decided that the strange type in his local launderette was worthy of a typeface in its honour, we were to observe how fast the digital revolution had progressed – the typeface became the typeface of the world for one year only in 1991 as easily available desktop font software made it possible for anyone to grab their fifteen minutes of typographic fame.

But it's design in three dimensions that provides us with a fitting end to this chapter. One English designer, when presented with the opportunity to design an autumn shopfront for famous Knightsbridge fashion store Harvey Nichols, chose to break the paradigm of display cases completely when he created a curving three-dimensional structure that appeared to flow in and out of the glass windows themselves. Thomas Heatherwick, the brains behind this idea, then continued to show that he was more than a one-trick pony by creating blue public squares in Newcastle and exhibitions constructed entirely of cling film.

EMIGRE №19:
Starting From
Zero

Heatherwick encourages all of us that it *really is* possible to attain a massive shift away from the expected to the unexpected.

So it's simple: to genuinely attain a paradigm shift all you need is a great client, a great idea, no preconceptions at all of what will be the 'right' solution, some luck, hide like a rhino for deflecting criticism and, above all, courage. That seems easy enough, doesn't it? Good luck.

Problem: Magazine design needs a shake-up to survive, at least once a decade.

Solved: For the 1980s Neville Brody, for the 1990s, David Carson.

These two architects of design revolutions in the 1980s and 1990s both chose the medium of editorial design to test their ideas out on their initially unsuspecting public.

Editorial is, of course, ideally placed for experimentation – it has to happen fast, it's out in the public domain, then another edition comes along and you've often got space to experiment, to make mistakes without getting fired.

Neville Brody made his main historical mark with the fashion/style manual, *The Face*. His tenure as art director turned most of the then preconceptions of editorial design upside-down by introducing his own hand-drawn elements to establish a clear typographic style (taken from 1920s and 1930s typography and drawn laboriously, pre-computer, with pen and ruler).

He began experimenting and simply continued unabated – his influence was so great that by the end of the decade he had produced a book of his work, held an exhibition at London's Victoria & Albert Museum and was known the world over.

Whilst Brody loved to experiment, he still included photos of band members and broadly respected the magazine traditions of header, intro and body copy. David Carson was to ignore any such conventions – untrained in graphics, all his experimentation happened live. Unfettered by any degree of layout rules, Carson deliberately turned editorial design upside-down with the magazines *Beach Culture* and *Ray Gun*. When he thought his writer's piece on Bryan Ferry boring, he set the whole text in unreadable dingbats. Every issue brought radical rethinks of all the rules of magazine design. By the publication of his first book, his influence was such that he could legitimately title it *The End of Print* and watch in paradoxical satisfaction as it sold in many tens of thousands around the world.

Whilst the work of each of these innovators is inevitably time-locked purely by the popularity they achieved during their key 'moment', both designers' influence on that which followed has been immense. We await with some interest the key magazine influence of the twenty-first century.

ALL DESIGNS THIS SPREAD
NEVILLE BRODY UK

BELOW
The Face cover no. 39
1983

BOTTOM
The Face 'Killer' cover no. 59
1985

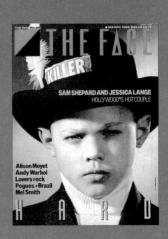

RIGHT
'Holidays in Hell' opener
1984

FAR RIGHT
'Avanti' opener
1986

BELOW
New Socialist cover
1986

BELOW RIGHT
Spreads from February, March issues
of *The Face* (utilizing same drop cap)
1985

HOLiDAYS IN H℮LL

You've trekked across the Himalayas, taken a train to Peking, gone topless at St. Tropez. You're been everywhere, seen everything and done it all twice. You're bored, jaded, blasé – but still useless. You want more than just a cheap holiday in someone else's misery. Next year, try Sumatra. Your pass will be valid until tax-day, after which you're on your own. Or Beirut, where you can sunbathe on the rockets fly overhead. Or how about Rio, or the Bronx, or even Amsterdam – all places that guarantee an extra frisson. We tell you how to get there, and how to die there.

avanti

A
ARENA

COMPILED BY STEVE TAYLOR, MICHAEL WATTS
STUDIO PHOTOGRAPHY DAVIES & STARR

STRONGER **VODKAS**...NEW
LOOK **BETTING SHOPS**...
MATTHEW HILTON'S **TUBULAR**
FURNITURE...**PAUL SMITH**
IN PARIS...THE MICRO-**CAMERA**
CHUNKY TYROLEAN FOOTWEAR...
SWISS ARMY KNIVES...THE
ELECTRONIC **ORGANISER**...

ARENA **10** WINTER

N℮W SOCIALIST

S T Y L E   W A R S

D A V I D   E D G A R   VERSUS
R O B E R T   E L M S

JUNE JORDAN: ISRAEL'S UNHOLY ALLIANCE
FEMINISM AND **CLASS POLITICS**

F A L L - O U T   O V E R   L I B Y A

THE glamourous liFe

arhol

ALL PROJECTS DAVID CARSON USA

FAR LEFT
Skateboarding contents page
1987

LEFT
Ray Gun extra large article
1993

BELOW
Ray Gun Bryan Ferry article
1994

BOTTOM
Beach Culture Tony Hawk article
1990

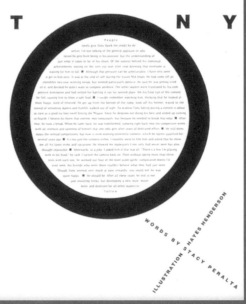

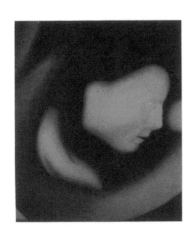

RIGHT
Ray Gun Frank Black article
1993

BELOW
Ray Gun Survical Research
Laboratories
1993

BELOW
Beach Culture
Hanging at Carmine Street
1991

BELOW RIGHT
Pepsi ads
WITH BBDO NY CIRCA 1994

The FUNNY BOO-HOO *problem*

It's the default setting of many creatives. Stuck for an idea? – use a funny. Like telling a joke to get an audience warmed up, there's no doubt that humour makes people warm to a person, a product, an ad. But what if it gets in the way of the real message and all we do is laugh at the joke, and forget everything else?

Like a good best-man's speech at a wedding, humour can really work. But as bad best-men the world over know, the jokes have to be appropriate and well-timed, otherwise it can all back-fire.

For centuries, designers and communicators have been using wit and humour to plant their messages in people's heads. Whilst a dependence on wit and whimsy may have burnt itself out by the end of the 1980s, there's no doubt that humour – at times legitimate, at times gratuitous – remains a powerful tool when used in the right hands and in the appropriate fashion.

Post-war graphic artists demostrated their joy at being able to bask in the mindless fun of commercial art; designers playfully mixed collage and humour in their layouts, which had a strong influence on a new

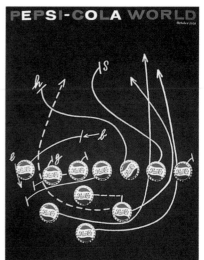

generation of designers. In New York, designers such as Robert Brownjohn, Ivan Chermayeff and Tom Geismar began a period of wholesale experimentation that still stands as a fabulous body of work forty years later.

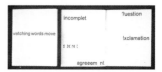

Whether it was the bizarre collage and engraving madness of Pushpin Studios or the meticulous typography of Herb Lubalin, this concentration of designers on the US East Coast had a profound influence on world design. On moving to London in the early 1960s, Brownjohn found more opportunities to ply his trade across many disciplines, whilst his fellow exile Bob Gill had established a close partnership with the men (Alan Fletcher and Colin Forbes) that would go on to form Pentagram.[1]

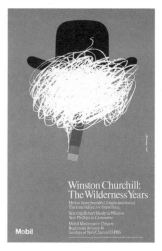

Gill's own particular approach to problem-solving is best characterized by his page from this 1976 calendar. When asked to submit a page, Gill's response was to track down the hairiest (and possibly smelliest) student he could find and persuade him to have his beard and hair chopped off bit by bit, with a photographer on hand to record the process. Gill simply reversed the pictures for his day-by-day picture diary. And it

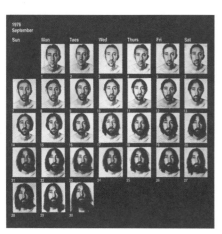

ABOVE TOP & ABOVE LEFT
Covers for Pepsi-Cola world
BROWNJOHN CHERMAYEFF
AND GEISMAR USA 1950S

ABOVE MIDDLE
Watching words move
BROWNJOHN CHERMAYEFF
AND GEISMAR USA 1959–60

ABOVE
Winston Churchill poster
CHERMAYEFF AND GEISMAR USA 1982

LEFT
Calendar page
BOB GILL USA 1976

ABOVE
National Portrait Gallery poster
PENTAGRAM UK 1990

RIGHT
IBM art poster
PENTAGRAM UK 1983

BELOW LEFT & RIGHT
CJS Plants corporate identity
THE PARTNERS UK 1985

CJS Plants
Plant Display
Unit 9
Poyntz Road
London
SW11 5BH
Tel 01-228 0333

always provokes a smile – we know it is ridiculous for hair to grow at that speed but it doesn't matter, it's funny, we let it go.

His ex-partner Alan Fletcher has become one of the world's finest exponents of the visual pun. Whether it involves forming snow blizzards of thumbprints or identikit pictures of Prince Charles out of other portraits for the National Gallery, Fletcher's is a rich and sophisticated language.

Producing one of his finest solutions, when asked to supply posters to 'mark time' in a blue-chip reception area before 'real' art arrived, he based his ideas and solutions upon famous quotations on art. The way he managed to turn simple words into amusing and playful solutions is arguably more interesting than the art that eventually replaced the posters. A great example of how far the creative mind can leap when given enough time, a bit of budget and relatively few restrictions.

The baton of wit has been passed on (within the UK at least) to The Partners, whose ability to infuse humour into many of the projects that they attract is neatly summed up by this piece for a landscape gardener. The starting place, as is often the case, is an English pun or saying, in this case the phrase 'green fingers' used for botanically-minded people. But what could have been clumsily treated is cleverly played – the green fingerprints appear on the fronts and backs of stationery, exactly where you would hold the paper. Even the white van has green prints by the side of the door handles.

"Every work of art is a child of its time."
–Wassily Kandinsky

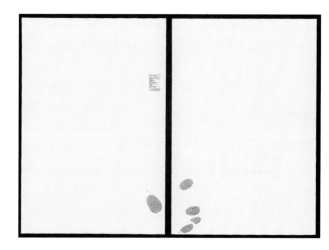

British designer John Gorham was one of the unsung heroes of finely crafted, witty British design for more than three decades. Whether through his work, his stints as a teacher or design consultant to his impressive list of clients, collaborators and ex-students, Gorham produced idea after idea that often looked completely different from those that preceded them.

He had no perceivable style that he felt he needed to fall back on and he displayed few or none of the modernist tendencies of his peers. His was straightforward, gut-level design – more likely to be influenced by a sweet-wrapper found lying on the pavement than whatever stylistic tic had gripped those around him.

Gorham's skill was to apply a witty, crafted twist to almost everything he worked upon; he found the humorous angle in things as theoretically tedious as a typeface catalogue (by making typefaces out of type and faces, for example).

Paradoxically, making something that *is* funny *seem* funny is probably the most difficult brief there is. Theoretically a dream poster brief, the poster for an American conference on humour received the obligatory 'banana skin' humour pun from the

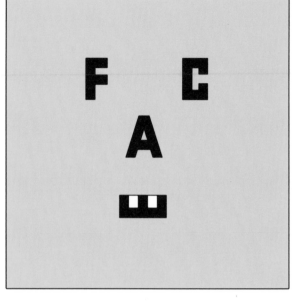

ABOVE
Face Photosetting symbol
JOHN GORHAM UK 1974

LEFT
Face catalogue cover
JOHN GORHAM/
HOWARD BROWN/PETER BLAKE
UK 1970S
Gorham and Brown imagined what the Gill family would look like if they had letters for heads

BELOW LEFT
AIGA humour show poster
M&CO USA 1986

appointed agency. It was given a witty twist by being terribly cropped by the printer, but the designers couldn't resist placing hand-written scribbles onto the artwork saying things like 'watch the crop, it's for the AIGA' and suchlike, rather over-doing the joke and turning it into pastiche.

It seems that humour is much more successful with unknowingly boring subject matter. As with comedy, most people laugh at the straight man, not the funny one. Laurel is the funny one, not Hardy.

OPPOSITE TOP
Nynex ads
CHIAT DAY MOJO USA 1991
The magnetic sheep is a teaser ad for the category 'Steel Wool'

OPPOSITE BELOW LEFT
Yellow Pages cover designs
JOHNSON BANKS UK 1998–2000

OPPOSITE BELOW RIGHT
Yellow Pages poster
AMV BBDO UK 1998

Letterheads

If it's out there, it's in here. **NYNEX** Yellow Pages

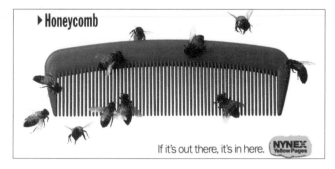

Honeycomb

If it's out there, it's in here. **NYNEX** Yellow Pages

Bulldozing

If it's out there, it's in here. **NYNEX** Yellow Pages

Hair Tinting

If it's out there, it's in here. **NYNEX** Yellow Pages

RIVETS

All you need for all you want

YELLOW PAGES
www.yell.com

So, on either side of the Atlantic it comes as no great surprise that products as dull as telephone directories should receive some witty work.

When Nynex decided to advertise their wares, they began with a strange-looking picture of a blue hare. This was a teaser.

Soon the body copy arrived, and we realized that it was an ad for hair tinting services found in the directory. Pun-meistering of the highest order and almost cringe-inducing (but hilarious just the same).

From letter-heads to cow-hides and honey-combs, Nynex and their agency Chiat Day Mojo repeatedly brought magic to what must qualify as one of the world's most boring subject matters. In the UK, all seventy-six editions in fifteen years of the Yellow Pages had the same dull old cover. In 1998 they realized a) they could change the covers each time a new book was printed, b) the directory was associated with the colour yellow and c) although it was really only the place that people went to in a panic about a plumber, there was actually a warmth of feeling towards the brand. So a series of yellow covers was developed, with comical pictures and references to categories (sunflowers for art galleries, fish for swimming instructors etc). Meanwhile, the ad agency had woken up to yellow too, and had responded with more silliness – pictures of frogs for the category 'rivets' – get it?

(Be careful with the Kaminomoto)

Toyota Spacio

Faced with a bizarre brief for an Asian tonic promoting hair growth called Kaminomoto (but unable by law to mention the words hair-tonic), The Ball Partnership produced a classic twist on the 'before and after' scenario by showing (in an extreme form) what the product might do to eggs and the like.

Another Singaporean agency, confronted with doing press ads for faceless and characterless (but well-built, safe and family-focused) Toyota cars, responded with an hilarious take on safety by featuring bubble-wrapped children, then echoed another car's home comforts with a set of dining room chairs neatly arranged in the form of a people carrier. The same rule – of boring being a great opportunity – seems to apply in packaging too. Wart ointment and battery packs seem that much more entertaining when transformed into animals and witch removal cream.

ABOVE LEFT
Kaminomoto hair tonic ad
THE BALL PARTNERSHIP
SINGAPORE 1980S

ABOVE AND LEFT
Toyota Spacio and Corolla ads
SAATCHI & SAATCHI
SINGAPORE 1999

BELOW
Boots Wart Remover packaging
LIPPA PEARCE UK 1992

BELOW RIGHT
Boots battery packs
LEWIS MOBERLY UK 1998

Corolla. For overprotective parents.

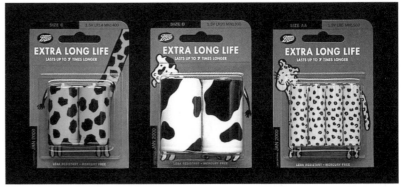

p-o-t-a-t-o

Humour, of course, has the ability to satirize, and this has been used to vicious effect by designers to lampoon politicians' errors over many years. Dan Quayle's infamous gaffe over the precise spelling of a root vegetable was immediately tortured by M&CO. The appearance by ex-British prime-minister Margaret Thatcher in the 2001 general election campaign enabled the Labour Party's agency to indulge swiftly in a bit of photo-collage whereby they affixed the hair of the ex-leader on to Conservative leader William Hague's head. American artist Robbie Conal has viciously portrayed decades of US presidents in his gruesome, 'melted-face' style of drawing.

Get out and vote. Or they get in.

Labour
www.labour.org.uk

IT CAN'T HAPPEN

HERE

But a personal favourite is this poster from the early 1970s, inspired by 'tricky Dickie' Nixon's manoeuvring over the Watergate scandal, with a large photograph of him, out of focus, and the accompanying (and now historic) phrase 'let me make myself perfectly clear'.

HAIL TO THE

THIEF

CONTRA

DICTION

"Let me make myself perfectly clear."

TOP LEFT
P-o-t-a-t-o postcard
M&CO USA 1992

TOP RIGHT
Hague/Thatcher poster
TBWA\LONDON UK 2001

ABOVE, RIGHT & MIDDLE RIGHT
American president series
ROBBIE CONAL USA 1997–2000

FAR RIGHT
'Let me make myself perfectly clear'
Nixon poster
SYNERGISMS USA 1971

The satirical skills of the retoucher's mouse can also make us recoil – these images from *Colors* magazine illustrated global views on racism by altering the racial identity of iconic figures, whether heads of state or Hollywood idols. But such skills are often applied to make a political point; no-one is completely sure where this photo composition of George Bush's face and a Muslim headdress originated, but as an internet 'meme' it rocketed around the globe so fast it appeared on placards in central Asian rallies within a week of its first viewing.

Interestingly, identity design remains largely impervious to the influence of wit – probably because a blue-chip faced with economic downturn may not want to present a relentlessly witty face to the world, especially if having to report negative growth or a slashed dividend to a group of disgruntled shareholders.

Whilst Paul Rand may regularly have been able to imbue his designs for Westinghouse and UPS with a degree of charm, most humour at identity level seems restricted to the province of the lesser client or one-man band.

A great exponent of this is Texan designer Woody Pirtle – whether it be for a construction company, a hairdresser or a copywriter, his skill is to turn a small black and white logo into something special.

In advertising, humour seems to provide the branding quick fix and the ability to establish companies very quickly in the minds of consumers.

TOP LEFT & RIGHT
Images from *Colors* magazine
TIBOR KALMAN USA 1993

ABOVE MIDDLE
George Bush/Taliban
BUSH FOR DUMMIES.COM 2001

ABOVE
Westinghouse and UPS logos
PAUL RAND USA 1960, 1961

BELOW LEFT
Aubrey Hair logo
WOODY PIRTLE USA 1976

FAR LEFT
'Hot Seat' Knoll poster
WOODY PIRTLE USA 1980

THIS PAGE
Outpost.com TV stills
CLIFF FREEMAN & PARTNERS
USA 1998

From pizza delivery men at boot camp, to tattooed children, to make-believe Turkish sports programmes, Cliff Freeman & Partners have come to be mischief vendors to the American public.

At a time when European advertising was passing through an especially dour and serious stage, Freeman's agency, on the other side of the Atlantic, started to work in a completely unhinged style that firmly re-established New York as the hot-bed of thirty seconds of silliness.

A great example of this are the ads run for

Outpost.com, a company that specializes in home and office computer supplies. At the height of dotcom fever, as its competitors frantically jostled for the real estate of people's memories, Outpost needed to get its name remembered.

So it ignored completely what it actually provided as a service and went right for the jugular of name recognition – burly men were filmed tattooing Outpost.com onto children's foreheads, viewers were warned that they would see a pack of ravenous wolves attacking a teenage marching band, gerbils were fired through holes in walls (or not, as the soundtrack let us know with cruelly timed 'clunks' as one gerbil after another hit the wall).

Outrageous, and outrageously funny. 'These commercials were designed to upset people or get their attention' said one of the creators at the time – 'kids, animals and violence, these are three sacred areas you never touch. We wanted to do that.'

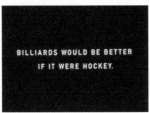

The stricture placed on scripts by twenty or thirty seconds of TV sometimes plays right into the hands of this type of comedy writer.

Approached more like sketches than actual ads, Fox Sports demonstrated their sports focus with this hilarious series of ads; firstly asking why one sport couldn't be more like another (and graphically illustrating it on screen), then emphasizing the importance of local sports in a region by showing the viewer how sport looks on screen in India, China and Turkey. Freeman's agency has been dubbed 'post-modern' or 'oddvertising',[2] but it doesn't really need a label, it's just funny. Critics might have queried the Outpost ads, but they added 15,000 new clients after airing. 'Silly' can also be successful too.

When we descend to the level of snack food, all remnants of taste are removed and the gloves are well and truly off as ridiculous humour is used to sell us the latest snack. In a clever double twist, the European campaign for the meat snack Pepperami is based on the line, 'it's a bit of an animal'.

Of course, it is, literally, a bit of an animal, but the line also sets up the angry meat stick character to behave abominably, at one point even eating itself, it is so hungry.

In Japan, a long-running campaign for Cup Noodle features a team of marauding stick-waving cavemen racing across the screen before they are chased back by an equally marauding woolly mammoth. Presumably the desired response is – 'it's easier to eat a Cup Noodle'.

The British equivalent recently featured a team of beer-bellied pub-goers (some might say the true target audience) in a bizarre spoof on the Sharks and Jets fight scene from *West Side Story*.

LEFT
Fox Sports TV stills
CLIFF FREEMAN & PARTNERS
USA 1997

BELOW MIDDLE
Pepperami TV stills
STILL PRICE LINTAS UK 1993

BELOW BOTTOM
Cup Noodle ad
TAKUYA ONUKI JAPAN EARLY 1990S

OPPOSITE TOP
Super Noodles TV stills
MOTHER UK 2001

OPPOSITE BOTTOM
Cinzano TV still
COLLETT DICKENSON PEARCE UK
1978

The 'just add water' approach to instant brand-building that humour can provide is very persuasive, and when, worldwide, down-to-earth products like instant noodles abandon any pretence at style for easy laughs, it's understandable. It's 'fits with the brand' as marketing men would say.

But an example from the archives show us that whilst the public may love your ads, as they did with this famous series for Cinzano starring Leonard Rossiter and Joan Collins, they may still prefer someone else's product (the sales of rival Martini went up).[3]

Unfortunately, being entertaining isn't always enough – people need a genuine reason to buy one product over another, not just the entertainment it provides in the ad breaks between the soaps.

Problem: Department stores aren't particularly funny places.

Solved: They are, if you're Takuya Onuki.

It's hard to envisage that Takuya Onuki's work for the Laforet store could exist in any other city of the world but Tokyo. Imagine, for a moment, a Bloomingdales ad featuring naked (except for their underpants) business men and women grouped around a flipchart. Or Selfridges running a poster of construction men with pixellated sculptures instead of heads. Unlikely, isn't it?

Onuki's bizarre take on the world has many potential patrons, but his long-running alliance with the Harajuku store has given the world an astonishing body of the weirdest and funniest images. Only the Laforet fishtank can be quite as full as the one below. Only Laforet could advertise their 'grand bazar' with a burning frying pan (see overleaf). Only Laforet would print their name on the end of your nose or in the smallest of small print.

Baffling, ironic, post-modernism or just downright silly? Who knows, and in many respects, who cares? As advertising moves away from its formal roots and towards art, it is the art of Onuki that will catch the eye and tickle your ribs.

THIS SPREAD
AND FOLLOWING SPREAD
Laforet department store posters
TAKUYA ONUKI JAPAN 1990–2000

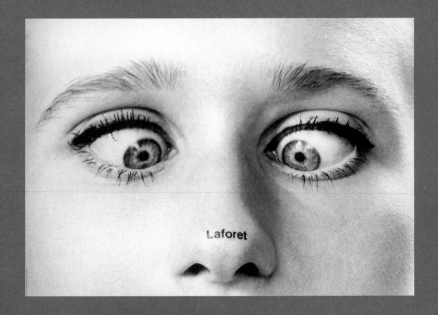

Laforet

The NOTHING SHOCKS ME *problem*

Whether it is decreased attention spans or just jaded visual palettes, communicators around the world often resort to shock tactics to get their message across. But how often are their tactics legitimate, and do they work? What happens if it's just shocking for shock's sake and has little to do with the actual product or service on offer?

Resorting to shock tactics is unsurprising: in an increasingly visually frenetic world, getting a message through the general level of noise becomes more and more difficult.

When dealing with illustrations of genuine plight the tactic is understandable and appropriate. When Luba Lukova placed a nutritional values chart inside the head of the Sudanese child, hers was a heartfelt plea – 'Africa is starving, please understand (and please help).' 'How much longer can we live here?' asks this poster of a plastic world filled with earth, split asunder.

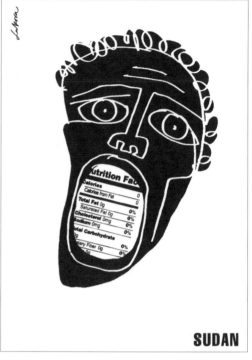

SUDAN

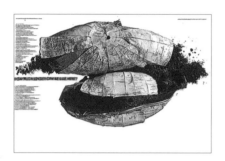

The sight of our world burst and mutilated is a shocking but compelling one. As attempts to illustrate world issues, then, these posters have more than adequately done their job.

But when we contrast them with a worldwide distributor of woollen and cotton clothes, Benetton, and their campaigns based on the harsh realities of humanity, we enter a much trickier area. Whilst the power of their campaigns featuring dying AIDS victims and new-born babies undoubtedly raised the profile of the company and generated nautical miles of press coverage worldwide, we are left with a nasty taste in our mouths and the overriding question 'What has all this got to do with woolly jumpers?'.

Benetton's strategy was further blurred by their parallel house style of squeaky-clean, beautiful children of the world, meticulously shot on pristine white backgrounds, smiling down on the horrors of the world on posters around them, apparently thinking, 'We're fine, we're beautiful, it doesn't affect us'.

The confusion levels ratcheted up another notch when the company started their magazine, *Colors*. This gave editorial *carte blanche* to an international team which, unshackled from traditional magazine requirements, was able to explore AIDS,

ABOVE
Sudan poster
LUBA LUKOVA USA 2000

ABOVE LEFT
'How much longer can we live here?'
Peace poster
YUKIO IKOMA JAPAN 1992

BELOW
Benetton Aids victim ad
OLIVIERO TOSCANI ITALY 1992

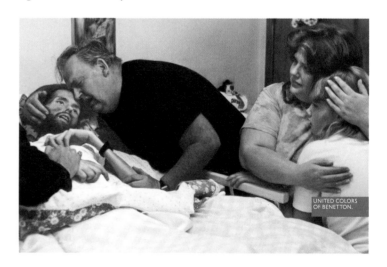

UNITED COLORS OF BENETTON.

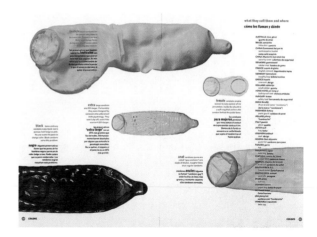

gang culture, the shape of the world's condoms, whatever they wanted. If Benetton's problem was 'make us appear much more than just clothes, make us appear like the moral guardians of the world' then that one was well solved. And into the annals of design history the layouts go, but not before we wonder what the point of all this was.

Clearly the ads had struck a chord – perhaps buying your socks from this particular shop really was an attempt by you, the consumer, to cleanse your soul of the horrors of the world via the 'caring' image of the Benetton brand.

But for the advertising at least, the end of its first era came when a campaign featuring American death-row inmates titled 'We on Death Row' was researched under the guise of journalists working for a weekly news magazine.[1] This may have been acceptable, but then the supplement was adapted for a worldwide advertising campaign that featured serial killers on the world's billboard sites.

Whilst one of its co-creators suggested that it succeeded in its goal of 'presenting a human view of the person the state seeks to kill', it met with a barrage of public and media criticism. Couple that with the outrage of the relatives of the victims of inmates now emblazoned on the world's poster sites and it hastened the departure of Benetton's creative director and the return to smiley, happy, cut-out people.

Public distaste for the departed creative (Olivier Toscani) even found extra voice in an anti-Toscani ad mocked up for a suburban bus shelter.

Benetton had shown that appropriating shock tactics can't be approached lightly. The itchy moral high ground they had taken was eventually going to be scratched, even if it took eighteen years.

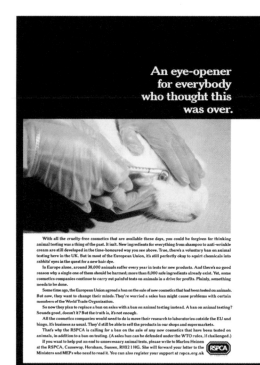

It seems that we are much more attuned to the horrors of the world when they are shown in 'legitimate' advertising appeals. Charities such as the Royal Society for the Prevention of Cruelty to Animals (RSPCA) have repeatedly gone for the visual jugular when trying to build attention-grabbing campaigns.

The skills of the world's ad agencies at 'shockvertising', whether it be crucified children or blood-soaked fur on the catwalk, have even led to many of the world's award schemes amending their rules for the entry of charity advertising. So powerful (and successful) had charity-based ads become that this ad for a rule change in a well-known competition felt compelled to lampoon the style of the sector with the line 'Here's a dead dog. Where's my award?'.

ABOVE TOP
RSPCA Eye Opener ad
AMV BBDO UK 1990S

ABOVE LEFT
Lady Mayoress Relief Fund
OMON AUSTRALIA 1989
Kings Cross was the drugs centre of Sydney at the time of this ad which explains the crucifix/cross reference

ABOVE
Greenpeace TV stills
YELLOWHAMMER UK 1985

LEFT
'Here's a dead dog...' ad
SAATCHI & SAATCHI AUSTRALIA 1991

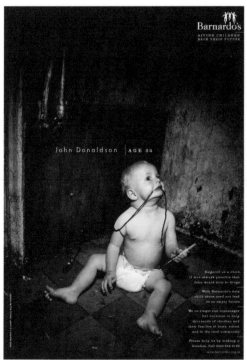

But, as ever, when appropriate, shock works. This campaign for Barnardo's cleverly showed us the plight of the future twenty-year-old drug-user or suicide victim by focusing on the child that they once were. The sight of a small child attempting to shoot up shocks our senses, we know it is wrong, we want to do something about it (problem solved). In a bizarre twist to their campaign, when told that their next ad had been banned from a particular magazine, they ran a picture of a perfect, smiling, bouncy baby which seemed just as shocking as the ads that had preceded it, because the reader was expecting something much worse.

That example worked because of its incongruity; sometimes shock succeeds more by stealth. When designing a poster for a competition notorious for its style-obsessed entrants the designer found a way to address his own personal dilemmas concerning the state of his profession by asking his four-year-old daughter to write the copy out for him. To see the childish scrawl of a series of existential questions places the viewer in a serious quandary: is he being critical or not? Is he questioning his own design by deliberately not designing it?

Designers have become adept at using images that at first sight seem innocuously beautiful before revealing hidden messages. Stephen Doyle's AIGA posters jar because we don't understand why he has crudely painted WAS on the rusty saw, and his image of books seems innocuous until we see that the bolt has been crudely drilled throughout both volumes, rendering them almost completely useless in the process.

ABOVE LEFT & RIGHT
Barnardo's campaign
BARTLE BOGLE HEGARTY
UK 1999–2000

BELOW LEFT & MIDDLE
ACD 'saw' & AIGA 'If A ...' posters
DRENTTEL DOYLE PARTNERS
USA 1994–5

BELOW FAR RIGHT
American Center for Design
100 Show Call for Entries poster
PENTAGRAM USA 1992

The poster shown right for an exhibition at the Stedelijk Museum in Amsterdam on Uruguay, Argentina, Brazil and Chile uses the visual vehicle of cake and cookie cutters. But it's more sinister than it seems – at another level the designer is criticizing the regime that he is meant to promote – he has used human hair and raw meat to fill his pastry shapes, not dough.[2] Other good examples of images that

shock, amuse and jar all at the same time are these for the British band Gay Dad.

The appropriation of the neutral traffic figure leaves us confused – there is no attempt to change the figure's shape or proportion, it is simply re-presented with the strangely dichotomous name of the band beside it.

And before the advent of celebrity copy approval, magazines were able to harness the power of subtle shock, such as this article from the turn of the 1970s predicting how the stars of the time might look when middle-aged. Now in the more litigious twenty-first century we marvel that anyone could have run such a piece (and how right – and wrong –

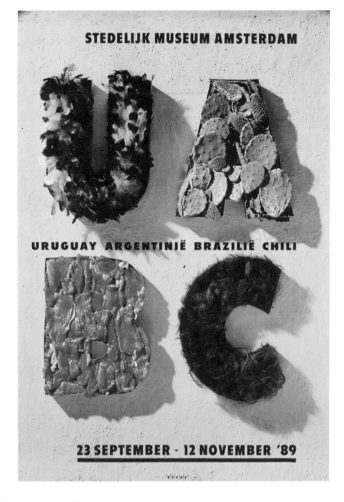

STEDELIJK MUSEUM AMSTERDAM

URUGUAY ARGENTINIË BRAZILIË CHILI

23 SEPTEMBER - 12 NOVEMBER '89

At present we neglect and dislike old people

some of the illustrators predictions had been).

But the global advertising industry remains the most effective user of subtle shock, none more so than in this

ABOVE
UABC poster
ANTON BEEKE
THE NETHERLANDS 1989

ABOVE LEFT
Gay Dad CD sleeve for 'Leisure Noise'
PETER SAVILLE UK 1999

LEFT
Sunday Times Magazine article
MICHAEL RAND UK 1970

French ad for the PlayStation games console. Only on second glance do we see that the figure on the worshipped cross above the bed is actually an all-action heroine, not Jesus.

This Australian surf-wear ad shows the product surviving undigested (unlike its owner) inside the stomach of a dead shark in a bizarre twist on the principle of product placement. And in the heady world of salad cream and mayonnaise, London agency Leo Burnett managed to shock, amuse and disgust, simultaneously, with their campaign which implies that this particular brand is so supreme in taste that it enhances the quality of all meals, even if they are left-overs in the sink or lost dogs. Truly disgusting (but truly brilliant). But distil shock tactics down to

one recurring ingredient and we are always left with the human form. Nudity and regularly-exposed body parts retain the capacity to surprise the prudes in all of us and designers and advertisers still capitalize on this to achieve the greatest reaction.

Ever since now vanished Welsh guitarist Richey Edwards of the Manic Street Preachers

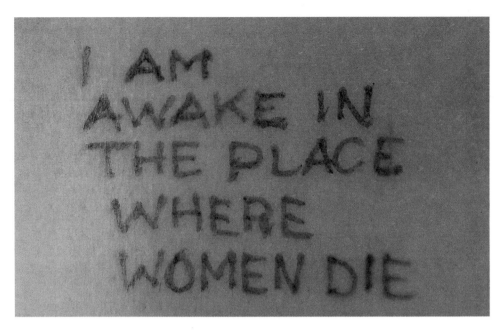

carved '4 Real' into his arm in front of a music journalist, designers across the world seem to have written and carved messages into themselves in order to gain attention. Jenny Holzer and Tibor Kalman mixed irradiated blood into printing ink to enhance the power of their series of graffiti confessions for *Süddeutsche Zeitung* magazine.

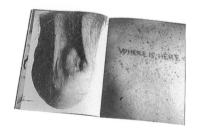

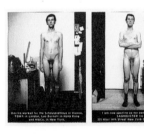

Austrian-born designer Stefan Sagmeister (high-priest of self-abuse in the graphic sense) reaches as regularly for his scalpel as others reach for their type books. Often utilizing the technique of carving type on his own body for promotional, polemical pieces or to publicize his talks within the industry, he has taken the notion of suffering for his art to a whole new and painful level.

Of course, when it comes to other sins of the flesh,

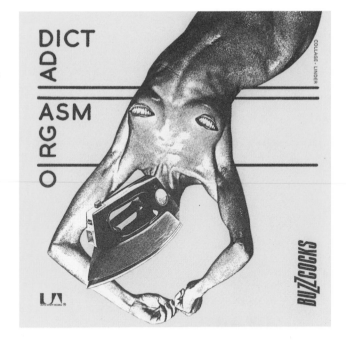

designers and advertisers have been trying to use the human (especially the female) body to sell us all manner of products for years. Whether it is breasts as type, as in this ad for Vogue.com, or talking breasts and an iron-like head in this seminal piece for Manchester punk band the Buzzcocks, the willingness of art directors to mess about

with bodies shows no sign of letting up. At least Anton Beeke lets both sides have an equal say; in this extraordinary triptych of posters for the Dutch theatre group Toneelgroep, Beeke has amplified the emotions (and indeed the organs) of both sexes for an astonishing poster set only accepted in the relaxed environment of a city like Amsterdam.

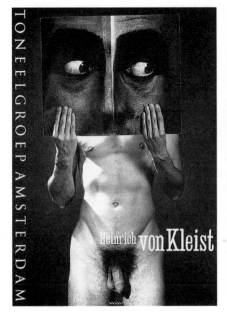

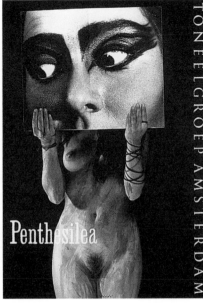

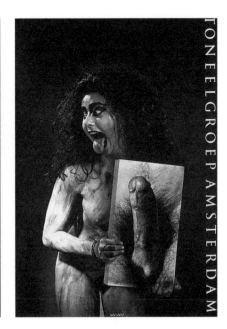

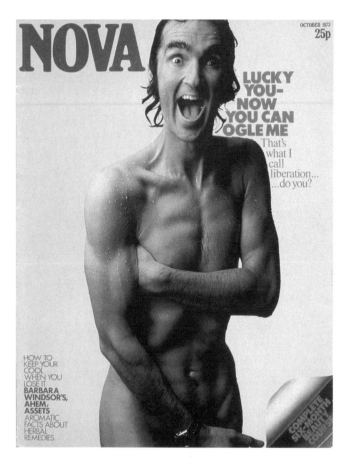

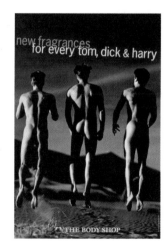

Only occasionally, as in this famous *Nova* cover and this Body Shop poster are we presented with the naked male form. The true default, the 'Times Roman' of art director settings, depressingly, still seems to be the naked or semi-naked woman. However degrading some might find Eva Herzogovia's wicked look, it seemingly tapped into the psyche of thousands of women as sales of Wonderbras rocketed (as did those of their competitors).

ABOVE
Tom Dick & Harry poster
THE BODY SHOP
UK 1995

LEFT
Nova magazine cover
DAVID HILLMAN
UK 1974

BELOW
'Hello Boys' Wonderbra poster
TBWA SIMONS PALMER
UK 1994

Instead of rejecting the image of the impossibly beautiful woman, womankind embraced her (and wanted to wear her bra).[3]

But perhaps we should leave the last word in this chapter to an undoubted master, Niklaus Troxler. Having experimented with mutilated arms and fingers as iconic devices for a series of theatre and jazz posters, when asked to contribute to an environmental poster series all he had to do was show us the stumps of Tote Bäume (Dead Trees) to make his point. Poignant and poetic, probably shocking, but definitely not gratuitous. And not a naked body in sight.

ABOVE TOP
Cecil Taylor Solo poster
NIKLAUS TROXLER
SWITZERLAND 1989

ABOVE
Irene Schweizer,
Buschi Niebergau,
Allen Blairman poster
NIKLAUS TROXLER
SWITZERLAND 1973

RIGHT
Tote Bäume (Dead Trees)
NIKLAUS TROXLER
SWITZERLAND 1992
*Asked to submit a poster
design to illustrate the plight
of the environment, Troxler
chose to illustrate an image
of dead trees. Shigeo Fukuda
called this poster a 'requiem
to our silent planet'*

Problem: Producing compelling ideas, when posters seem to have lost their power.

Solved: The haunting images of Makoto Saito.

There are few greater exponents in the world of shock tactics than Japanese designer Makoto Saito.

But his is not a world of gratuitous imagery, of obvious references, or of clear and simple communication. His images are oblique and complex, thick with meaning.

His poster for a Buddhist altar manufacturer just uses a photograph of a bone and a few pieces of type. But the bone has been sprayed blue, and the type reads 'I am the ancestor of the future.' And no-one can forget this piece once they have seen it, such is its power.

Nor do his images for his other clients easily leave the memory – 'The Cross' (shown opposite) features five posters of parts of one body linked by thin coloured lines which are designed to be presented together in a crucifix shape.

His use of collaged photos and surreal compositions give his work for galleries and retailers enormous power.

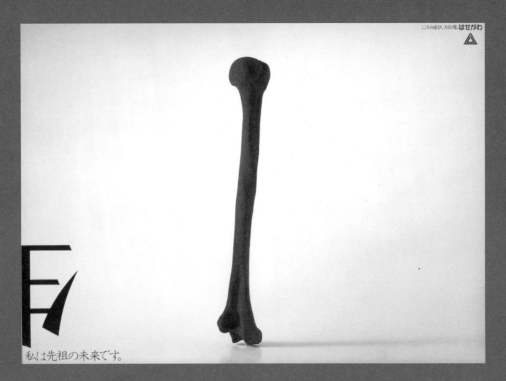

ALL POSTERS BY
MAKOTO SAITO JAPAN

ABOVE
Dance Hall posters
1986

LEFT AND BELOW
Hasegawa posters
1985

OPPOSITE PAGE
Image Mirror II
'Parts of the Body – The Cross'
1988

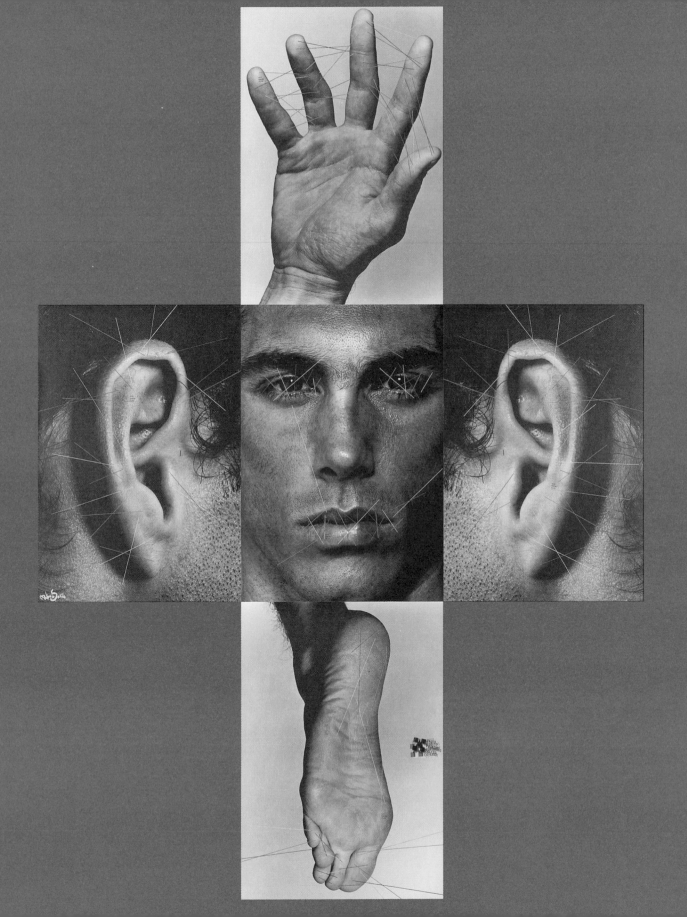

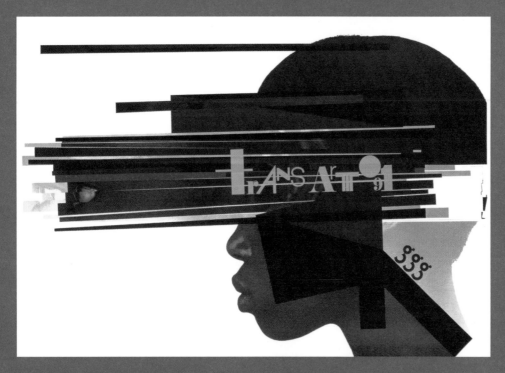

Whilst western clients would probably object to the lack of prominence given to his patrons' logos, Saito's Japanese clients seem to be more than happy to see him as a master image-maker. As he moves from one dislocated view of the human form to another, he beomes the creator of disturbed dreams that enhance products and brands more by oblique association than by any direct reference.

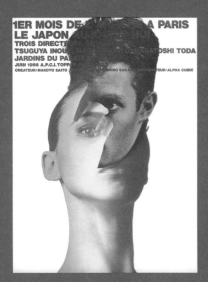

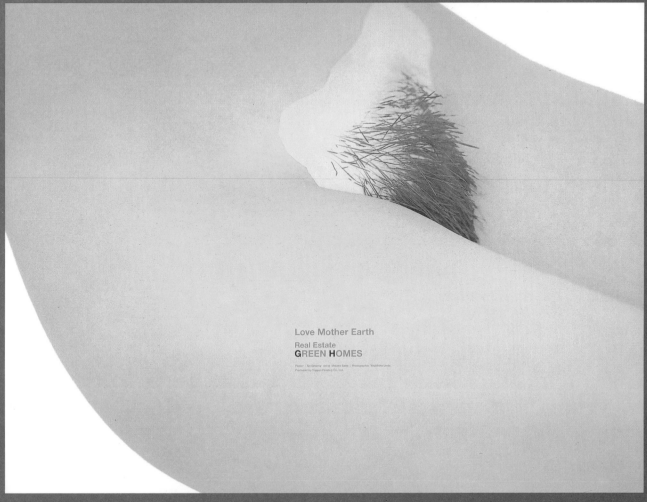

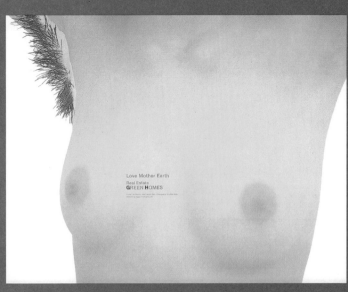

OPPOSITE TOP LEFT AND RIGHT
Trans Art 91 GGG gallery poster
1991

OPPOSITE FAR LEFT
Poster exhibition in Paris
1986

OPPOSITE RIGHT
Virgin Japan poster
1991

ABOVE AND RIGHT
Love Mother Earth posters
2001

The EVOLVE OR REVOLVE *problem*

Very few ideas, brands or identities survive unchanged forever – something eventually has to give. But inertia often sets in and a client won't trade what they have for a radical change. 'There's so much goodwill in our name', they plead. 'People know that typeface as ours', they claim. So, many hours are spent discussing the degree of change. Surprise, surprise, it's always much easier to muddle through and evolve a brand or corporate identity than to stare into the abyss of revolution. Is it always the correct decision?

Once it was simple. You had an idea, you started a company, you picked a few names out of the dictionary that you liked, rang a graphic designer and got them to bash out a logo and, hey presto! you were legitimate. You were in business.

Things have changed. There may be compelling reasons for companies to radically revise their identity but the barriers to change have become considerable. More often than not, they are more comfortable with the known than the unknown.

While it may frustrate their magic-marker wielding consultants, most established companies often quite rightly feel their name, their reputation, their image has to be worth something. 'If we were that bad, surely we would have gone out of business', comes the common observation.

Of course it doesn't take a lot for an incoming chief executive to bring in a few contacts from a previous life 'to have a little look at where we might take the brand'. After many months of analysis and graphic soul-searching, they reach the sticky bit, usually aided with a few visuals.

'Our choice, gentlemen, is this – we either go through radical revolution and re-name ourselves SYNERGISTICON (holds up board) or we take our current logo, re-draw it slightly and brighten the blue a shade.' Well, it takes quite a ballsy executive to stand up at that point and make a case for SYNERGISTICON, doesn't it?

No surprise then, that the world's brand consultants regularly rack up fees equivalent to the GDP of Guadalupe,[1] tweaking a logo here or mending a logo there. Having been persuaded to remove their 'T' logo in the face of similar marks in Spain (Telefonica) and Hong Kong (Hong Kong Telecom), British Telecom introduced a radical change in the form of the now infamous piper symbol. The idea at the core of the piper symbol, that of listening with a cupped hand then speaking through his pipe, was relevant then and still is now to a communications business. Some argued that its sinuous curves were liable to

date fast, and many of the users of the symbol within the company came to dislike the mark. But after a while a logo becomes just another logo, losing its impact and becoming 'the thing in the corner of the ad next to the telephone number and the web address'.

Ten years after its introduction, an identity review by a different branding

BELOW
Hong Kong Telecom logo
HENRY STEINER HONG KONG 1978

BOTTOM LEFT
BT logo
WOLFF OLINS UK 1989

BOTTOM RIGHT
British Telecom identity
BANKS AND MILES UK 1984

agency came to the unsurprising conclusion that people had got accustomed to the piper; it should be kept, the size of the piper should change slightly and BT should amend the shade of the red and blue. Oh, and that'll be several million[2] in implementation fees, thanks very much.

Interestingly, one of the most famous logos of all time, for IBM, was itself an evolution of a blocky serif piece of type previously used as a useful piece of shorthand by the company known as International Business Machines.

The designer, Paul Rand, took his time, experimenting with different lined versions for a couple of years before finalizing the version we now know. Rand's sway over his client was such that he even had the opportunity a few years later to amend his original proposal and change the famous stripes. (Imagine trying that now: 'Hey, you know that logo I did for you a few years back? I'd like to tweak it slightly if you don't mind.')

The strength of Rand's work lay in the consistency and energy he put into the applications of the identity throughout a relationship which spanned many decades, treating each toner cartridge or ribbon box with the same respect as an annual report cover.

Sometimes there is logic in incremental change. Federal Express, for example, was referred to for years by their nickname, FedEx.

When they finally got around to reflecting this in their identity, they did so with skill and subtlety, even incorporating an arrow symbol within the 'e' and 'x' of the new mark (can you see it?) and keeping their old name in full underneath, just in case.

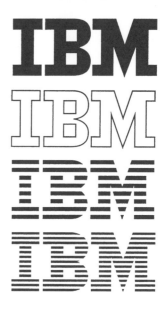

It is an example of the 'evolve' problem that comes through the process with flying colours, with the name that everyone used anyway, and a better symbol to boot.

The merger of the two oil giants BP and Amoco provided a different opportunity for the image-makers to ply their art. In BP's case, theirs was already a much-meddled-with symbol. Whilst Shell's approach has been to review and adapt their marque steadily over the years, BP's has been more schizophrenic. They had investigated amending their shield device in the 1970s, only to conclude that they shouldn't change and only to click the 'italicize' button on the symbol in the 1980s and come out with a slanted version. A merger with Amoco necessitated another review – somehow they had to imply that BP no longer stood for British Petroleum, that it stood for something altogether more in keeping with a transatlantic alliance of, well, oil companies, but ones that really did care about the environmental aspects of oil. So we have (cue fanfare) a new environmental flower device, the same colours (only brighter), and a board of directors keen for us to understand that the B and the P no longer stands for petroleum from Britain but 'Beyond Petroleum'. Having re-launched in a blaze of publicity the company hastily distanced from the positioning (perhaps realizing how troublesome it could become).[3]

Some companies have even managed to develop a boomerang version of evolve/revolve. The North American Space Agency (known more commonly as NASA) had developed, a flying planets and stars symbol (known as 'The Meatball') for badging their spacecraft.

TOP LEFT
BP logo
FLETCHER FORBES GILL
UK 1968–70

TOP RIGHT
Shell logo developments
1900–67

ABOVE
BP italicized mark + application
ADDISON UK LATE 1980S

LEFT
BP 'flower' identity
LANDOR USA 2000

RIGHT
NASA logo – 'The worm'
DANNE AND BLACKBURN USA 1974

BELOW MIDDLE
Revised logo – 'The meatball'
JAMES MODARELLI USA 1959

BELOW
The NASA seal
USA 1990S

BOTTOM LEFT
British Airways identity
NEGUS AND NEGUS UK 1970S

BOTTOM MIDDLE
British Airways identity
NEGUS AND NEGUS UK 1970S

The advent of the space race in the 1960s brought with it a desire to modernize, and resulted in a famous symbol (often referred to as 'The Worm') being developed by Bruce Blackburn. The worm came to symbolize space travel itself – modern, flowing, sinuous, a continuous line. A logo designed to work well on television, in space, wherever.

Corporate American identity design had its role model, and needed no further prompting.

Like IBM before it ('put stripes in it, that'll make it look computerized'), the worm created a new benchmark to which designers could refer when they were seeking to appear 'new' and 'technological'.

And if it was good enough for our boys blasting off into space then heck, it would be perfect for your railway, travel agency or nightclub.

But then something odd happened. Having gone for radical change, moving from the tin robot symbol to cutting-edge modernism, NASA decided internally that actually they wanted to go back to their roots. In a bizarre about-turn, their new chief executive switched back to the old mark, citing 'heritage' as the reason.[4]

Perhaps we'll see BP revert to their shield in a few years time, having seen their new flower wilt in the greenhouse-effect sun. Who knows?

Nowhere is corporate paranoia more evident than when a national airline decides its identity is ripe for review. For a carrier with an average reputation, racked by strikes and industrial action, British Airways spent much of the 1970s looking just that, average. At one point a designer had persuaded them to remove

the word 'airways' from their fuselages and just become a generic term. After all, it was clearly a plane, so why bother to state the obvious? But BA seemed to lack the razzmatazz of its global rivals.

LEFT
British Airways identity re-design
LANDOR USA 1984

BELOW
Stills from British Airways TV ad
SAATCHI & SAATCHI UK 1990

The pace picked up in the 1980s when the airline, just privatized and keen to re-present itself as the newly-christened 'world's favourite airline', ruffled a lot of British designers' feathers by asking a San Francisco-based design consultancy to 'evolve' the airline's identity.

Unfettered by parochial views about what 'British-ness' really stood for, Landor distilled the world-view of the UK's identity pretty well – classical-looking type and stripes, silvery-grey colours plus blue and red and, of course, a royal-looking crest (with the words 'To fly to serve' incorporated within).

Whilst the reality of the crest was that at more than twenty paces it looked like a squashed beetle, the 'cigarette pack' identity coincided with a period of unprecedented growth and success for the airline, backed up by a series of ground-breakingly triumphant advertising campaigns and a gung-ho period of boom in the UK and world economies.

Then, in the caring-sharing 1990s, the gung-ho started to look a bit gung-ho-hum, a bit out of step, smacking slightly of an imperial past better forgotten.

More and more, the company discovered that the proposition of 'the world's favourite airline' worked best when they showed the people of the world as their client base. So as the many colours and races of the world appeared increasingly in their advertising, it came as no surprise that a design idea that developed this was tabled for their identity. At the front of the plane was the classic evolutionary identity fudge, a slightly redrawn piece of type and the older speedwing design softened into a ribbon device.

But for the aeroplanes' tails they had a fantastically brave idea, at least on paper; a genuine revolution in identity and branding. The proposal was to recognize the airline's global constituencies by devoting forty different tailfin designs to the patterns and designs of the people of the world.

Wherever the airline flew, there would be a pattern from that destination. Delft patterns from The Netherlands, Aborigine bark-paintings from Australia, and so on.

There were two significant problems with this proposal. The re-design took place just as the airline's financial fortunes took a nose-dive; and there was the recognition problem. Somewhere along the line, something significant seemed to have been missed: air traffic controllers and pilots depend on the aircraft's tailfins to identify one huge piece of dangerous flying metal from another.[5]

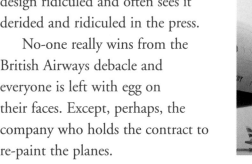

Overnight, British Airways and their design consultants had apparently been expecting the world's airport staff to become conversant with brand identity theory and to be able to differentiate Dutch glazes from Outback dot-paintings.

So what happened? They went back to a swooshy Union Jack device that had previously been dedicated to the troubled Concorde fleet and the nation's commentators seemed happy to use the tailfin designs as a suitable scapegoat for the company's business ills. Perhaps airlines (like countries) end up with the identities (or leaders) they deserve.

In the political maelstrom of identity change, there are often compelling reasons to stand still and fiddle with what's there. If the fiddling makes something valuable a little bit better, or something flawed correct, then maybe it's valid. It's the minor (and expensive) change because of fear and bad advice that makes identity design ridiculed and often sees it derided and ridiculed in the press.

No-one really wins from the British Airways debacle and everyone is left with egg on their faces. Except, perhaps, the company who holds the contract to re-paint the planes.

Problem: An identity once designed to clarify now isn't clear.

Solved: Evolve the bit that is known, revolve the rest.

The mid-1980s identity developed for the Parc de la Villette, a cultural park in the north-east of Paris, managed to sum up neatly the area's major elements. The green triangle symbolized the park as a whole, the red square the science museum and the blue circle then unbuilt music centre. As the park established a reputation for its varied avante-garde activities, the symbol was a perfect reflection of the 1980s graphic zeitgeist.

But one issue remained unsolved. While there was scope within the original identity to reflect the needs of the three major players, as the park developed and needs changed it became frustrating for the green triangle (the 'Parc') to find itself always associated with the park's main attraction, the red square (the Science Museum).

By the late 1990s, the organization found itself engaged in a sort of feudal war as the museum, music centre and park dropped the original logotype and used their own versions of the original mark, with varying degrees of success.

The park authorities attempted to develop the green triangle for their own use, with dubious results – for each of their productions they would receive sponsorship and the lines of sponsors' logos

BELOW, BELOW LEFT,
OPPOSITE RIGHT
La Villette design applications
GRAPUS FRANCE 1986

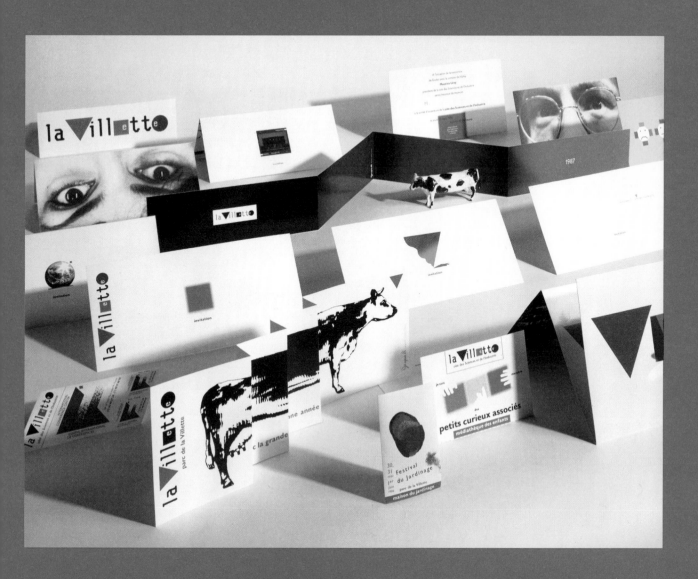

Parc de la Villette leaflet covers
VARIOUS FRANCE 1998–9
These covers, all by different designers,
illustrate how the original scheme had
begun to break apart after a decade

would often vie for prominence with the name of the park. The solution was to take the triangle shape and build it into a bar that could be used on the side of any piece of communication, allowing the park to 'own' its many events without competing with sponsors' messages.

   With the controlled use of one typeface and the introduction of simpler, more arresting imagery, the park itself now had a recognizable and unified house style flexible enough to match the variety of its events.

THIS PAGE AND OPPOSITE
Parc de La Villette logo evolution,
poster applications, TV stills
JOHNSON BANKS UK 2000–01

SAISONS

2001

PROGRAMME AU 01 40 03 75 75

JARDIN DES CULTURES

PARC LA VILLETTE

Try as they might, some companies just can't create a viable image for themselves for a different, younger generation who don't believe them, don't like them and would never, ever buy anything from them. So they proceed by stealth and create new, 'junior' brands under assumed names and hope that no-one will notice. Does it work?

Once it used to be called The Product Life Cycle. Lots of dull marketing books refer to how products and services are born, go through difficult teenage years, mature and then, well, expire. Consequently many brands (especially of the global variety) now spend millions every year on becoming the brand of choice for whoever the next generation will be. There's just too much riding on them to allow them to simply slink off and expire the way the product life-cycle seemed to suggest.

But some brands don't seem to be able to make themselves seem new again. They try, of course, but often a younger, sassier audience can see straight through it. A brand like Diesel might have kept itself on the cutting edge of cool for most of the 1990s, but consider what happened to Falmers jeans, or Gloria Vanderbilt – they went the way of all fashion clothing, when being 'in' simply went 'out'. Calvin Klein needed Brook Shields once but didn't when her star had faded.

Girls bought Charlie perfume once. They don't any more. They buy Tommy Hilfiger. And Diesel and Tommy continually pursue the hottest agencies in the world to keep themselves at the very edge of coolness, otherwise they and their brands will disappear.

The marketeers behind Charlie must have known that the nine-year-old girl's perfume of choice, like her taste in the 1970s for Donny Osmond and in the 1990s for boy bands, was likely to change and so may have planned for the future accordingly.

But for other companies, it's a bit more difficult.

Within the super-competitive drinks market, it's often almost impossible to change a brand's positioning overnight – the Colas are continually tweaking their local and global marketing campaigns to try and stay, if not one step ahead,[1] at least in tune with the next generation of brown-sugar-syrup drinkers. Pepsi spent billions worldwide masterminding a change in their livery from blue, red and white to blue, with supporting PR stunts and activity seemingly affecting sales by a negligible amount but achieving, in their eyes at least, some clear blue water between themselves and their red-branded competitor.

Interestingly, Coca-Cola in the US once tried a new version of a soft drink reputedly aimed at the Generation X 'slacker' market, called OK Soda.

BELOW
Diesel ad campaign
KESSELSKRAMER
THE NETHERLANDS 2001

BELOW LEFT
Calvin Klein Jeans
IN-HOUSE AGENCY USA 1980

BELOW RIGHT
Pepsi blue ad
AMV BBDO UK 1996

This wasn't a re-think of Coke, but a radical attempt to try and produce a tangy soft drink which deliberately side-stepped typical major brand values, tapped into a generation then described as 'millenarian, depressed, cynical, frustrated, apathetic, hedonistic and nihilistic', and sold itself with lines such as 'don't think there has to be a reason for everything' and 'what's the point of OK? Well, what's the point of anything?'. While its grunge design style and use of underground comic-book artists for pack designs gathered many design plaudits, its core message didn't really hit home and it was quietly shelved a year after its launch. Perhaps its parent decided that the grunge-skateboard-tangy-drinks market was a little more niche than they had thought? We will never really know; perhaps even trying it in the first place indicated a level of bravery not usually seen in this sector (or a level of cynicism never previously brought to life as a product before).[2]

But the perils of sitting on a traditional brand and presuming that everything will be fine are severe – consider the UK retailer, Marks & Spencer. Rather than reacting to the growing pressures of worldwide brands arriving on the high street with their innovative point of sale, snappy advertising and fast reactions to the requirements of the consumer, M&S stuck to their guns, left their shops alone and counted the profits.

Until, that is, the profits nose-dived and then all hell was let loose – only after carnage in the boardroom did they call in the designers and advertisers to create the Emperor's new clothes, and this from a company that had never previously advertised. Whether naked Rubenesque women posing by windows would be sufficient to save the brand remains to be seen. But it surely comes as no surprise to anyone that a company from whom your Grandma and your Mum bought their clothes was going to struggle to bring in younger customers until they began to make clothes for their daughters and granddaughters too?

ABOVE
OK Soda packaging and stickers
WEIDEN + KENNEDY USA 1994

RIGHT
Marks & Spencers poster
RAINEY KELLEY/Y&R UK 2000

One area where it seems to be particularly difficult for companies to appeal to a youth market is within financial services and commodity products such as power services. Long-established financial organizations like the British-based Prudential and Abbey National, after finding out that their brands simply didn't reach that new and elusive 'youth market', simply decided to launch sub-brands under completely different names.

So Egg was hatched to specialize in financial services, and Cahoot was created as an on-line offer from Abbey National. Both chose to subtly endorse their projects with small print that re-assured the sceptical punters that they were from legitimate companies, honest. Both will presumably monitor how their new offspring fare before deciding whether they should go to proper school or not, but with the dotcom bubble well and truly burst, they will have to perform well to avoid being sent home for good.

Whilst the rise of the internet was the probable driver for these brands, the drive for direct services and consequently the need to sub-brand probably began in the UK with First Direct, a telephone-only banking service. Then part of Midland Bank, it seemed logical that this piece of information should be hidden in the small print since it might dissuade a new generation of customers from using them.

And in their design and advertising, they created a fresh and unusual idea for a company that genuinely separated them from the competition. Of course, once the parent company had been bought out by Hong Kong & Shanghai Bank a few years after First Direct's inception, lo and behold! the HSBC logo appeared on the First Direct collateral.

In 2001, after the merger of global insurance giants Royal Insurance and Sun Alliance (re-named Royal & SunAlliance), the company realized that their 'direct' service (ie. using phone and web) was not doing as well as it might. Having tried a new livery but no new name, they took the plunge and renamed and re-launched their direct division with the oddly memorable name, MORE TH>N. By including the greater than/ more than symbol within the mark (the '>' sign), they were able to do a

TOP
Egg TV still
HHCL UK 2001

ABOVE
Cahoot press ad
EURO RSCG WNEK GOSPER UK 2001

LEFT
First Direct identity
WOLFF OLINS UK 1988

BELOW
MORE TH>N logo, poster
JOHNSON BANKS/
BRAND GUARDIANS
UK 2001

rare thing – begin ownership of a character on a keyboard previously viewed as merely generic.

Royal and SunAlliance's desire to test a sub-brand was based on hard research that suggested that their core master-brand was not 'youthful' enough to compete for the investment dollars of a new market – there was good reason for the change, in other words. And who knows, if MORE TH>N is successful, they might even consider moving more of the master-brand's portfolio under the new brand's jurisdiction.

Sometimes changes seem mysterious to say the least. For example, Scottish Power decided at the height of dotcom fever that they wanted to create a sellable electronics division and their 'regional' name was holding them back.

Therefore, Thus. As with Abbey National and Cahoot, they felt the need to explain the provenance of their new offshoot by initially including the name 'formerly part of Scottish Power' on their advertising, but still it seemed a mystifying move. OK, Scottish Power was not really going to set the world alight as a brand, but to re-do everything with a name like that, with some strange type and three little dots?

Whether creating Thus will 'mark a new momentum in the company's development' remains to be seen[3] but it is a good example of how difficult name-changing and name creation has become – many of their favoured names had probably been registered. Cybersquatters spent the latter half of the 1990s registering web names wholesale, then merrily selling them on to the highest and most desperate bidder.

Obtaining original and memorable names (difficult) and the worldwide registration thereof (really difficult) plus the currently magical dotcom suffix (practically impossible) has turned the naming game into a logistical minefield.

One approach is to use internet suffixes as part of the name. The Italian brand Theex only made any kind of sense when you used the .it Italian suffix (Theex.it), and the snappily titled Russian dating site cleverly used the Russian

ABOVE TOP
MORE TH>N ambient ad
JOHNSON BANKS UK 2001

ABOVE MIDDLE
Thus corporate identity
999 DESIGN UK 1999

suffix (.ru) for its name, iam.ru. The UK-based lifestyle site for women, 'be me', made no sense at all when written down (beme.com) and relied on the sophistication of its visitors to 'decode' the URL.[4]

Such is the confusion surrounding dotcom names the recent realization that the island of Tuvalu's internet suffix was .tv led to pandemonium as companies scrambled to register .tv names, not knowing if anyone would ever understand the suffix or not.

As more names become registered worldwide, companies have to develop strategies to deal with the situation. It sounds weird, but it's true: the world is running out of names.

For many years, car companies have been stock-piling names for their cars and carefully registering them worldwide, just so they are prepared for their next global launch and ready with their next Micra, or Vectra, or Mondeo, or Shogun. As these names can often sound a little odd, to say the least, some car manufacturers cling desperately to their numbering strategies, such as BMW with its 3, 5, and 7 series, or Audi with its A3, A4, A6, A8 system.

The number route avoids the problem of picking a car name that could mean something very unfortunate in a different language (such as the 'Nova' which sounds suitably 'new' in English but translates as 'doesn't go' in Spanish). Its inherent weakness, though, is that the company is always having to communicate that theirs is a new 5 series on the road (even though there are 5 series BMWs dating back twenty years that are still on the road).

And then there is the most ridiculed sector, that of the invented name. Now that we see some of the problems of naming, it explains why consultancies, naming agencies and sometimes companies themselves fall back on something made-up because then they know they can at least register it.

So we have the 'sounds like something but isn't really' category, like the new name in the UK for The Post Office, 'Consignia'. Or the 'vaguely Latin/Greek but not quite' category, such as Diageo, the name for the merger of Guinness PLC and Grand Metropolitan PLC. Or the 'stick two words together and let's see if it flies' approach best summarized by Accenture, a merger of the words 'accent' and 'future', the new name for what was formerly Andersen Consulting.

Netscape: BEME.COM First place for women on the web

ABOVE
Beme logo & web page
WOLFF OLINS UK 1998

BELOW
Consignia logotype
DRAGON INTERNATIONAL
UK 2001

BOTTOM RIGHT
Diageo logotype
WOLFF OLINS UK 2000

OPPOSITE TOP LEFT
Q8 lorry
WOLFF OLINS UK 1985

OPPOSITE MIDDLE RIGHT
Accenture logo & ad
LANDOR USA 2000

Consignia
The new name for The Post Office Group

DIAGEO

Or the 'it means something if you think about it long enough' type best exemplified by what was Standard Oil, 's' followed by 'o', or Esso for short. The strangest example of this must be the re-named Kuwait Petroleum, who were persuaded to take the admittedly memorable moniker Q8 (ie. Ku-eight? Get it?). This would be fine, of course, if it weren't for the fact that most of Q8's business is done in non-English-speaking countries where, for example, kuu-otcho (Italian) or kuu-agt (Dutch) doesn't really get the phonetic message over.

MONDAY:

ABOVE
Monday: logotype (PWC Consulting)
WOLFF OLINS UK 2002
This new name for Price Waterhouse Cooper's consulting division was launched to a sector still reeling from the Accenture re-naming. Some internal PwC observers immediately dubbed it 'Blue Mundane'

BELOW
Do Co Mo identity
NTT JAPAN LATE 1990S

BOTTOM
Tomato Bank identity
SHIGEO KATSUOKA
JAPAN 1989

Accenture is only distinguished by the rather touching fact that all the names expensively put to them were rejected (including, reputedly, 'Global Curves' and 'Mind Rocket') by their consultants and the final name was actually dreamt up internally by an Oslo-based partner in the firm, who won a golfing weekend in Australia as a prize for his wordsmithing.

Then there are the simply weird and wonderful names like Do Co Mo, the mobile brand of Nippon Telecom. Do Co Mo is at least helped by the fact that they are operating in a fast-moving, youth-orientated market, and sounds just about right for their target. And of course its verbal appeal – 'Do Co Mo' simply sounds great when you say it, regardless of your native tongue.

Another example of that distinctly Japanese twist on naming is the fabulously named Tomato Bank. Yes, that's right, a bank called Tomato. While this might appear a ridiculous name to the stuffy financial institutions of New York, London and Frankfurt, in Tokyo there's no problem. And the symbol? A tomato stuck onto the beginning of the word, of course. Diageo falls into a long list of names

often ridiculed by the press, but Consignia created a category of derision all of its own by not only choosing a strange name, but then placing that next to a symbol of questionable provenance, which has been regularly 'outed' in the satirical magazine, *Private Eye*, devoting a regular column to Consignia-symbol look-alikes sent in by its readers.

The company themselves then put the cat amongst the pigeons when the same chief executive who had launched the name as one that 'describes the full scope of what The Post Office does in a way that the words "Post" and "Office" cannot' had to admit soon afterwards that 'Consignia? The name doesn't actually mean anything'.[5]

By 2002 their chairman had announced publicly that they were going to revert to their previous name, The Post Office. Mmm, that doesn't sound too bad, does it?[6]

Perhaps the problems of name change and name creation will see a return to simple, ordinary names like Eddie Stobart, the British truck haulier who has achieved huge levels of branding for his own company by following the simple strategy of writing his own name in six-foot-high letters on the side of his massive fleet of lorries and driving them all over Europe.

Or consider the deceptively simple decision of Australian brewer, Lion-Nathan. Having decided, seventy-five years ago, that they wanted to introduce a new beer to their range (a range that totalled one at the time), after months of discussion and scenario planning they decided to rename the old beer, 'Toohey's Old'.

And the name for the new beer? You guessed it, Toohey's New.

Finally there's a naming strategy that makes perfect sense.

OPPOSITE PAGE
Consignia look-alikes as featured in *Private Eye* magazine
PRIVATE EYE UK 2001

ABOVE
Eddie Stobart lorry
EDDIE & WILLIAM STOBART
UK 1970S–PRESENT DAY

RIGHT
Toohey's Old and Toohey's New pack designs
LION-NATHAN AUSTRALIA 2000

Problem: Nobody wants to buy your sweet sticky orange-flavoured drink any more. You're not cool.

Solved: Re-package your product, then re-invent yourself as an irreverent anti-brand.

Whilst most of this chapter has shown companies and brands attempting to relaunch themselves and often doing it wrong, this case study concentrates on a relaunch which went spectacularly right. An example of design and advertising working well together. An example of unfettered creativity and the power it has to create something that people really love.

This is how it once looked, a rather dated-looking pack that sold averagely well but certainly wasn't setting the soft drinks market alight. Faced with possible extinction, Tango had one last chance for a new life.

Step 1: A new look. Although it doesn't look as radical now as when launched, the new Tango can created quite a stir with its irreverent style and bizarre illustration of an opened orange. It broke soft drink packaging conventions by using black, all combining to offer something dramatically new.

But where the relaunch really took off was in Step 2: Its advertising. From the launch ad showing a huge fat orange man slapping someone around the face, to bizarre ads for new products hinting at masturbation, to huge helicopter numbers for the launch of blackcurrant Tango, to parodying print ads for Euro 2000 (the soccer tournament), the Tango positioning has been one of anarchy and anti-branding, the brand that doesn't care, that likes to have a laugh.

And laugh we did, whilst consuming millions of gallons of the sticky stuff in the process. Whilst its original relaunch agency, HHCL, may no longer be in charge of the brand's advertising, the legacy they created will be hard to follow.

ABOVE
Original Tango packaging
UK 1980s

LEFT AND OPPOSITE
Tango re-designs and line extensions
WICKENS TUTT SOUTHGATE UK
1990s

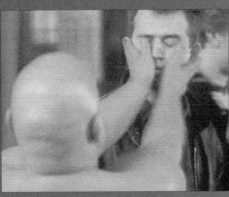

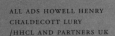

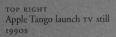

ALL ADS HOWELL HENRY
CHALDECOTT LURY
/HHCL AND PARTNERS UK

LEFT
Tango re-launch TV stills
1991
The re-launch television ad featured an almost naked fat orange man who appears and slaps the Tango drinker around the face to emphasize the power of the drink's flavour. The idea proved too successful and had to be amended – when it was found that schoolchildren were copying the ad and slapping each other around the face throughout Britain's playgrounds

TOP RIGHT
Apple Tango launch TV still
1990s

ABOVE RIGHT
Blackcurrant Tango launch TV still
1996

OPPOSITE PAGE
Euro 2000 press ads
2000
These ads merrily criticized the barrage of sponsorship advertising accompanying a major football tournament by proudly being a sponsor of nothing at all

OFFICIALLY A DRINK DURING EURO 2000

OFFICIALLY A DRINK DURING EURO 2000

OFFICIALLY A DRINK DURING EURO 2000

It's claimed that we are all subjected to thousands of marketing messages a day. Can you remember even a hundred of the ones you received today? Probably not. Why not? Because we've trained ourselves to filter out all bar the absolutely essential. Pity, then, the designer or communicator charged with getting information over in a way that the public will absorb, not ignore.

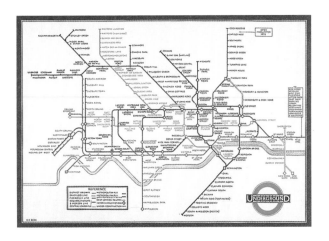

LEFT
London Underground map design
HARRY BECK UK 1931

ABOVE
Underground map before
FH STINGEMORE UK 1920S

BELOW
Metropolitan Transportation
Authority map
VIGNELLI ASSOCIATES USA 1970

Some of the greatest steps forward made in communication design in the twentieth century came from surmounting the most difficult of information design problems. When an out-of-work engineering draughtsman called Harry Beck[1] decided he would devote his spare time to devising a simpler way to understand London's then tortuous underground railway map, he probably didn't realize that he was almost single-handedly inventing a whole new category of design.

Beck had identified a seemingly intractable problem: how to simplify something that by the 1920s had become a tortured spaghetti of train routes criss-crossing London. In one geometrically inspired swoop, Beck suggested a solution based on 45- and 90-degree angles. Although his map sentenced generations of visitors to think that Charing Cross and Embankment stations were some distance apart, rather than just 300 yards, in almost every other respect it was a work of genius. His was just a clear and simple mindset – 'I need to get around London more easily and it would be better if the lines were less cluttered.'

Although initially rejected, in 1933 a trial run was printed and the design was soon adopted by the public because it solved such a significant problem – that of navigating the capital.[2] Here was essential information made impossible to reject.

Seventy years later, Beck's map has reached iconic status and has been emulated all over the world, but not always with the same success. New York-based arch-modernist Massimo Vignelli produced a strictly 45- and 90-degree version for the then newly-formed Metropolitan Transit Authority

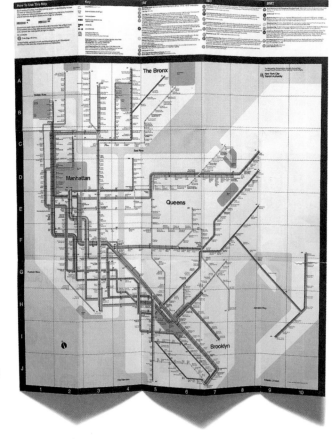

ABOVE
'The Map',
MTA USA 1989

BELOW TOP
Charles de Gaulle airport signage
ADRIAN FRUTIGER FRANCE 1973–6

BOTTOM
Melbourne Exhibition Centre signage
GARRY EMERY DESIGN AUSTRALIA
1995

which neatly summed-up the rigid corporate design of the early 1970s – clean, beautiful and fairly functional but a bit cold, and strangely unemotional. Actually using the map, rather than just framing it on the wall and admiring its beauty, was quite a challenge.

It only took the New York MTA nine years to replace the first design with what seems like a huge jump backwards to an almost photographic negative of what Vignelli had tried – replacing angles with real curves which followed the true path of the tracks.[3] But only eight more years passed before the definitive attempt was produced with a name to match ('The Map').

Alas, 'The Map' hardly comes across as 'The Greatest'; any attempt to simplify has been lost in a sea of complex curves and boxes.

The examples above are a simple crystallization of the issues faced by what we have now come to call the information designer – that of helping users navigate their way around a space, whether real or virtual. Visitors to an airport, museum or website all face the same problems – they need information and guidance as quickly as possible about where to go and how to get there.

Whilst Beck's map gives us the historical precedent for the simplification of complex material, airports have long been seen as the benchmark from which information design stems. Ever since Adrian Frutiger designed a special typeface in black on huge yellow signs with massive numerals for Charles de Gaulle Airport in Paris, the die has been cast for terminals and public spaces worldwide; only in recent decades have designers begun to experiment with large scale signage that didn't correspond to the Charles de Gaulle model.

The worldwide adoption of Frutiger's problem-solving has its benefits, of course. Regular plane travellers have become versed in the language of reading signs in what is often a stressful environment – when jetlagged and carrying heavy bags and/or screaming children. Many studies have shown that black type upon yellow is one of the most legible combinations for signage (NB. signage, not words – if this page were designed on yellow you'd soon see it's almost

painful to look at small words on an
expanse of the colour). The airport
approach (luckily not always the yellow)
has been appropriated throughout the
gallery, theatre and museum worlds to aid
navigation throughout their buildings.

   Famously, some have added other
elements. For example, this highly-
acclaimed signage for the Rijksmuseum in
Amsterdam introduced pictograms taken
from the museum's collection to enliven
what could otherwise have become another
dour 'slab' system. As it is, within the
scheme you begin to understand that if you
follow the angel, you will be able to ascend
and descend (albeit in a lift), whilst the
clouds denote the path to the toilets. The
idea also serves to reinforce the artistic
icons that the museum holds in the minds

of its visitors, continually stressing the depth and history of their collection.

   The same firm had developed their Rijksmuseum approach after their
ground-breaking scheme for a hospital in Westeinde that featured the path of a
bouncing ball around what was a typical hospital space. The hospital, which

often changed layouts
and rooms at very short
notice, also received a
functional 'slab-system'
including a set of
interchangeable
symbols, copyright-free
(for non-commercial
projects only).

   A hospital in Japan
managed to add
humour and warmth
to the signage of a
stressful environment;

ABOVE
Rijksmuseum signage 1985

LEFT AND BELOW
Westeinde Hospital signage 1980

BOTH STUDIO DUMBAR
THE NETHERLANDS

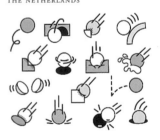

the information within the scheme by Kenya Hara is applied on to white, washable, soft plastic which immediately helps to reassure any worried inhabitant or visitor (and enhances the impression of a perfectly clean and sterile environment as well).

Many of the principles of three-dimensional navigation can also be carried over into the world of web design. As this new discipline struggles to find its feet in the face of sluggish browsers and lengthy download, the elements that users have come to treasure more than anything else are speed and the ability to navigate the space easily. Early website structures, often produced by programmers rather than designers, assumed that their visitors knew that

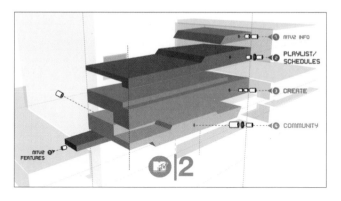

websites work in tree-like forms and tended to include buttons like 'up' and 'down' rather than 'backwards' and 'forwards'. Luckily, sense soon prevailed and designers began to think about their sites in terms of the way the visitors, not experts in HTML, would approach them.[4]

The website for MTV2 takes the approach of turning the whole site into a kind of 3D object where the visitor can choose which floor, or area, to access. This makes the

experience clearer and also makes navigation a memorable part of the design. Users of the British Design Museum's site spin a cube device that helps them decide in which direction to turn their attentions next (as though they are simply walking around the museum itself).

However progressive these sites might seem, there are many that ignore the simple

TOP
Umeda Hospital signage
KENYA HARA JAPAN 1999

ABOVE
MTV 2 website
DIGIT UK 2000

FAR RIGHT
Design Museum website
DEEPEND UK 1999

laws of navigation (tell people where they are at all times, let them self-orientate as much as possible, never assume any knowledge on the part of the visitor, never add more clutter than is absolutely necessary). Whether it be distracting banner ads, whirling animations or links that make no sense, many sites seem to be designed more for the creator's portfolios than the actual end-user.

Clarity, simplicity and readability are the simplest rules for solving the information-rejection or information-ignorance problem. The issues of readability can occur in the most glamorous and most mundane of places.

The record sleeves shown right seem like simple, dramatic type layouts isolated on a page of this book, but their primary application was for DJ's within a dark nightclub. To solve the problem of aiding recognition (and avoid the embarrassment of spinning the wrong disc), the information is clearly laid out in the most legible way possible and the 'livery' of the record label is firmly entrenched in the user's mind.

At the more mundane end of the spectrum, the principle of readability at all costs has led to some of the most interesting (and most detailed) typographic work of the last twenty years: for telephone directories.

The problem is this – the producers of these massive 1,000 page documents need to stuff as many small lines of type in as possible to save on paper costs. But they can't print the information in type that is completely illegible. So what do they do?

In the case of the US phone books, the re-design of the then-used typeface, Bell, to a narrower weight with specially-designed characters, allowed the entire book to be set in four columns, not three. The same information took up less width whilst still being legible, and made enormous savings on paper.

When the UK Yellow Pages realized they had to improve the legibility of their entries, but get more information into the same space because of ever-

ABOVE
Deconstruction record sleeves
FARROW DESIGN UK 1995

LEFT
Bell Centennial font design
MATTHEW CARTER USA 1975–8

OPPOSITE BOTTOM
UK road signage system
KINNEIR CALVERT
UK EARLY 1960S

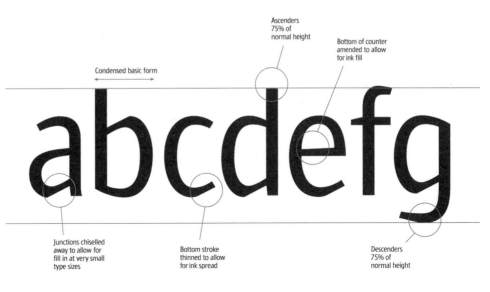

Condensed basic form

Ascenders
75% of
normal height

Bottom of counter
amended to allow
for ink fill

Junctions chiselled
away to allow for
fill in at very small
type sizes

Bottom stroke
thinned to allow
for ink spread

Descenders
75% of
normal height

ABOVE
Old Yellow Pages
typesetting (enlarged)

RIGHT
Yellow Pages font design
JOHNSON BANKS/THE FOUNDRY
UK 1998

BELOW
Contrast of old and new setting

Bennett R.M, 54 Drumalig Rd............... Carryduff	812278
Benson S.S, 96 Thornhill Rd,Rock.................. Pomeroy	758257
Benson T, 19 Cannagola Rd,Portadown...... Annaghmore	851435
Berry J.D, 41, Brootally Rd,Lisagally................Armagh	522355
Berry N.D.& Sons, 41 Tullyraine Rd............... Banbridge	62767
Berry W, 20 Chapelhill Rd,Tynan................... Caledon	568384
Best R.D, The Cairn,14 Brankinstown Rd........... Aghalee	651222
Bethel W, 36 Point Rd................................Banbridge	62455
Bethel Wm, 6 Island Rd...............Newtownhamilton	878345
Biggerstaff Norman, 84 Diamond Rd......Dromore(Dn)	692555
Biggerstaff R.S,	
57 Upper Quilly Rd,Banbridge...........Dromore(Dn)	692419
Bill John, 802 Antrim Rd........................ Templepatrick	432673
Bingham Barney, 28 Carnew Rd................ Katesbridge	71329
Bingham D.W,	
68 Ballymartin Rd,Templepatrick..................Ballyclare	352272
Bingham Edward,	
65 Annaghilla Rd,Augher................................Ballygawley	68287
Bingham Jsph, 14 Lackan Rd,Ballyroney...... Rathfriland	30364
Bingham Noel, Ballinsaggart Rd................ Ballygawley	68444
Bingham R,	
203 Sevenmile Straight,Crumlin............... Templepatrick	432236
Bingham S, 38 Tullycorker Rd,Augher.................. Clogher	48353
Birch J.A,	
Mill View Farm,8 Abbacy Rd,Ardkeen...............Portaferry	28030
Birch S, 1 Keadybeg Rd,Mountnorris................. Glenanne	507314
Birney F, Tullanaglare............................Irvinestown	21480
Birt E, 137 Mullaghboy Rd.........................Bellaghy	386738
Birt Michl.E, 10 Bogashen Rd............... Portglenone	821354

Bennett R.M,54 Drumalig Rd...............................Carryduff	812278
Benson S.S,96 Thornhill Rd,Rock..............................Pomeroy	758257
Benson T,19 Cannagola Rd,Portadown...................Annaghmore	851435
Berry J.D,41, Brootally Rd,Lisagally...............................Armagh	522355
Berry N.D.& Sons,41 Tullyraine Rd...........................Banbridge	62767
Berry W,20 Chapelhill Rd,Tynan................................Caledon	568384
Best R.D,The Cairn,14 Brankinstown Rd.......................Aghalee	651222
Bethel W,36 Point Rd..Banbridge	62455
Bethel Wm,6 Island Rd.................................Newtownhamilton	878345
Biggerstaff S.J,57 Upper Quilly Rd,Banbridge.....Dromore (DN)	692419
Bill John,802 Antrim Rd...Templepatrick	432673
Bingham Barney,28 Carnew Rd..............................Katesbridge	71329
Bingham D.W,68 Ballymartin Rd,Templepatrick.........Ballyclare	352272
Bingham Edward,65 Annaghilla Rd,Augher...........Ballygawley	68287
Bingham Jsph,14 Lackan Rd,Ballyroney...................Rathfriland	30364
Bingham Noel,Ballinsaggart Rd.............................Ballygawley	68444
Bingham R,203 Sevenmile Straight,Crumlin........Templepatrick	432236
Bingham S,38 Tullycorker Rd,Augher............................Clogher	48353
Birch J.A,Mill View Farm,8 Abbacy Rd,Ardkeen.......Portaferry	28030
Birch S,1 Keadybeg Rd,Mountnorris............................Glenanne	507314
Birney F,Tullanaglare...Irvinestown	21480
Birt E,137 Mullaghboy Rd.......................................Bellaghy	386738
Birt M,10 Bogashen Rd...Portglenone	821354

lengthening telephone numbers, they started experiments with the now publicly-available typeface that the US directories had adopted.

But this typeface couldn't cope with the demands of setting the lines of type very closely together. So this time another font was developed which was narrow, had huge chiselled gouges in it to allow for the effects on the type of the crude printing used for directories, and featured drastically truncated ascenders and descenders (the tops of t's and h's and the bottoms of p's and q's). This allowed lines to be set perilously close to each other, again saving whole forests of trees in the process.[5]

Probably the ultimate test of this chapter's theme, information rejection, is official information. If the road signs of a country don't immediately inform a visitor which direction to take as they drive off a ferry or away from the car hire depot, what side of the road to drive on or where the motorway is, they have failed. And if they fail it has an immediate impact on the perception of those signs, and ultimately on that of the country itself.

The road signage system meticulously developed by British designers Jock Kinneir and Margaret Calvert in the early 1960s not only provided a role model to the world of how to explain crucial information in the most demanding of circumstances, they unwittingly branded a nation at the same time. It's only when trying to navigate another country's system that a driver realizes how ingrained their own system has become to them. Just driving across a European border reveals that an arrow meaning 'straight on' could point upwards or downwards depending on whether you are in Italy or Switzerland.[6]

The images above show how we come to depend on these visual codes. If we re-design a British sign in the style of the US Highways agency, it looks wrong to a European viewer but right to a North American, and vice versa for Route 66. Most of us take letterforms and information for granted, yet as soon as we play with those perceptions, we immediately know that something is wrong, and that the reliability we ascribe to road signs is affected (regardless of how well they work).

ABOVE
Theoretical highways signage
JOHNSON BANKS UK 2002

OPPOSITE TOP LEFT
Speed Kills poster
SAATCHI & SAATCHI
NEW ZEALAND 1994

OPPOSITE TOP RIGHT
Student project on the car
CHARLIE SMITH
GLASGOW SCHOOL OF ART UK 1999

OPPOSITE MIDDLE LEFT
London Transport Helpline poster
BMP DDB UK 1998

OPPOSITE RIGHT
London Zoo Regent's Park poster
ABRAM GAMES UK 1975

OPPOSITE BOTTOM LEFT
'The Tate Gallery by Tube' poster
THE FINE WHITE LINE UK 1987

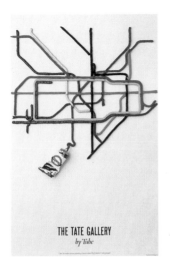

THE TATE GALLERY
by Tube

The power of the information style is so strong that some have appropriated its vernacular as a unique way to deliver their own messages. As part of a protest piece against cars, student designer Charlie Smith used the language of the street, of road markings and bicycle lanes, to make the point that for every one car there could be ten bicycles on the road.

A New Zealand-based advertising agency turned the whole road into an ad for safer driving.

Abram Games appropriated the language and lines of Beck's map and cleverly introduced the underground symbol as well in this classic poster advertising a famous London park.

It seems that the variations on the theme are endless – the posters shown left, twist the language of lines into those for telephones in this 1998 information poster, or change the tube lines into lines of paint for this famous 'Tate by Tube' example.

Simon Patterson, who was nominated for the Turner Prize in 1996, twisted the underground icon to

LONDON

REGENT'S PARK

Underground to Baker Street, then Bus 74

his own ends when he produced a version of the map (itself heralded as 'an icon of 1990s art') that replaced the names of stations with the names of famous philosophers, Hollywood actors, popes, painters etc. Patterson's genius was to make even his intersections function by using the likes of Kirk Douglas on both the 'Hollywood' and the 'Artists' lines.[7]

Patterson has often let his closet designer sensibilities show in other works, such as this piece based on a Delta airline flight-path, or the attendees

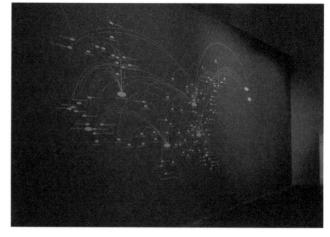

of the Last Supper arranged in football formations, hand-painted on to church walls (with Christ in goal in both instances and Judas coming once off the bench).

So, as we have seen, information, when properly presented, can affect the way we get to work or around a museum, and even how we perceive a country.

But in the 2000 US presidential election, the confusion caused by a new ballot paper may even have affected who got the world's most powerful job when the form re-designed by Theresa Le Pore led to a complete re-count of the votes cast in Florida. Many felt that the re-design led to confusion as to where to punch the hole, as voters tried to vote for Al Gore but voted for ultra-right-wing Pat Buchanan by mistake. Many then punched another hole, trying to correct their error but technically 'spoiling' their ballots in the process.

The designer, in her defence, stated that she was actually trying to make it easier to use. But the re-design and the 19,000 spoilt ballots that resulted as voters tried to correct their mistaken vote for Buchanan meant that, after months of legal wrangling, George Bush was proclaimed the winner in the state (an announcement since proved to be almost certainly erroneous).[8]

Now, that's a sobering example of the power of bad information graphics don't you think?

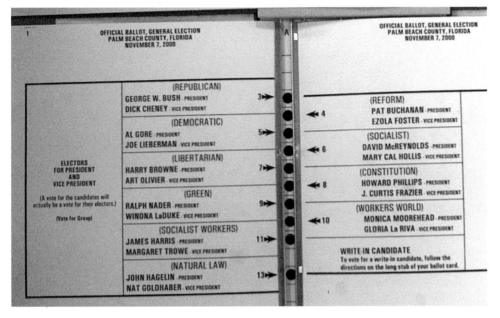

Problem: How to illustrate powerful and disturbing personal facts and observations.

Solved: Use the impersonal language of information graphics.

A recent trend amongst student designers has been towards more personally-focused design work, centred more on the designer as author and observer than problem-solver in the traditional sense.

Interestingly, as a whole generation has turned inwards for its inspiration, it hasn't chosen expressive graphic forms to show us its feelings but the pared down, neutral voice of information design.

One designer, briefed to investigate possible symbolism for the United Kingdom, decided to ask friends and relations from across the country to draw the outline of Britain. When compiling his results he grouped together the drawings by region; it became fascinating to see that London-based respondents made the south of England proportionately huge and were almost incapable of rendering Scotland within their drawings, whilst the Scottish participants were the most able to draw the island's outline accurately.

Another student chillingly chose to record forty-eight years of civil airline disasters not in any sensationalist way but in the form of a map of the world, simply plotting the location of the discoveries of black boxes (the indestructible flight recorders recovered from the wreckage of most crashes).

A class at the Glasgow School of Art devoted themselves individually to the bizarre mapping of their relationships, bone-breakages and personal hang-ups. One plotted her personal phobias against others in her family in order to track for how long and to what extent the phobias continued through life; one accident-prone girl mapped the extent of her own bone breakages and double joints onto a life-sized layout, then removed her outline simply leaving her body detailed only by sets of concentric circles.

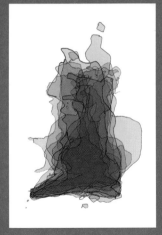

ABOVE
'What is Britain?' student project
SAM WALKER
KINGSTON UNIVERSITY UK 1998

LEFT
Black Box diagram
JEREMY COYSTEN RCA UK 1999

BELOW
'Here am I, where are you?'
ANDI McCRINDLE
GLASGOW SCHOOL OF ART UK 2001

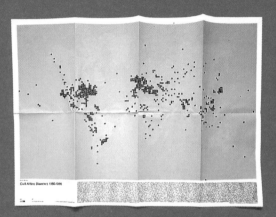

THIS PAGE
Phobias project
NICKY WRIGHT
GLASGOW SCHOOL OF ART
UK 2001
*This project maps one student's
personal fears and phobias against those
of her mother and her grandmother.
The duration of the phobia is shown
by the diameter of the circles*

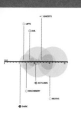

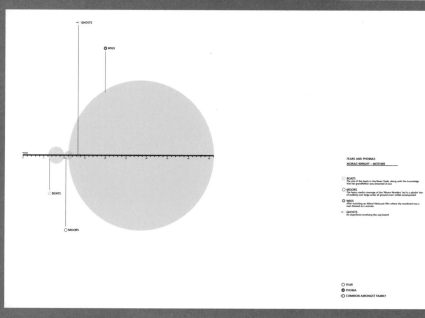

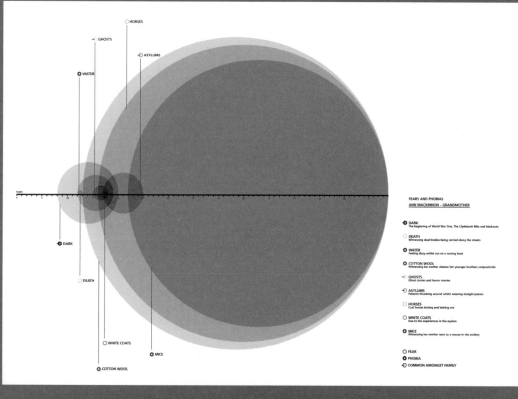

KEY

Friends through education

Nursery School —— Fanoola
—— Charlotte

Primary School —— Valerie
—— Lorna
—— Lynette

High School —— Wendy
—— Emma
—— Kirsty
—— Laura

—— David
—— Derek
—— Andrew
—— Craig

Art School —— Craig
—— Andy
—— Kieran
—— Sarah
—— Jodie
—— Sarah

Family

—— Mum
—— Dad
—— Susanne

—— Gran
—— Grandpa

—— Aunt Jane
—— Uncle Ken
—— Andrew
—— Iain

—— Uncle David
—— Aunt Maureen
—— Yvonne
—— Debbie

—— Aunt Pat
—— Uncle Ray
—— Caroline
—— Philip

—— Grandpa Long Distance
—— Gran Long Distance

But in a neat return to the beginning of the chapter, this designer chose to map the relative closeness of her friends, family and art college group, making a poignant and mysterious map of her first two decades of life in three layouts and coloured lines. She has represented herself by the ever-present straight lines throughout. We can see her relationship with friends, family, even tutors, how they enter and leave her life at different times. An amazing set (and an amazing memory).

How close do you get?
Where are you? I am here ——

Moira	Laura	Felix
Joe	Louise	Joe
Greame	Natalie	Georgina
Simon	Emma	Holly
Jodie	Sarah L	Jenny
Sarah	Jane	Barrie Tutor
Andy	Fiona P	Steve Tutor
Kieran	Fiona H	Sharon
Sarah M	Lisa	Steven
Stephanie	Jaqueline	Jamie
Craig	Caroline	Michelle
Dan	Vidar	Lisa
Niel	Anita	Susie
Ryan	Rhonda	Joe Tutor
Andy N	Wendy S	Elaine
Julie	Nicky	Fiona C
Mandy	Jade	Kate
Wendy		

THIS SPREAD
'How close do you get?'
SARAH-JANE CASSELLS
GLASGOW SCHOOL OF ART
UK 2001

FAMILY

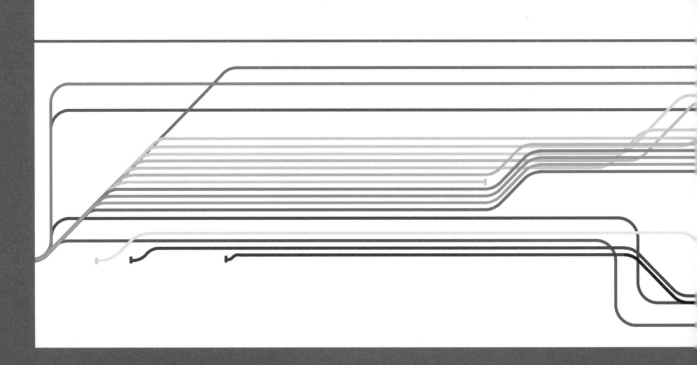

FRIENDS

ART SCHOOL

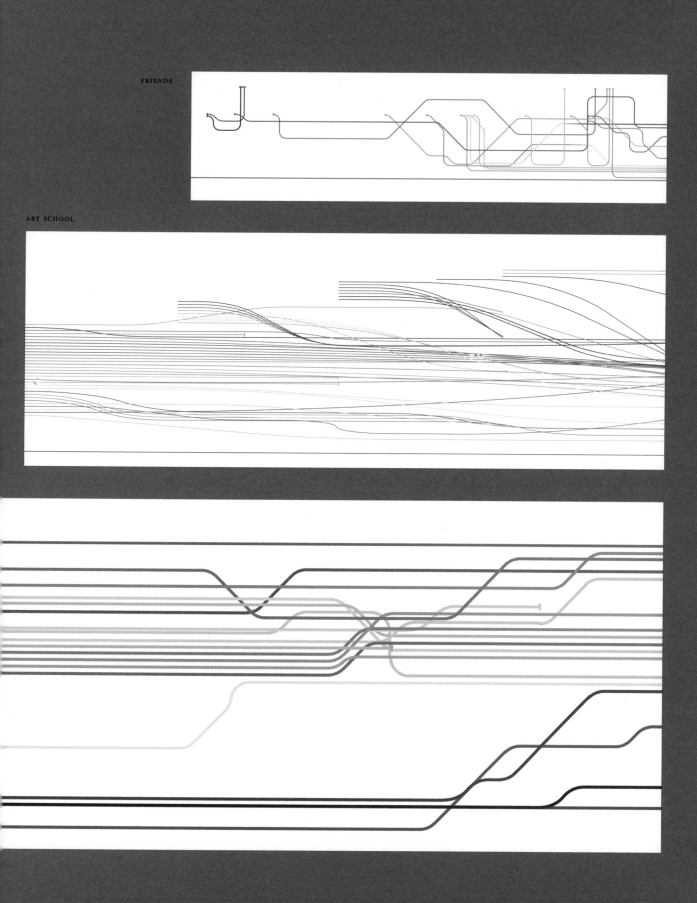

Can creatives produce potent work
for a cause they don't believe in?
Do you have to smoke to do great
cigarette ads? When does a creative
person's ethical responsibility
kick in and the client's kick out?
And why does political advertising
often produce such great work
– is it the ultimate product to sell,
the ultimate demonstration of the
communicator's skills?

Throughout the twentieth century, politics and communication have been inextricably linked. Wars have been fought and lost, backed up by propaganda campaigns. Student riots have been sparked off and recorded worldwide by the political or quasi-political image.

Designers and advertisers have always been involved in these developments. And sometimes creatives will have been asked to produce work which they could, or perhaps should, not have believed in. But can they simply plead poverty, close their eyes and get on with it? Surely there is a point at which personal beliefs must come into play and where 'commercial art' becomes un-commercial and even unethical.

The first well-known examples of propaganda date from the First World War, when, spurred on by various versions around the world, the famous Kitchener poster came about for the British war effort (to be copied and lampooned for the rest of the century). Poster artists on all sides were called in to ply their skills in the services of their countries. And the tradition continued into the 1920s as Russian Constructivism tested its theories on images of civil war.

But it is the rise of Nazi Germany that illustrates the problem at the core of this chapter. The poster designs of Ludwig Hohlwein rightly hold pride of place

UND DU?

in the world's poster archives but they pose awkward problems – we stand back and admire their beauty in communicating the strength and power of the fledgling Third Reich, but we can't divorce them from the unhappy associations with the 'client'. When producing her ground-breaking propaganda films, Leni Reifenstahl introduced cropping and editing skills that were to have a lasting effect on world cinema, but her beautiful and powerful images were produced to promote a violent dictatorship.

Many see in Albert Speer's starkly powerful exhibition, banner and logo designs the beginnings of post-war corporate identity schemes (rigorously controlled repetitive elements with a restricted palette of colours and layouts). Did he close his eyes to the horrors around him? And how different is Speer's predicament to that of a contemporary designer producing posters for a regime that suddenly falls foul of the establishment?

Luckily, the same era provides us with some clues for a 'right' way to proceed, with the work of John Heartfield (formerly Helmut Herzfelde) who produced anti-Hitler posters in Germany itself before fleeing to Britain in fear of

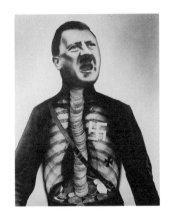

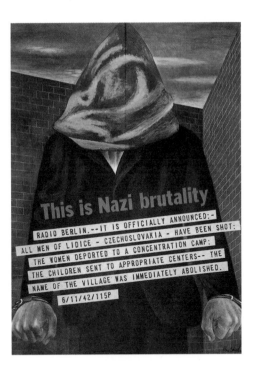

his life. His image of Hitler's neck full of coins stands with Abram Games's 'Your Talk May Kill Your Comrades' and Ben Shan's concentration camp poster as one of the most compelling of the war.

But still, where does that place Holwhein? To use the defence heard many times at the Nuremburg war-crimes trial following the war, he 'was just following orders' and it wasn't his fault that his then masters were soon to be war-criminals.

Until the Nazis began to demonstrate their true colours, you could argue that he was simply extending the classic poster tradition for a client, which at that point had restored pride to a previously depressed nation.[1]

Whether we like the moral circumstances surrounding them or not, Hohlwein, Reifenstahl and Speer's work stands the test of time because in their purest form they were fine examples. We just happen to abhor what they actually stood for.

The language of the protest came back into its own during the 1960s, when a new generation railed against all manner of foes, from American presidents, to police aggression on the streets of Paris. Whether pasted up billboard-style as an anonymous protest against the state, or as a critical piece of bedroom furniture, the poster once again became essential propaganda. The change of heart over Vietnam by the American people is easily tracked in the posters of the time, which give voice to the ever-growing disquiet of a nation pitted against an unbeatable enemy in an unwanted war.

In the UK in the late 1970s, the Conservative opposition party ran a hugely significant poster campaign claiming that 'Labour isn't working', aimed at a nation then racked by industrial action and rising unemployment. Many well-read neutrals knew that actually the monetarist plans of the Conservative party

TOP LEFT
'Adolf, the Superman: Swallows gold and talks tin'
JOHN HEARTFIELD
GERMANY/UK 1932

TOP RIGHT
'This is Nazi brutality'
BEN SHAN USA 1943

ABOVE
'Your talk may kill your comrades'
ABRAM GAMES UK 1941

RIGHT
'SS'
ATELIER POPULAIRE
FRANCE 1968

LEFT
'Labour still isn't working'
SAATCHI & SAATCHI UK 1979

BELOW LEFT
'Pregnant man' poster
SAATCHI & SAATCHI UK 1970

BELOW
'New Labour New Danger'
M&C SAATCHI UK 1997

BELOW RIGHT
'Four years of Labour and he still
hasn't delivered'
YELLOW M UK 2001

BOTTOM RIGHT
'Tory Cuts'
TBWA\LONDON UK 2001

would, in all likeliness, increase unemployment substantially (which is exactly what happened). But the fact that it was a brazen piece of work doesn't stop it from being one of the most famous posters of the century, whatever problems there were with the accuracy of its message.

When returned to government, this right-wing administration pursued, in their eighteen years of power, some of the most powerful political advertising ever seen, conveying the core messages (that the Labour opposition would tax you to hell or that the then new leader Tony Blair was the red devil in disguise) with single-minded efficiency (albeit ultimately unsuccessfully).

The left-wing Labour party was left to fight against the various government policies on a campaign-by-campaign basis. Only when replaced by a now more middle-of-the-road Labour party were the Conservatives thrown into disarray, and thus far unable to strike back coherently.

The most potent and historically interesting image of the British 2001 election only ran once, when an ex-intern at the Conservatives' old agency (Saatchi & Saatchi) posted a parody layout of their famous 'pregnant man' ad to the leader of the opposition. It used a picture of a pregnant Tony Blair accompanied by the line 'Four years of Labour and he still hasn't delivered'. The Conservatives' new agency, Yellow M, was then forced to run the ad, even though the original inspiration was by a rival agency.

The Labour party, re-elected in 2001, chose to pursue a tactical strategy – reputedly their new agency had developed up to 40 posters which could be 'wheeled out' for any eventuality. Unfortunately, this led to a slightly piecemeal campaign, with vastly

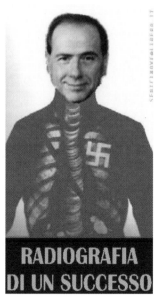

varying styles of execution (veering from reportage, to pastiche film humour, to straightforward tax-cut shockers). But at least in the UK political parties can appoint agencies that agree with their policies, each then having a relatively free reign. In some countries government control of the media has become so strong that this level of freedom of speech is genuinely endangered.

In the 2000 Italian election, candidate Silvio Berlusconi flooded Italy with images of his grinning visage next to bland promises (such as 'a concrete promise: less tax for all', 'safer cities' etc). Unfortunately for the would-be premier, rumours that the picture was somewhat out-of-date (and hence slightly misleading about the precise extent of his follical challenge) led inexorably to a proliferation of easy jokes and graffitti ('a concrete promise: more hair for all') and then vast website resources devoted to spoof posters of Berlusconi as a Klingon, Che Guevara, the Pope and the most evil of them all, Darth Vader.

One wonders why the opposition parties did not simply attack the dubious record of the Berlusconi empire, but the truth is probably that against a mogul with such control over the vast majority of Italian media, the guerrilla activity (and low cost) of the internet suited them just fine. In the end, Berlusconi turned the campaigns to his advantage by offering a prize for the best one.[2]

What is clear from the previous cases is that successful political advertising is related to the persuasions of the agencies concerned. The Conservatives used the Saatchi

LEFT
'Red tape' billboard
BOASE MASSIMI POLLITT
UNIVAS PARTNERSHIP 1984

BELOW
Silk Cut poster
SAATCHI & SAATCHI UK 1987

BOTTOM RIGHT
Health Education poster
SAATCHI & SAATCHI UK 1970

BELOW LEFT
Lucky Strike packaging
LOEWY USA 1940S

brothers in their various agency guises because they were famously right-wing, while the socialist examples above were carried out by confirmed left-wing London agencies BMP DDB and TBWA. It's when we move away from politics and look at these agencies' other work that things get a bit more confusing.

For example, Saatchi & Saatchi have for years produced a campaign for Silk Cut cigarettes, which on the face of it has produced very fine examples of advertising. But how do the creatives feel advertising the biggest known cause of cancer?[3] Are they also just following orders? Strangely, when just a fledgling agency in the early 1970s, Saatchis made one of their

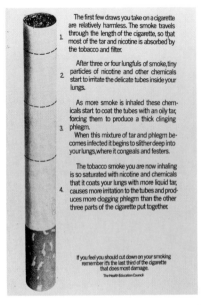

first breakthroughs with work for the Health Education Council illuminating the dangers of smoking to the public.

Agencies and designers have long worked for ethically dubious clients, but history tends to view the work with strangely tobacco-tinted spectacles, especially the work that broke barriers before government's or surgeon's health warnings started appearing. Raymond Loewy's re-design

of the Lucky Strike cigarette pack is often heralded as a design classic but few designers now would happily acknowledge or publicize their involvement in cigarette-pack design. The classic, ground-breaking advertising produced for Benson & Hedges in the 1970s by London agency Collett Dickenson Pearce (CDP) rightly occupies centre stage in terms of advertising history but these ads also encouraged a whole new generation that it was cool to smoke.

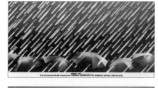

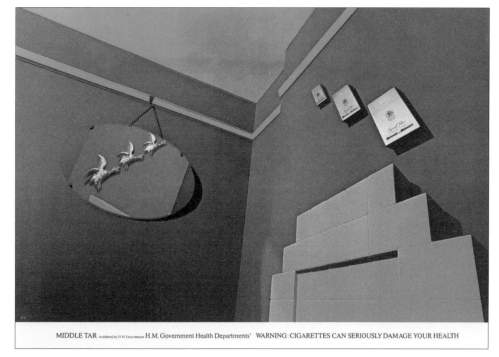

MIDDLE TAR As defined by H.M. Government H.M. Government Health Departments' WARNING: CIGARETTES CAN SERIOUSLY DAMAGE YOUR HEALTH

Presumably these agencies then saw no contradiction in their position. But placed in context with their many examples of social 'cause' advertising, this writer finds an ethical dilemma – agencies that can produce a charity ad one minute, then a cigarette ad, then an ad for a political party must have a 'moral compass' that is severely faulty. The Nuremberg defence doesn't apply for the anti-moralists, as we shall call them. They would respond that all they are doing is responding to whatever that particular client's problem is. That is their job, not to comment politically upon it. But that undermines the whole profession – if you are going to work for ultra-capitalist clients *and* do charity ads, it seems to this writer at least that the two simply don't mix; selfishness and selflessness make unsuitable bedfellows.

And with the next generation of communicators demanding higher levels of ethical responsibility from their employers, it's an issue which increasingly will appear on the agenda.

ABOVE
Benson & Hedges posters ads
COLLETT DICKENSON PEARCE
UK 1977–80

RIGHT
Anti-smoking poster
HALL ADVERTISING LTD UK 1978

WHY DO YOU THINK
EVERY PACKET CARRIES A GOVERNMENT HEALTH WARNING?

Problem: What best sums up a nation: its flag or its symbols of government?

A nation's flag usually provides the perfect visual summary of a nation. The speed and regularity with which graphic designers turn to their flags to make positive or negative points, simply reinforces the original design's message. Most countries will point to their flag as the most potent symbol of their identity – the United States turns to its flag in times of need, either as a kind of comfort blanket in the recent aftermath of terrorism, or as a potent outlet for hatred for anti-Vietnam campaigners thirty years earlier.

Other designers turn to their flags to make straightforward nationalistic points or to protest: Niklaus Troxler used the simplicity of flags and their colours to make the suggestion to join the EU – but his image of his native flag being overlapped by a 'European' version could incite patriotic emotions.

Whilst the Stars and Stripes generally has enough graphic simplicity and meaning to come out on top, the hijacking of the Union Jack by ultra right-wing supporters and arch-royalists in Britain has meant that 'the waving of the Union Jack' has layers of complex meaning.

The British Government does not display the Union Jack on its letterhead, simply a Royal crest, leaving the fluttering flags to its airline and football fans. It may seem strange to outsiders, but the *four* countries of the 'United Kingdom of Britain and Northern Ireland' are not all symbolized by the *three* flags combined to make the Union Jack.

Some countries, notably Germany, France and Canada, have attempted to deal with the potential confusion between state and flag by coming to some sort of compromise, where some, if not all, of the elements are echoed somehow in the visual identity of their governments. The German administration identifies itself with an eagle and a thin strip of the flag to maintain a link, the French government has the tricolour of the flag but adds the human silhouette of Marianne into the mix.

Canada, in one of the simplest systems developed, uses small versions of the flag and the maple leaf in the corner of its corporate-logo-like solution.

Other countries may be summed up by flags but yearn to change them, seeing them as symbols of a past they wish to leave behind.

ABOVE
Show magazine cover
HENRY WOLFF USA 1963

LEFT
Breakdown of the Union Jack
UK 1606
Top to bottom: The St Georges Cross, flag of England; St Andrew's Cross, flag of Scotland; St Patrick's Cross, flag of Ireland; Union Jack. The Welsh dragon is not incorporated because the principality was already united to England before 1606

BELOW
Canadian government identity
JIM DONOAHUE CANADA 1960

BELOW
French government identity
AILLEURS EXACTEMENT FRANCE 1999

BELOW AND RIGHT
German Federal Government identity
METADESIGN GERMANY 1997

BELOW LEFT
Swiss Book Design poster
PIERRE MENDELL GERMANY 1994

BELOW RIGHT
Visual application to join the EU –
membership for Switzerland
NIKLAUS TROXLER
SWITZERLAND 1996

Die
Bundesregierung

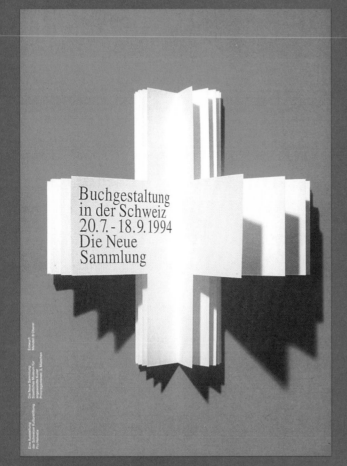

Buchgestaltung
in der Schweiz
20.7. - 18.9.1994
Die Neue
Sammlung

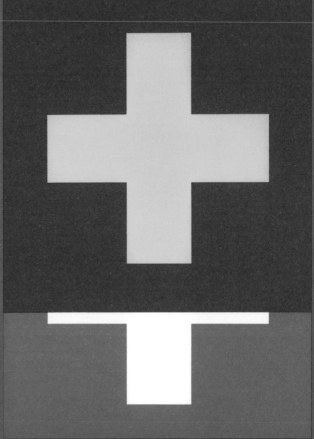

The Australian media regularly publish proposed flag re-designs that will rid them of their colonial or chequered past in the way that South Africa has done. And when Australia eventually finally becomes a republic, they will be able to abandon what is to many of them an embarrassing link to the history that their flag represents, and to recognize their visual (and constitutional) independence. In the meantime, regular competitions are held to propose possible designs for when the revolution finally comes (or for when enough blue-rinsed royalists finally pass away).

When asked to suggest solutions to the problem faced by the European Community's circle of stars flag (ie. what happens when more members join), world achitecture and brand guru Rem Koolhaus simply shredded the member states flags into an amazing multicoloured bar-code design that threw Europe's broadsheet papers into disarray.

But one of the neatest short-term solutions to the problem of summing up nation and state came about in Romania once they had finally deposed their much-hated leader, Nikolae Ceausescu.

The most potent symbol of the turbulent time became simply the Romanian flag with Ceausescu's royal seal removed – the removal of that little bit of nothing neatly summing up a nation's anger and relief.

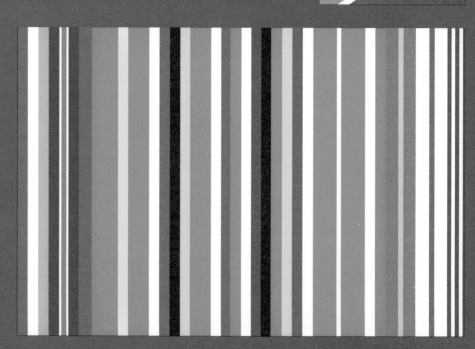

The CAN'T LEARN, WON'T LEARN *problem*

Designing for education sounds pretty boring, doesn't it? Can't we talk about the new ads for Diesel instead? No, we can't. Because this is important. It may be difficult and unglamorous, but the power of an educational poster, effective exhibition, or breakthrough in children's books can win over the coldest hearts and minds.

Politicians always talk about education, education and then education because they know it's something that we all care deeply about. Yet because this is a notoriously under-funded sector, few design or advertising agencies concentrate on this area. Most need moneyed blue-chip clients to survive, but seeing a fourteen-year-old understand a piece of real science rather than the science of his or her new trainers not only rewards the creative, it enhances our world.

Providing inspiration and knowledge for the public as a whole has historical precedents that go back hundreds of years – the Great Exhibition of 1851 was a potent symbol of Victorian Britain, demonstrating its manufacturing skills to the world. There is no coincidence in the fact that many items from the exhibition became the backbone of the collection of what decades later became the Victoria & Albert Museum (whose carved stone entrance carefully promises *inspiration* and *knowledge* to the visitor).

A theoretically temporary structure, the Eiffel Tower was built to commemorate another international exhibition, and only escaped demolition in 1909 because of its value as a telegraph antenna. With the first half of the twentieth century thrown into turmoil by two world wars, it wasn't until the immediate aftermath of the Second World War that the responsibilities of a world adjusting to peace brought out the best in the world's communicators.

Abram Games, FHK Henrion and Hans Schleger, having made their names as propaganda artists, were able to apply their persuasive skills to the British nation. Lester Beall applied his 'people-orientated' approach to a series of classic American public information posters, guiding them through issues such as supplying electricity to urban areas and providing power for farms.

Rather than overload his audience with information he chose to educate with the simplest palette and almost brutally reduced shapes, a design role-model

ABOVE
This child found a 'blind'
ABRAM GAMES UK 1945

BELOW
Rural Electrification Administration
posters
LESTER BEALL USA 1937–41

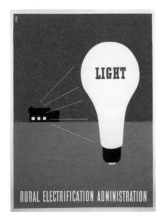

regularly returned to by contemporary designers.

Josef Müller-Brockmann's seminal series of posters for road safety in Switzerland also stands as a benchmark for graphic mass education – simple but incredibly powerful with their minimal use of two or three elements, they have rarely been bettered in terms of clarity of message.

The post-war period also saw the return to importance of the public exhibition. Bizarrely, one of the UK's most visited exhibitions ever took place in 1946 at the V&A. Over two million people visited a significant exhibition entitled 'Britain can make it!', making this still the most attended exhibition in the museum's history (although some consider this a 'freak' explained by a war-torn British public deprived of any visual stimulation throughout the war years).

The public enthusiasm for large-scale, educative material was borne out by the enormous success of the Festival of Britain of 1951, which between six and eight million people visited over five months. Here the die was set – collaboration between the greatest designers and architects of the era producing set-piece displays to impress the visiting public. It also illustrated to governments the emotional aspects of such large-scale attractions – psychologically it helped the UK population begin to believe that they could leave the ration-book era behind and look forward to some degree of prosperity.

As world fairs became increasingly popular, US-based innovators began to demonstrate their skills. The Museum of Modern Art in New York staged the classic 'Family of Man' exhibition in 1955, celebrating humankind through the museum's extensive collection of the relatively young art-form of photography.

American designer
Will Burtin produced
two landmark projects
at the end of the 1950s
for the pharmaceutical
company, Upjohn. The
first was a concerted
effort to produce a 3D
representation of a

LEFT
Upjohn Human Cell exhibit
WILL BURTIN USA 1958

MIDDLE LEFT
Upjohn Human Brain exhibit
WILL BURTIN USA 1960

BELOW RIGHT
Excerpts from *Powers of Ten*
CHARLES AND RAY EAMES
USA 1977

BOTTOM LEFT AND RIGHT
Visions of Japan
Victoria & Albert Museum London
TOYO ITO JAPAN 1989

human cell which a visitor could enter and walk around (Burtin 'finished' the
model himself because his scientific advisors could not agree on the precise shape
of a cell blown up to this size).

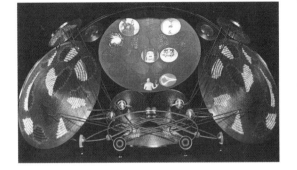

Such was the success of this
piece that it became the
benchmark for interpretive 3D
objects of the future. Burtin
followed this with another
classic, a brain exhibit that used
lights, images and colour to
show visitors how a thought is

created. Charles and Ray Eames showed their versatility by diverting from
furniture design to produce film classics such as *Powers of Ten*. This landmark
film, still shown in science labs the world over, illustrated the degrees of scale
that mankind is part of. Constantly referred to, referenced and ripped-off ever
since, this product of a time before computer animation still seems astonishing.

It travelled from outer space (a distance of 10^{+25}
metres away from earth) to the inside of a peaceful
picniker (10^{-18} metres),
moving at a distance
of the 'power of ten',
thus giving us the title.

The idea of the
immersive environments
that Burtin established
and the Eameses
explored in their multi-
media projects still

continues to this day. Still much discussed and referred to was the landmark piece in 1989, 'Visions of Japan', which managed to make the visitor really feel that they were actually experiencing Japan, rather than simply walking along the leafy pavements of South Kensington.

And although criticized for its cost, the Millennium Dome still attracted six and a half million people to a site designed as a kind of sequel to the Festival of Britain, fifty years later. Some of the educational aspects became lost to the power of corporate sponsors keen to establish their branded 'seals' of approval, but many of the zones such as 'Work', 'Play' and 'National Identity' will live long in the memories of those who visited.

While these are prime examples of the huge, set-piece blockbusting 'permanent' exhibition, the ability to educate with a piece that can also travel successfully has become a significant problem to solve. Burtin's ground-breaking pieces did occasionally travel, but with some difficulty – conversely this piece on Dutch Design for the public sector from the late 1970s featured plexiglass figures holding examples of work on exhibit, which could easily be compressed down into waiting packing-cases, ready for their next tour venue.

Some ideas solve the 'temporary' brief in their very simplicity, such as this waiting room at Grand Central Station in New York, designed by Drenttel Doyle Partners and dedicated to the Nineteenth Amendment to the US Constitution. Doyle and his design team turned the whole floor of a gallery over to a massive typographic edict on women's right to vote, with a simple stand-alone element as a compelling focus featuring photographs, tracts and buttons of the suffrage movement.

Another design showcase for Grand Central was created by Casson Mann and invited passers-by to

TOP LEFT
National Identity Zone,
Millennium Dome
APICELLA ASSOCIATES/
CARIBINER UK 1999

MIDDLE LEFT
Dutch Design for the Public Sector
travelling exhibition
STUDIO DUMBAR
THE NETHERLANDS 1978–2000

BOTTOM RIGHT
Nineteenth Amendment exhibition
DRENTTEL DOYLE PARTNERS
USA 1995

take an oversized seat at a dining table of design treasures. It was also carefully engineered to split into two smaller sections which could then tour the globe independently.

This design for 42nd Street featured chairs hung along the billboard in an attempt to engage passers-by in the project

concerning the redevelopment of the area.

Of course, all the above examples solve the 'can't learn' problem by creating amazing experiences that cannot fail to engage a visitor or pedestrian. But 'won't learn' poses different problems, the classic one being that of the bored teenager. Whilst the world's museums know that adults and under-eights are relatively easy to entertain, it gets a lot trickier in the teens.

Museums have devoted significant time and energy developing digitally-based displays, knowing that an increasingly wired-up young visitor might be more interested in staying in their museum than pestering a long-suffering parent to leave as soon as possible. Both the

ABOVE
Great Expectations exhibition,
New York
CASSON MANN UK 2001

ABOVE LEFT
42nd Street 'Everybody' project
M&CO USA 1993

LEFT
Digitopolis, Science Museum, London
CASSON MANN UK 2000

OPPOSITE TOP LEFT AND RIGHT
Science Museum, London
The Basement, The Garden
BEN KELLEY, CASSON MANN UK 1995

OPPOSITE MIDDLE
The Garden of Dunes,
Parc de la Villette, Paris
ISABELLE DEVIN/CATHERINE RANNOU
FRANCE 1987

OPPOSITE BOTTOM LEFT
Cité des Sciences et de l'Industrie,
Parc de la Villette, Paris
ADRIEN FAINSILBER FRANCE 1986

OPPOSITE BOTTOM RIGHT
Investigate, Natural History Museum,
London
PENTAGRAM UK 2000

London Science Museum and the Cité des Sciences in Paris have pioneered interactive and digitally-based displays that can genuinely compete with the games consoles and the satellite TV at home.

At the new four-storey Wellcome Wing in the Science Museum, one floor is dedicated to digital technology and is carefully constructed to echo the warps and wefts of digital data, allowing the visitor opportunities to criss-cross the space at their leisure rather than following any pre-determined path. Along their journey they can scan their head in three dimensions, play all the instruments in a four-part electronic orchestra or programme a set of robots in a bizarre game of electronic catch.

The London Natural History Museum, not to be outdone, developed a hands-on area for the mythical 'eight and up' sector when they opened 'Investigate', an area specifically designed to allow inquisitive minds to run free

with their own computer terminals, trays of objects to be examined and their own magnifying glass. They even included a small outdoor courtyard with assistants on hand with magnifying glasses so that children could peer at the caterpillars on the leaves.

The subject-matter of some recently-developed buildings and installations is deliberately targeted at

an even older audience. Daniel Libeskind's new Jewish Museum in Berlin attracted 300,000 visitors simply to walk around the space before any exhibits were put in, because the architect had so successfully managed to suggest the plight of the Holocaust victim purely in terms of its architecture. Visitors cannot enter the museum through a normal entrance (it has no door).

They enter the adjacent (traditionally-styled) museum and then walk through a disorientating tunnel lit only by the occasional light, echoing the harrowing entrance of many refugees to the camps themselves. Libeskind plays games with the corridors and walls throughout to make the visit feel like no other – even when thrown out into the garden, trees are planted on top of huge concrete pillars, nearly out of sight of the visitor.

A recently-developed Holocaust exhibition at the Imperial War Museum in London has even had to publish a cinema-like '15 years or over' health warning because the contents are so disturbing. Faced with a huge pile of shoes taken from concentration camp victims or the cart used to carry dead bodies through the ghetto, many visitors have found the experience simply overwhelming.

The decisions made in the late-twentieth century to build

ABOVE
Jewish Museum, Berlin
DANIEL LIBESKIND GERMANY 1998

LEFT AND BELOW
Holocaust Exhibit,
Imperial War Museum, London
DEGW/AMALGAM UK 2000

OPPOSITE PAGE TOP & BOTTOM
Washington Vietnam
Veterans memorial
MAYA LIN USA 1982

g the possessions of the dead

d or sent for slave labour were taken to a group of barracks nicknamed
staffed by prisoners who sorted the goods and searched for valuables.
d to Germany for re-use. The workers in 'Canada' could, at great risk,
ets, or valuables to bribe guards. This provided the basis for an
that saved many lives.

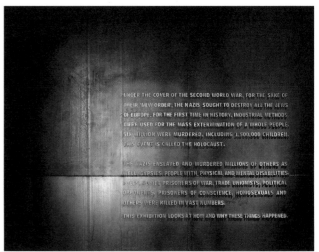

UNDER THE COVER OF THE SECOND WORLD WAR, FOR THE SAKE OF
THEIR 'NEW ORDER', THE NAZIS SOUGHT TO DESTROY ALL THE JEWS
OF EUROPE. FOR THE FIRST TIME IN HISTORY, INDUSTRIAL METHODS
WERE USED FOR THE MASS EXTERMINATION OF A WHOLE PEOPLE.
SIX MILLION WERE MURDERED, INCLUDING 1,500,000 CHILDREN.
THIS EVENT IS CALLED THE HOLOCAUST.

THE NAZIS ENSLAVED AND MURDERED MILLIONS OF OTHERS AS
WELL. GYPSIES, PEOPLE WITH PHYSICAL AND MENTAL DISABILITIES,
POLES, SOVIET PRISONERS OF WAR, TRADE UNIONISTS, POLITICAL
OPPONENTS, PRISONERS OF CONSCIENCE, HOMOSEXUALS AND
OTHERS WERE KILLED IN VAST NUMBERS.

THIS EXHIBITION LOOKS AT HOW AND WHY THESE THINGS HAPPENED.

permanent memorials to the excesses of war and educate the next generation so that they do not make the same mistakes are admirable, and are best illustrated by Maya Lin's classic Vietnam memorial in Washington, DC. Her competition entry bowled the judges over, and bowls visitors over, by being brutally simple –

a chevron of marble planted in a grassed space, with all the American soldiers' names carved in the surface. But Lin's genius was to arrange the names not in alphabetical order, but in the order in which they died or were reported missing in action.

In this way, the visitor experiences the staggering number of names as they search through, looking for their relative, sometimes completely disorientated, leaving many overwhelmed.

ABOVE AND ABOVE LEFT
Pfäfferli + Huber Pharmaceuticals
poster campaign
ERNST BETTLER SWITZERLAND 1959

Some choose to educate by more subtle means. Although he is now becoming recognized as one of the founding fathers of the 'culture-jamming'[1] form of protest, Ernst Bettler's way of revealing to 1950s Switzerland that Pfäfferli + Huber AG (a pharmaceuticals company) had Nazi roots was astonishingly subtle.

When commissioned to design a set of fiftieth anniversary publicity posters he suggested four in total. And into each one he echoed the shape of the letters

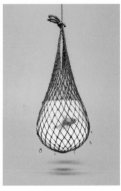

'N', 'A', 'Z' and 'I' through the image photographed (the only surviving 'A' poster is shown opposite). It was only when the posters were put up randomly around town that his client realized that their embarrassing roots had been revealed. There was public outrage. Only six weeks later Pfäfferli + Huber were out of business, thanks to the underground information campaign of Bettler.[2]

When the target market won't come to you, sometimes the trick is to go to them. In the mid-1990s, the British Design Council experimented with a set of posters and accompanying teachers' guides aimed at raising awareness of design within schools by using 'wrong' images on posters in order to prompt responses. Learning from this original set, a new pack was developed and targeted specifically at the trickiest group, bored fourteen-year-olds.

The idea of the set, entitled 'The Big Zipper' and co-produced with the BBC, was to encourage teenagers to feel valued, to feel that they had important ideas of their own and that they *were* capable of great ideas too. Armed with the posters, blocks of Post-its and work-sheets, thousands of schools and youth groups around the country set about attacking the tasks set by the piece, hopefully inspiring in the process the next generation of Dysons and Bransons.

Perhaps The Big Zipper will provide a way forward for the future. Rather than viewing educational materials as necessary, low-cost commodity items, government departments around the world may slowly realize that bright, engaging and fun 'tools' can help produce bright, engaging and fun people too.

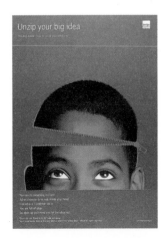

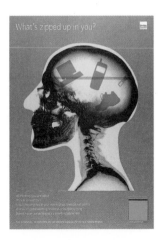

Problem: How to bring design and art to life for children.

Solved: Think like Bruno Munari.

Bruno Munari's life and work crossed over into all areas of visual art, from painting to sculpture, from photography to conceptual art, but one area to which he returned thoughout his life was designing for children.

He was one of the pioneer designers of interactive children's books, and his books stand as the finest design examples, using multiple flaps, die-cut pages, transparent paper, whatever it took to generate the feeling of a circus performer on one spread or fog in a town on the next.

He ran workshops for children, encouraging them to see things in a new way. He could make the lines on stones turn into art in a way that anticipated by decades artists such as Andy Goldsworthy. He designed rubber cats and made forks dance in their own special sculptures.

Best of all, when faced with producing books for children before they began to read properly, he created a magical set called 'pre-libri' (pre-books) which devoted themselves to textures and materials and introduced small children to the idea of books.

Somehow Munari managed to keep that childlike way of seeing throughout his life. He made learning brilliant, not boring. His ideas will continue to inspire for a long time to come.

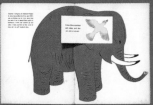

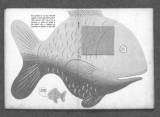

ALL PROJECTS BRUNO MUNARI ITALY

LEFT
'Who's there? Open the door!' 1957

ABOVE
'Jamais contents' (never happy) 1946

OPPOSITE TOP LEFT
'ABC by Bruno Munari' 1960

OPPOSITE LEFT
'Nella notte buia' (in the dark night) 1956

OPPOSITE RIGHT
'The Circus in the Mist' 1969

OVERLEAF
'I Prelibri' (prebooks) 1980

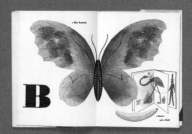

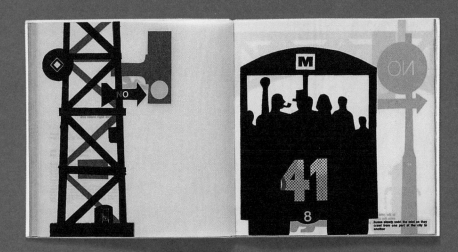

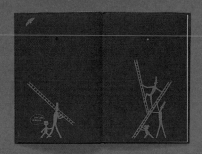

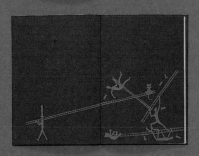

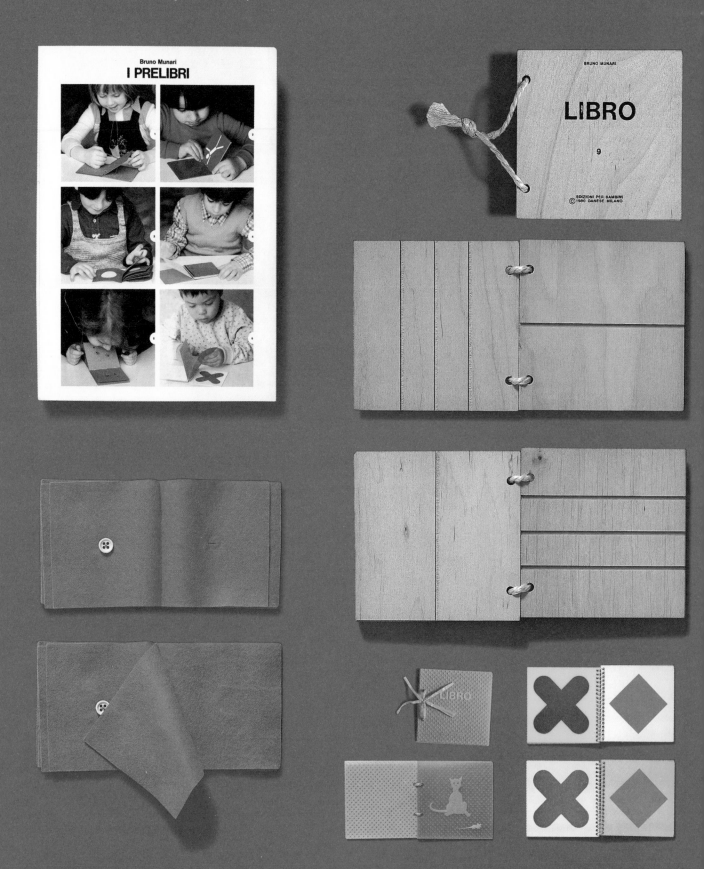

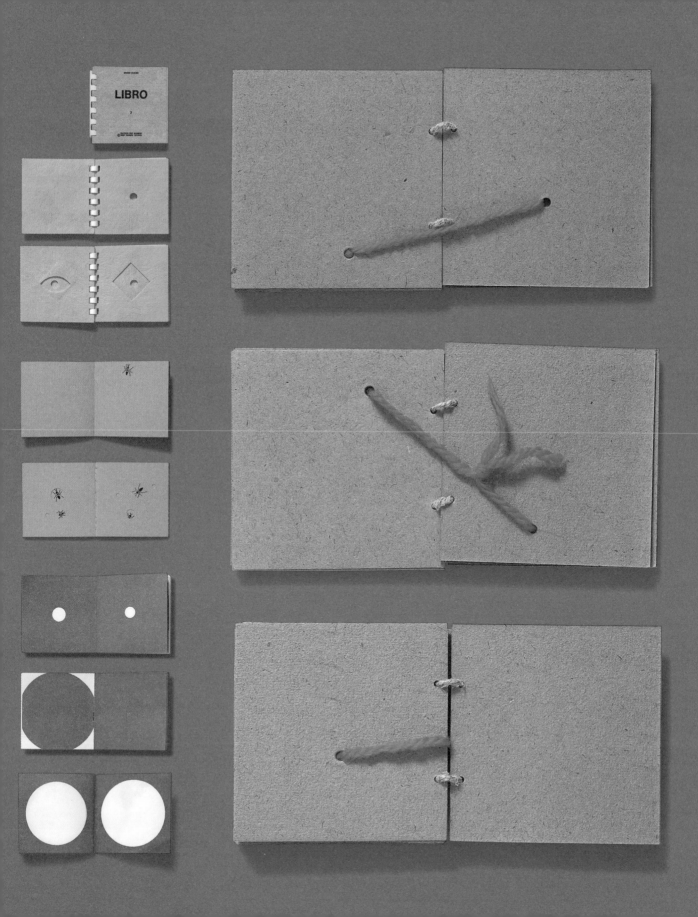

The OLD CAN BE GOOD *problem*

To make something seem like it's been around forever, even when it hasn't? Now there's a challenge. It helps if a product or service has legitimate heritage and the designer or communicator can latch onto something genuine. Sometimes, though, they are asked to 'create' history out of thin air, and this may not work – customers can be cannier than you think.

Sometimes 'age' or 'tradition' is just part of the brand and there's no getting away from it. This *Emigre* cover by Rudy VanderLans makes a point of taking an ancient 'blackletter' typeface and rendering it as a coarse-edged pixellated outline, but it's a cruel joke at the expense of our notion of what makes 'heritage'.

All the exhortations of legions of design consultants will not convince clients with hundreds of years of heritage (such as Coca Cola) to change their identity – the last time their's was looked at, the designers were careful simply to clean up what was already there rather than create anything new.

Even a sector like motoring moves slowly, especially at identity level. Look at the Ford logo a bit more closely – it's really old-fashioned, isn't it? No-one would enter a room now with that and say that it sums up the image of a global, twenty-first-century mobility provider? Like the other great example of Swirls-'R'-Us, Coca-Cola, the Ford logo belongs to a different century but has resisted any attempt to change because it carries with it such emotional and historical baggage, no one would dare touch it.

Perhaps it would take a prolonged, deep global recession to really hurt a company like this, and that might provide the vulture-branders with enough ammunition to prepare an attack. Perhaps, but unlikely.

For products that are umbilically tied-up in their heritage cord, it takes a brave advisor to wield the scissors. That's why, when trying to re-create the glory days of their 1960s motoring, Jaguar, in their modern guise, have deliberately created a car that echoes the shape and feel of their 1960s classics. The market for vintage guitars is booming, not with young guns just starting their first band (who frankly couldn't afford them) but with forty-somethings playing air guitar in their bedrooms, trying to re-create lost youth by buying the pieces of spruce and mahogany their heroes played back then, hoping for a little bit of reflected glory.

A classic example, of course, is Harley-Davidson – the design of their bikes hasn't really changed for decades (still not appreciably fast, still not particularly comfortable) but their fans don't care because they are buying into a piece of American history. And with painstaking care, their design advisors in Chicago (Harley riders themselves) have lovingly re-created, and wallowed in, the design opportunities that this presents.

LEFT
Emigre 14 magazine cover
RUDY VANDERLANS USA 1990

BELOW
The worldwide language of Coca Cola
USA 1887 ONWARDS

BELOW MIDDLE
Ford logo circa 1900
and a proposed re-design
PAUL RAND USA 1966
*Rand proposed this re-design
but it was rejected by Henry Ford
as 'too radical a departure'*

BOTTOM RIGHT
Harley-Davidson brochure
VSA PARTNERS USA 1990S

How Harley will communicate their newly-designed V-Rod bike (with modern designs, less of that shuddering vibration and finally the ability to go faster than an old station-wagon) within the 'retro' language they have carefully maintained remains to be seen. But with hundreds of back orders before it has even shipped, perhaps that doesn't matter.

Perhaps the Harley brand can embrace something new without turning into the type of modern bike brand that its hardened acolytes abhor.

The launch of the 'new' VW Beetle in the late 1990s sent minds back to the classic Beetle, and whilst the launch ads themselves carefully steered away from overt references to the car's classic provenance, a solution to a student brief to market the car seemed to sum up where the advertising could have gone. The new Beetles are pictured suckling at the chassis of the old camper-van, neatly encapsulating the old and new in one picture. A 'real' ad that did run picked up on the historical theme when a new type of people carrier

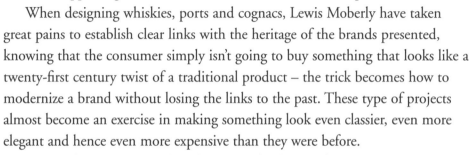

was pictured as jelly appearing out of the mould set by the classic VW 'combie' thirty years previously.

Sometimes 'retro' seems the only possible solution to a problem posed by traditional clients for whom appearing 'modern' is for once the least desirable option on the table.

When designing whiskies, ports and cognacs, Lewis Moberly have taken great pains to establish clear links with the heritage of the brands presented, knowing that the consumer simply isn't going to buy something that looks like a twenty-first century twist of a traditional product – the trick becomes how to modernize a brand without losing the links to the past. These type of projects almost become an exercise in making something look even classier, even more elegant and hence even more expensive than they were before.

When The Partners developed a series of pub signs for Courage Brewers, they resolved the problem of how to produce a large quantity of different signs in a short period by establishing silhouettes as their linking device, allowing several different illustrators to work on the project at the same time. The use of the historical vernacular also allowed the design to neatly straddle old and new, with enough historical references to hang happily outside a sixteenth-century tavern without attempting to look centuries old, which would have been inappropriate outside a more modern pub.

One packaging solution developed for an organic olive oil simply fooled many purchasers into thinking that they had purchased old fermented oil,

with its earthenware bottle, irregularly fitting wax stopper and one-colour label. But no, this was simply olive oil, cleverly packed to look naïve, old and a real 'find', doubtless selling much better in the delicatessens of the world as a result.[1]

In one famous instance the British supermarket Asda, wanting to develop its sales of its own line of wines and spirits, needed to package the liquors in a way that suggested that it was equal to the 'real' brands it shared space with. Packaging in a plain, generic way would have seemed too cheap an aping the style of the brand leaders would have been problematic, potentially litigatory and definitely self-defeating for the design agency, looking to re-define the sector in tandem with a brave client. They settled on an

ABOVE
Courage Brewers Pub signs
THE PARTNERS UK 1989

LEFT
Joy Olive Oil
MICHAEL·NASH UK 1997

BELOW
Asda vodka/Scotch

admirable strategy in the end, creating clear identities for each product and presenting them as modern versions of old classics. The vodka avoided the semi-heraldry of the brand leader and presented a simple illustration. The bottle looks different, but not cheap and cheerful. The whisky doesn't attempt to appear to be

nine hundred years old but uses a simple image of the Scottish Highlands to establish a more appropriate tone. And the results? In the first year, sales jumped by 100 per cent, and they remain on the shelves fifteen years later.

Reference rather than adherence to heritage worked in that case, but some are happy to plunder the archives of design history to make a particular point, or just to revitalize a forgotten way of working. Fashion designers regularly return to the history of dress design for new inspiration, so why shouldn't designers turn the clock back to old work they admire and simply re-use it in a modern context? Paula Scher's admiration for a famous mid-1930s Herbert Matter poster became the inspiration for a new poster for Swatch (the Swiss connection being a neat link).

Henrik Werkmann's typographic experiments in the 1920s have been re-modelled for a new audience by typographers such as Alan Kitching and Vince Frost – the simple fact that the type is not particularly computer-compatible makes the rustic charm of the wood type even more attractive in a time of glossy, perfect, computerized finishes.

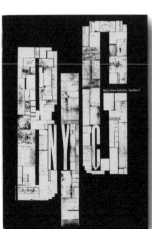

Designers such as Seattle-based Art Chantry have produced a huge body of work based on historical references, often for single- or two-colour projects, screen-printed and deliberately crude, with re-used material from magazines and ancient clip-art.

Chantry himself has proved again and again that he can keep modulating the way he works into new and significant styles, and along the way his work has sometimes tapped in to the graphic zeitgeist (such as his 'tool' series) so powerfully that it has spawned a legion of imitators.

The attraction of a retro style can, however, sometimes trap its proponents in a corner. Whilst the designer of the Swatch poster has taken great pains to show that she has moved on from her retro 'stage', designer Charles Spencer Anderson's work has, for twenty years, been based on the style of old clip art and a relatively fixed colour palette.

His artwork has even become purchasable with archives on CD or the internet – 'Want to design like Charles? – Buy the portfolio!'. Perhaps he has accepted his fate and is playing to (and selling) his undoubted strengths, but he may be pigeonholing himself in the process.

Sometimes a revival of a style can affect a whole decade of work. Kick-started by a renewed interest in the drawings of Aubrey Beardsley and the Viennese Secession movement, an Art Deco revival and copious amounts of mind-altering drugs, a huge amount of western design during the late 1960s and early 1970s seemed to be inexorably influenced by Deco style,

with decorative borders, drop-shadow type and pastel colours cropping up constantly. Later in the 1970s, the desire to painstakingly re-create Victorian typography took a hold of packaging design, imbuing the whole period with the feeling of Victorian soap powder packets.

ABOVE RIGHT
The Night Gallery Cabaret poster
ART CHANTRY USA 1991

ABOVE
Frank Yankovic CD
CHARLES ANDERSON USA 1990S

ABOVE LEFT
CSA Archive
CHARLES ANDERSON USA 1990S

LEFT
Crabtree and Evelyn packaging
PETER WINDETT UK CIRCA 1980

RIGHT
Levi's press ads
BBH UK 1996

BELOW MIDDLE
Commes des Garçons menswear
JAPAN 1990S

BELOW LEFT
Original Delta Airlines identity
USA

BELOW RIGHT
New Delta Airlines identity
LANDOR USA 1990S

Viewed now, some will probably recoil in horror from this seemingly gratuitous recycling of ideas. But just as in fashion and music, what seems terrible to us now will one day be re-examined and recycled, whether we like it or not.

As with the guitar-buying example at the beginning of this chapter, perhaps the influence of an ageing population will affect the way we view that which we see as 'old'. If we now tolerate our rock stars continuing touring into their 50s, perhaps the endless revisiting of former styles is inevitable.

Only recently, Rei Kawakubo of Commes des Garçons made ageing models the stars of her catwalk show, and Levi's used a series of press ads that prove that old can be bold, not boring.

Whilst the new-business executives of the world's design companies will hate me for saying it, some things may be better left well alone. For years American airline Delta flew happily in shiny aluminium planes, with slightly outmoded typography simply saying 'Delta' down the side. As it happens and in a bizarre twist, by the time they finally succumbed to the advances of the report-wielding revisionists, their corporate look had become strangely groovy again.

Across the world, designers were using square, blocky sans serif type much like the Delta logo on club flyers and record sleeves. They were trendy again – it's true, your identity really can come back into fashion if you leave it

long enough. So what did they do? They changed it, of course. Enter, stage left, a bland corporate typeface, and a bland corporate look. Exit old livery stage right.

Just as they began to be different from the rest, they became the same again.

Perhaps the moral here really is to ignore the admonishments of your advisors – whatever you

have may eventually come back into fashion.

Remember though, it may be a long wait.

Problem: Newer isn't always better.

Solved: The art of looking older by Sedley Place.

With their founders committed to the craft skills of drawing, building and writing, it's unsurprising that Sedley Place has built a portfolio of projects that look as though they've been around forever. And they are very happy with that.

Any dalliances on their part with whatever seems 'modern' to their London design counterparts have been swiftly airbrushed from their own particular history – this is a company that specializes almost entirely in the past, in discovering heritage, often creating it from scratch.

When approached by Truman's breweries in the 1980s to help with their then appallingly-liveried public houses, Sedley Place's reaction was to go right back in time and recreate the pubs of people's memories, not the pubs of plastic back-lit frontages. Typefaces were painstakingly hand-drawn, individual signs lettered and enamelled, furniture specially designed.

Years of careful work resulted in pubs that looked the way that pubs should be.

The ability of several of the partners to work with meticulous detail has drawn them into the drinks sector, where their ability to create designs for bourbons or whiskies that look irrefutably ancient has been grabbed by the marketing men. Even global brands like Smirnoff have received the Sedley touch – just a simple stretch of the

ALL PROJECTS SEDLEY PLACE UK

TOP
Truman Breweries fascia, 1970s

ABOVE
Truman Breweries brass plaque from the redesign 1980s

LEFT
Smirnoff Red Label re-design 1999
The new bottle is shown on the left

BELOW
Smirnoff Black Label range extension 1996

OPPOSITE PAGE
George Dickel Whisky labels 1988
The 'new' label is the lower one. The original label was made to look like a cheap cowboy souvenir by the redesign

Our "Charcoal Mellowing" process begins with hard sugar maple to make charcoal. We pile it into ricks, set fire and wait till they're charred just so. Then we pack the charcoal ten feet deep into our mellowing vats. Finally, the whisky starts its slow, easy journey down through the charcoal. What trickles out is the finest whisky that was ever aged in a charred oak barrel.

CG – 16.247.12.02

BOTTLED AT THE DISTILLERY

EST'D. 1870

GEORGE
Dickel®
TENNESSEE
Sour Mash
WHISKY
OLD Nº 12 BRAND

DISTILLED AND BOTTLED ONLY BY
GEO. A. DICKEL & CO., TULLAHOMA
TENNESSEE
45% ALC/VOL (90 PROOF)

MADE IN TENNESSEE

George Dickel wouldn't settle for less than the smoothest drinking whisky that ever was. He set up down Tullahoma way because the freestone water here is sweet, pure and iron-free. Also, only Tennessee Highland hard sugar maple trees would do for making the charcoal he needed to mellow the whisky. Over a hundred years ago George Dickel Whisky was known as the original smooth Tennessee Whisky. Still is.

CASCADE HOLLOW

*B*ack in 1870, George Dickel had a dream. He'd produce the SMOOTHEST Tennessee Whisky around. So on a choice piece of land in Tullahoma, using only the pure SWEET WATER from CASCADE SPRING, he began. George developed his own unique process he called 'COLD CHILLING'. With that know-how, and the finest grains available, he perfected the way TENNESSEE WHISKY was made. And because George's own methods are used today there's no smoother sippin' whisky than Dickel in all of Tennessee or anywhere else.

16.247.12.03

BOTTLED AT *Cascade Hollow* DISTILLERY

EST'D 1870

GEORGE
Dickel®
ORIGINAL
TENNESSEE
Finest Quality Sippin'
WHISKY

SUPERIOR Nº 12 BRAND

DISTILLED AND BOTTLED ONLY AT
CASCADE HOLLOW
TULLAHOMA–TENNESSEE USA
by GEORGE A. DICKEL & CO.
45% Alc/vol (90 Proof)

TULLAHOMA TENNESSEE

GEORGE A. DICKEL

*G*eorge Dickel believed that to make the best TENNESSEE whisky, there was one ingredient he needed most–TIME. First he took one full week to prepare the grain. Followed by a nice long spell of 'COLD CHILLING'. The extra step that made George's whisky so smooth. Then slow 'SWEET MAPLE MELLOWING'. Finally, he sent it to age and capture its RICH COLOR in charred, white oak barrels. Over a hundred years later, we still take the time,– and folks still agree "THERE AIN'T NOTHIN' BETTER"

bottle here and a smaller label there have subtly transformed the brand from looking a little bit 'bargain basement' to being the market leader again.

It's not just to drink that the partners always turn – the ability to design and produce bas-relief heraldry is hardly on the curriculum of the world's art schools – but these designers have the patience and knowledge to produce this detail, such as the stamps above.

Within corporate branding, prior to its submersion into the Diageo empire, Grand Metropolitan received the most elegant of identity solutions when they were given their own set of hallmarks which became

their corporate symbol (their own particular hallmarks of quality). The chain of inns that traded under the prefix 'dragon' managed to look established on day one, courtesy of a hand-sculpted, enamelled dragon applied across every piece of paper, menu and sign, cleverly doubling as an ampersand when needed.

But rather than shout about their achievements, they prefer to stay a well-kept secret, shying away from publicity, content in the knowledge that those who really want to know will find them – as they say themselves, 'a lot of what you see around you can be traced back to the same place'.

DRAGON INNS & RESTAURANTS

ALL PROJECTS SEDLEY PLACE UK

TOP LEFT AND RIGHT
Royal Mail definitive stamps 2001

ABOVE
Grand Metropolitan symbol
CIRCA 1987

LEFT AND OPPOSITE
Dragon Inns & Restaurants identity
1992

The OVER-DESIGNED *problem*

Sometimes design and art direction just get in the way. If someone's spent too long agonizing over a layout or picking a typeface, the viewer can often tell. And if it looks tortured in any way it's less likely to make someone believe in it or want to buy the product.

So how do we solve this problem? If an ad or poster is screaming out 'DESIGNED' at you, there must be a way to make it look un-designed.

It's no coincidence that clothes that look weather-beaten regularly come back into fashion – sometimes it just doesn't feel right for something to look slick and expensive. More and more television and film shows are shot with hand-held cameras because it just looks more real that way – hospital dramas before the advent of the Steadicam were so much more pedestrian.

Within communication, the same rules apply. Sometimes, if the hand of the designer becomes invisible it lets the message come through that much more strongly. And as a reaction to the stylized and slick graphics that often crop up each decade, the use of everyday forms (the vernacular) often finds a way to return to make its mark and grab our attention.

Historically, it has taken little to persuade designers to grab the everyday, especially if it helps them with the problem. This logo for a film about an inept secretary is made that much more powerful because the designer chose poorly-typed words to communicate her ineptitude. Minale Tattersfield used the language of early computing to make up the letter forms of the 1970s computer company Baric (and even managed to make the usually dull typing-style guide a delight in the process). The same firm produced a logotype for a clothes shop which appears to be stitched into the page; and we often see a logo in reverse where it looks even more like a 'found' piece of type, and nothing to do with a designer at all.

Obviously cherry-picking examples from the archives is easy in retrospect, but what these examples share is a timeless quality – because they manipulate the language of the everyday, it becomes almost impossible to date them successfully (especially astonishing is the fact that the film logo is nearly fifty years old).

BELOW
Private Secretary Film logo
BOB GILL USA 1956

BELOW LEFT & RIGHT
Baric identity + typing guide
MINALE TATTERSFIELD PROVINCIALE
UK 1970

BOTTOM LEFT
Browns clothing identity
MINALE TATTERSFIELD UK 1977

BARIC COMPUTING SERVICES LIMITED

The use of vernacular forms can really engage us because they can catch us unawares.

In an emotional appeal to potential nurses, a series of press ads were devised to look exactly like nurses' or doctors' folders, open and complete with typewritten body copy and paper-clipped photos. Reprinted in this book they have a fair degree of impact,

but they were designed to fall within the pages of glossy magazines and supplements, where their 'warts and all', down-to-earth feel would stand out from the superficial gloss around them.

Using this emotional 'pull' can enhance the simplest of ideas. This mailer for a memorial service for Alabama veterans appropriated the language of US government telegrams (embossed type, badly typewritten text, dogtags) to illustrate how some people had received information on dead relatives – here the power of the piece which arrives like any mail-shot creeps up on you and its message stays with you forever.

The next step (attending the memorial) seems relatively simple after the recipient has got over the stress of receiving the mailer in the first place.

An earlier campaign for Olympus cameras

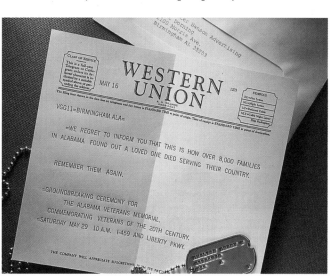

LEFT
Olympus Cameras press ad
LOWE HOWARD-SPINK UK 1995

BELOW LEFT & RIGHT
VW Polo Automatic
ad campaign
BMP DDB UK 1997

OPPOSITE TOP, RIGHT & MIDDLE
Restaurant Florent boards/postcard/ads
M&CO USA 1987–90

OPPOSITE BOTTOM
COR Therapeutics annual report
CAHAN & ASSOCIATES USA 1998

used a similar technique – by eschewing the glossy slickness of a traditional camera ad and instead using contact sheets seemingly dropped on to the page, with found type, we are drawn into the message, rather than left admiring (or not) the more traditional 'blown-up photo' approach.

These ads for the Volkswagen Polo automatic car seem like nothing at all. All we are presented with is a series of photos of discarded shoes on what could be any roadside. At first we are left bewildered – what have old sneakers got to do with mid-range German-built automatic cars? Then it begins to dawn on us as we notice that all the shoes are left-footed, leaving us to

realize that our left feet (in Britain where the campaign originates) will have nothing to do (there being no clutch to operate). So we may as well chuck our left shoes away.

On paper this would have seemed like a fairly mundane brief ('do some ads for an automatic version of a mid-priced, mid-ranged, mid-everything car'). It's the use of the everyday that makes the ad's charm even more appealing.

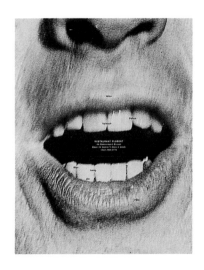

Sometimes using everyday forms comes about as a result of budgetary constraints. The early design work for New York meat-packing district Restaurant Florent was to be produced for tiny design fees. So the designers returned with layouts illustrated with symbols and pictures clipped from the phone book or Yellow Pages, or menus written out on battered old menu boards. Clip-art of a stomach was appropriated to illustrate exactly what particular restaurant delicacy would be digested where, or what bit of food would stick to which teeth.

Obviously, this type of design, especially within the fashion-related restaurant business, is asking the viewer to engage in the joke – 'are you hip enough to realize that we are deliberately "un-designing" this?, it asks. Probably many would not get the joke and assume that it was a bad restaurant that couldn't afford a 'proper' designer. But then they wouldn't be the appropriate diners, would they? The language of 'un-design' becomes a kind of entry code into a different world, only available to the code-crackers themselves.

Sometimes the desire for reality goes so far that we get into quite confusing territory. This report for a company producing anti-coronary drugs (COR Therapeutics) looks like a badly-designed newsletter or science journal. The typeface choices fall outside what we would term 'good taste'. The layouts are deliberately humdrum, word-breaks are poor and pictures un-engaging. But it was designed by one of the world's finest design groups, deliberately creating a document that to all intents and purposes looks as though it could have been created by the in-house designer. It's confusing, but it accepts that if it looks as 'undesigned' as possible we may be more likely to read it.

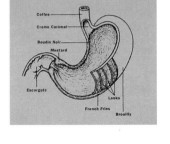

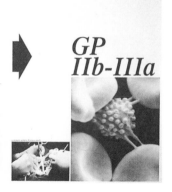

With the advent of accessible desk-top publishing for all levels of companies, everyone has the ability to create something that looks slick and competent, and often they do. It's no surprise that, faced with slick and competent, we feel obliged to turn back to ugly and unbalanced (but ultimately, more believable).

Whilst the designers of the COR report may have stepped too far into 'ugly' (by their own admission[1]), they have been exploring the possibilities of vernacular for some time. The plastic type used outside motels provided the ideal messaging style for a document themed around coming off the internet highway. A poster for their own talk looks like a hand-painted Tijuana bill poster. The complexities of 'I/O bandwidth interface solutions' are brought down to a human level in the style of children's books, propelling the client on to the front page of *USA Today* in the process.

The vernacular tends to be associated with protest and underground messages because of its in-built subversion. In the

ABOVE TOP & MIDDLE
Xilinx annual report
CAHAN & ASSOCIATES USA 1997

LEFT
Lecture poster
CAHAN & ASSOCIATES USA 1996

often stuffy world of government, resorting to hand-scribbled messages and graffiti-covered rubbish bins is an extreme route to use.

For the UK's Design Council, years of patiently explaining their activities didn't seem to have had much effect. The decision was made to base a report and accompanying set of posters on startling facts, or polemical statements, all buried within a surrounding photographic image. So a statement concerning the loss of British designers overseas is moulded into the top of a drain (to invoke the 'brain drain'). The environmental hazards of nappies are illustrated by a fossilized example in a museum case. Rubbish bins are filled with computers then graffitied with the sobering fact that 90 per cent of computers are simply thrown away.

Sometimes vernacular design can be taken to a new level, especially when a designer or advertiser is trying to make the viewer really feel what it is

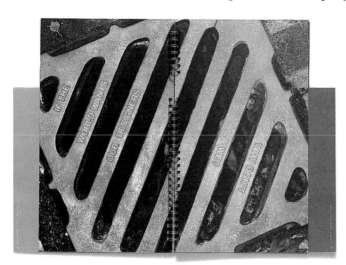

NAPPIES TAKE

CENTURIES TO

DECOMPOSE

like to suffer from a disease, or just to walk through a city. Often photographs or words alone aren't enough, and other approaches have to be tried to give the viewer or reader a greater degree of insight.

To illustrate an article on what it feels like to surf blind, American designer David Carson placed the first few words in white at the top of a black spread, but then placed the subsequent pages in a completely different section of the magazine. The reader is effectively lost within the magazine, and begins to share some of the feelings of the visually-impaired surfer.

British design group Tomato created a one-hundred-page book based entirely on the two authors' journey through New York, the words and the type on the page evoking their memories and feelings in a powerful jumble that immediately sums up the chaos of the city itself.

Multiple Sclerosis is a notoriously difficult condition to explain to the non-sufferer; most often associated with shaking symptoms, the condition additionally affects the brain and vision, jumbling up the way the sufferer looks at a page. So in 1999, the unprecedented step was taken of negotiating a deal with a newspaper to take the final artwork of a page of the paper and repeat it on the following

ABOVE
'Surfing blind' article opener,
Beach Culture magazine
DAVID CARSON USA 1991

LEFT AND BELOW
'Skyscraper I love you'
TOMATO UK 1994

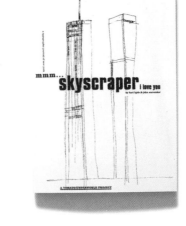

page in a horrendous jumble, thus allowing the reader some insight into the plight of the MS sufferer. A sister agency had pulled off an analogous trick some years earlier when they filmed an anti-drink-driving campaign through a succession of empty beer glasses to illustrate the danger of over-imbibing.

Whilst it's true that this chapter has shown many strong examples of everyday language used to make a serious message more powerful, there's no doubt that in the right hands the everyday can also become simple, straightforward fun.

A catalogue for fashion house Dolce & Gabbana poked fun at the norm by arriving with a cover of fruit, ribbon 'handles' and wrapped in orange gauze. In a promotional mailer for their agency, London agency Mother used the timing of the piece (coinciding with a significant football tournament in Europe) to 'celebrate' that infamous British export, the football hooligan.

They took the form and language of plastic model kits and created (very nasty) plastic hoodlums which could be used to terrorize the recipient's desk top. The level of detail was significant, even showing the right type of terrace chant to be produced by the vile figurines.

Of course, the language of the everyday can, and probably will, simply be absorbed into mainstream design and advertising as an 'acceptable' alternative, and hence may lose some of the freshness that explains the appeal of many of the examples in this chapter.

But until the world returns to a glossier, more glittering time, there's no doubt that the honesty of vernacular design will stay with us for some time.

Problem: How do you build up a cohesive portfolio of work that has a recognizable style?

Solved: Don't bother, just concentrate on a recognizable attitude.

Graphic Thought Facility exhibit a cerebral approach to problem-solving, combined with a love of the found and everyday, that enables them to stand outside design trends and pursue their own agenda.

For a stylish book dedicated to a decade-by-decade history of typographic trends, they were happy to be given the 1970s and equally happy to explore all forms of embroidered type, seemingly impervious to the looks of horror that this idea would have prompted in most of the world's design studios.

Whether it be Post-It notes re-photographed or Electro-Luminescent Car Components (see overleaf), they will find a way to use it in their work. For an exhibition catalogue containing printed elements of several different sizes, they simply comb-bound it along one edge and gloried in the odd juxtapositions that came about as a champagne label fell across hand-written notes or pre-printed glossy images.

For a book collaboration with design commentator Stephen Bayley, they used different typographic treatments for each sixteen-page section of the book, sometimes changing typeface several times within a chapter – completely against any conventions of book design but so much more interesting because of it.

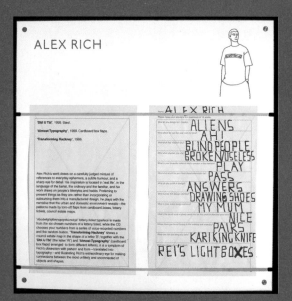

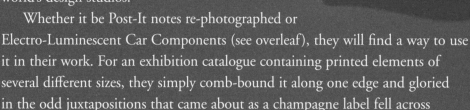

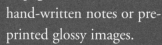

ALL PROJECTS BY GRAPHIC
THOUGHT FACILITY UK

OPPOSITE TOP
Divider spread from
20th century type, remix
1999

OPPOSITE BELOW
LEFT AND RIGHT
'Stealing Beauty' exhibition
graphics and catalogue
1999

ABOVE LEFT
General Knowledge, Stephen Bayley
2000

ABOVE RIGHT
Antoni & Alison poster
1994

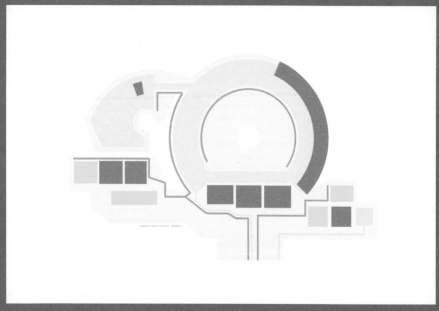

ALL PROJECTS BY GRAPHIC
THOUGHT FACILITY UK

TOP LEFT
Electro-Luminescent Car Component, off

MIDDLE LEFT
Electro-Luminescent Car Component, on

limited edition screenprints
2002

ABOVE, BELOW AND OPPOSITE
Elements from electrical signage/
exhibition graphics for Digitopolis,
Science Museum, London
2000

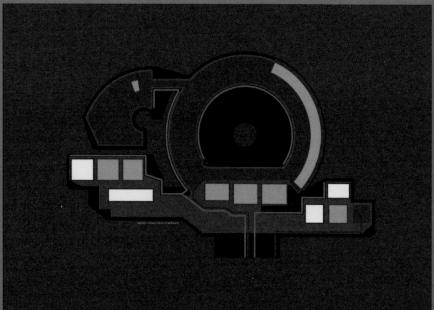

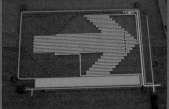

forms of electronic messaging within their exhibition graphics for the
London Science Museum led to an almost laboratory-like investigation into
the possibilities of electronic paper, and its ability to be customized as a
carrier of graphic information.

As visual jackdaws clutching their printer's ink manuals, GTF's great
skill is to show the world that design can be friendly, odd, wrong and yet
right, all at the same time, and all the better because of it.

DIGITOPOLIS

How does
digital technology
affect you?

Discover what makes digital technology
so useful. Explore its power and look
into the digital future.

intel®

Sponsor

GFA agfa

Sponsor

The GROUNDHOG DAY *problem*

People working outside design
and communication expect the
profession to be infinitely varied,
with new problems to solve
almost every day. But practising
professionals know that they
are often faced with re-interpreting
essentially the same elements,
and often the same brief, over
and over again.

It might be that nothing has really changed since the last time the project happened. It might be that a slightly lazy client has just found the brief from a year before and simply changed the dates. There are a lot of reasons for the groundhog day brief but all require the creative to tackle what seems like a repeat performance of something they have already done.

So we have this bizarre conundrum where highly-trained professionals, primed to attack a different brief in an interesting way, find themselves attacking the same brief in a different way, searching for new solutions to old problems.

How do you solve a problem like this? You could just ignore it. Some designers set themselves a limit – Tibor Kalman wouldn't allow himself to tackle essentially the same brief more than three times, claiming short attention span and the desire to try new things as the reason to decline a project. But few communicators have the luxury of turning down work on the grounds of impending boredom.[1]

For designers of annual reports, groundhog day occurs with monotonous regularity. Some take the simple view, and design the reports as a set so that when placed in a line, several years' documents look clean and consistent (such as this triptych of covers for the British Land Registry, or this set below for Cummins).

Not feeling restricted enough by the annual repetition of information, Heinz and their agency managed to narrow the brief even further by featuring only tomatoes (at the time 1,200 Heinz products used tomatoes). For fifteen years they did tomatoes – tomato as sauce, as hero, as pie chart. It was almost as though they were glorying in the tightness of the brief and its intentionally masochistic angle. 'We will make this work again' was their hummed mantra as they prepared another layout with a circular, red element within it.

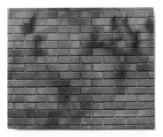

TOP
British Land Registry report covers
CDT UK 1991–2

LEFT
Cummins report covers
PAUL RAND USA 1976–86

In 1993, the Chicago Board of Trade exceeded its 1990 world trading record by over 24 million contracts—setting a new world record of 178,773,105 contracts traded. By providing the deepest, most liquid markets at the lowest possible cost for both its members and its customers, the CBOT has established a new level of success. This new volume record demonstrates customer confidence in our markets.

But it is in the face of repetition that some designers do their best work. In their seven-year relationship with the Chicago Board of Trade, the Chicago-based VSA Partners led the world in annual report design by setting themselves the task of designing radically different documents each year, always looking for new ways to sum up the vibrancy of their client. All the unwritten rules about linking one year to the next were shattered as the designers moved on to greater and greater heights, with the willing consent of their client. One year they bound a completely differently-sized book within the smaller document. The cover of another shouted 'open' on its front page, and 'close' on its back, emulating the beginning and end of a frenzied day's trading and filling the pages in-between with dramatic layouts and pictures echoing the daily drama of the trading floor.

Pharmaceutical and biotechnology clients may not seem to offer the perfect area for innovation in terms of design, but that is precisely what the Californian agency Cahan & Associates has achieved with its work for the likes of Geron.

Whilst most companies might view this sector as dull, Cahan manages to examine each brief from many different clients' perspectives and draw out human stories or compelling facts that can bring such dry technology to life.

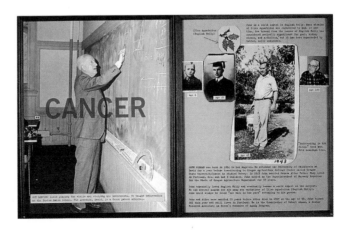

ABOVE
Chicago Board of Trade annual report
VSA PARTNERS USA 1991–4

RIGHT
Geron annual report
CAHAN & ASSOCIATES USA 1997

Magazines have long been the true home of the groundhog day problem. Whilst the day-to-day of laying out a magazine will always remain humdrum, the very limitations, the endless repetitive print cycle, the monthly rhythm seem to have proved a breeding ground for some of the finest designers of the last century. Magazines, for all their faults, provide the regular opportunities for experimentation rarely allowed in mainstream design and art direction.

The first master of magazine design to show a willingness to tackle one hundred continuous pages on a monthly basis was Alexey Brodovitch. Having established himself at *Harper's Bazaar* in the mid-1930s, Brodovitch was the first to show how pace, power, contrast and cropping could be used alongside fine photography within the monthly grind of a magazine. Here, for the first time, was a magazine art director taking meticulous care over the appearance of over one hundred consecutive pages of paper.

The baton was passed to the German magazine *Twen* in the 1960s, then *Nova* in Britain. Both magazines showed each month how scale and drama could make ideas burst out of spreads with exceptional power. The designers of both publications broke all the known rules within the theoretically repetitive world of editorial design and set the tone for modern magazine design.

It was not until the innovations of Neville Brody and David Carson in the 1980s and 1990s (see page 102), though, that modern magazine design caught up.

The series of covers produced by George Lois during his tenure at *Esquire* magazine again illustrates

the skills of someone at the height of his powers, persuading his publisher time and time again to take what at the time seemed huge risks with subject matter. With the civil rights movement gaining momentum, Lois decided the time was right to make boxer Sonny Liston his black Santa for December.

For another cover he appeared to fire arrows into Muhammed Ali, for another he showed Richard Nixon being pampered by make-up artists.

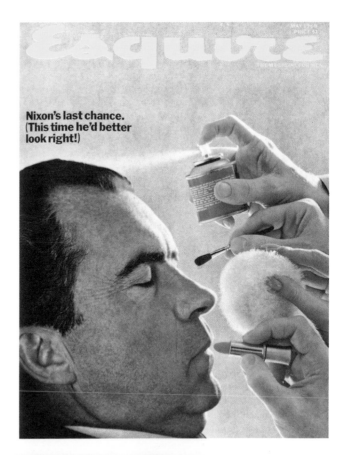

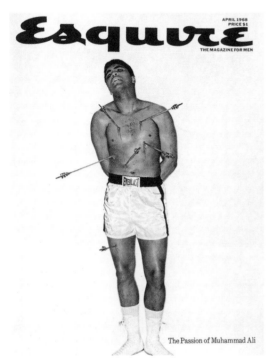

The Passion of Muhammad Ali

One of the designers who paved the way for much of the 'second coming' of modern editorial design was the Italian-born Fabien Baron. While Baron cut his teeth on Italian *Vogue*, he early established his skill at combining meticulously detailed typographic headers with powerful photography. On moving to the USA, he continued his innovations at *Interview* magazine and then *Harper's Bazaar*, uncannily echoing the movements and aesthetic of Brodovitch, the man to whom he is most often compared.

Meanwhile, in the UK, faced with producing weekly covers (at the same time as doing the contents) for a weekend newspaper supplement, Vince Frost established the ground rules swiftly with a generous A3 format, small text and lots of white space in which to place a photographed

image, itself shot on white, giving the impression of the object simply sitting there on the page. By imposing these rules on the style of layout and photography, Frost allowed himself more time in the hectic weekly schedule for the tricky bit, the generation of the best idea for each week's theme.

American designer Fred Woodward took the restrictions of the bi-weekly music-based *Rolling Stone* magazine and simply separated out the main sections of interest from the more laborious grunt

work. Whilst the layout of the main magazine is relatively straightforward, Woodward saves his best tricks for the lavish opening spreads at the beginning of feature sections. Often simultaneously utilizing many of the USA's finest photographers and illustrators, Woodward's genius has been to take the same double-spread format and endlessly vary his palette of type and colours several times an issue, twenty-five times a year. Like Frost in the UK, once he has

established the rules (in this case, really just the physical size of the magazine, a heading of some sort, perhaps a short introductory piece of type and a photo or illustration) he is off and running. Type made up of twigs, one-hundred-year-old cowboy type crashed together in retro-psychedelic heaven, headings twisted and contorted into any shape he fancies, his is work unshackled from any preconceptions of how magazine layouts should be.

As we've seen, to the best editorial designers repetition presents a straitjacket that is a great challenge to work within.

In some instances, it's clear from the outset that an idea must have the inbuilt ability to vary endlessly within the same basic rules. This is especially apparent within TV design – the symbol for MTV is no pin-up in the logo stakes but it is the station's ability to constantly mutate the mark's applications (driven by its teenage audience's expectations of constantly-changing stimulation) that is the true mark of a brand that has managed to reinvent itself constantly for twenty-five years.

In the UK, an original set of idents for BBC2 illustrated how the diversity and breadth of the BBC's alternative channel could manifest itself. For the first time in the UK, these were idents as art. As a storyboard, a giant metal number 2

OPPOSITE TOP
Italian *Vogue* Nureyev opener
FABIEN BARON ITALY 1989

OPPOSITE MIDDLE
Independent magazine covers
VINCE FROST UK 1995

OPPOSITE BOTTOM & ABOVE
Rolling Stone spreads
FRED WOODWARD USA MID 1990S

dropping like a knife into a table-like surface must have looked quite dull, but as eight seconds of film it takes some beating (and the channel implicitly recognized the power of the original films by continuing to use them for ten years). Another one, perfectly simple in its execution, sees paint drop sideways across the screen, seemingly defying gravity.

The power of the original idea is amplified by the fact that the BBC's in-house designers have been able to take it and develop a series of idents for several years now that have served to strengthen the original brief.

Sometimes, poster designers take the repetitive brief as a chance to build a yearly series of related works. This also helps greatly in their communication because if the public's eye is tuned to the previous year's design, there will already be a degree of familiarity with that which succeeds it. The German master of this technique is Gunter Rambow – within his posters for publisher S Fischer he simply mutate the original idea, year-on-year, to maintain consistency but also to signal that this year's event is different from the last. We can imagine the pleasure

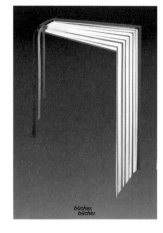

ABOVE
BBC2 channel stings
LAMBIE-NAIRN UK 1990

LEFT
S Fischer posters
GUNTER RAMBOW
GERMANY 1976–94

OPPOSITE PAGE
Slamdance film festival posters
ADAMS MORIOKA USA 1996–9

SLAMDANCE

WHERE THE WILDERNESS MEETS THE GARDEN

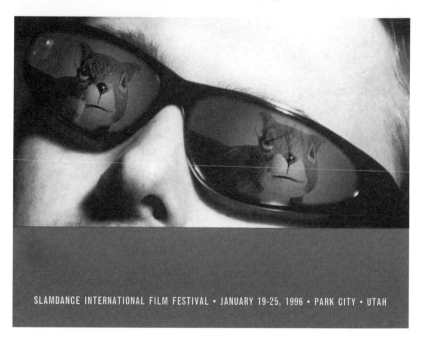

SLAMDANCE INTERNATIONAL FILM FESTIVAL • JANUARY 19-25, 1996 • PARK CITY • UTAH

that the art director takes from developing such a related series that has extended over a number of years – somehow much stronger as a linked group than separate items.

Californian postmodern-über-minimalist Adams Morioka's skill with recurring client the Slamdance Film Festival is to produce designs year after year that are new and fresh, but still related to the previous years.

One of the greatest groundhog day briefs of all time, however, has to be the dreaded Christmas card. Every September or October, in design and advertising agencies worldwide, the inevitable conversation is repeated – 'so who's doing the Christmas card this year then?'. This is, of course, when the communicator should be seen to come into their own; it should be a chance to show off, to impress clients, friends and peers.

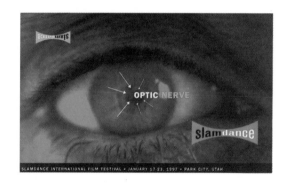

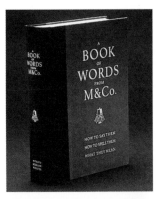

Well, not really. Were a global edict to go out banning the design of any new Christmas cards for evermore, thousands of designers worldwide would breathe a huge sigh of relief. Approaches vary to this, the most dreaded of briefs – the 'make your recipients so confused or guilty they'll never forget us' approach (M&CO) or the 'sidestep the problem entirely and send origami' approach taken by NB Studio. One renowned London design firm (The Partners) came to the conclusion, probably very wisely, that after the ten-year torture of producing an annual book about themselves that doubled as a

Christmas message, they would simply stop when they got to ten, do nice cards for their clients and simply not send one of their own at all.

Sometimes, repetition can be fortuitous. Milton Glaser's famous logo for New York rightly became a twentieth-century classic.

But when asked to provide a visual in the aftermath of the World Trade Center bombing for *New Yorker* magazine, his solution was simply to revise his original mark to say 'I LOVE NY MORE THAN EVER.'

After seeing his original, pre-copyright symbol copied across the world, Glaser had the chance to remind everyone of the provenance of the original mark, whilst making a very poignant point about his home town in the process.

TOP LEFT AND ABOVE RIGHT
M&CO Christmas cards
M&CO USA 1986, 1989

MIDDLE LEFT
Christmas card
NB STUDIO UK 2000

LEFT
Lewis Silkin Christmas cards
THE PARTNERS UK 1986

OPPOSITE
I Love NY + I Love NY More Than Ever
symbols
MILTON GLASER USA 1975, 2001

I ♥ NY

I ♥
NY
MORE
THAN
EVER

Problem: How to control a visual style for a television station.

Solved: Stop controlling, start creating.

The '2' symbol designed in 1973 for the public television station WGBH TV in Boston USA by Chermayeff & Geismar seemed, on the face of it, a straightforward, simple one.

But when the development of the identity passed to the station's in-house design team, few could have realized that this east-coast television minnow was going to become a world-wide trailblazer for developing innovative and ever-changing iterations of the same digit.

In a suite of designs destined to be emulated decades later around the world, the station's team subjected the humble number 2 to a bizarre series of treatments. From birthday cake to bunny's friend, from goal-kicking practice to wooden toy, everything was possible. The 2 even became an eleven-foot tall '2-mobile' which travelled the state on fund-raising duty.

From these humble origins in Massachusetts, television design had a new role model, and one which approached its own groundhog days with obvious glee at its self-created freedom.

ABOVE
WGBH TV logo
CHERMAYEFF & GEISMAR USA 1973

THIS SPREAD
WGBH indents and applications
CHERMAYEFF & GEISMAR (CONCEPT)
AND WGBH IN-HOUSE DESIGN TEAM
(APPLICATION) 1975–85

The Ascent
of Man

About
the House

WGBH TV
Boston

Happy

Easter

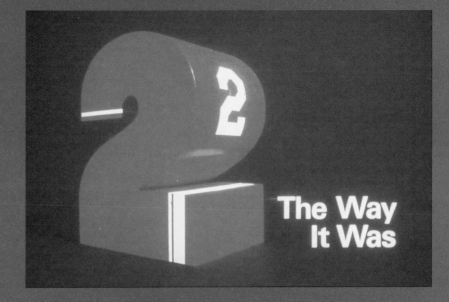

2

The Way
It Was

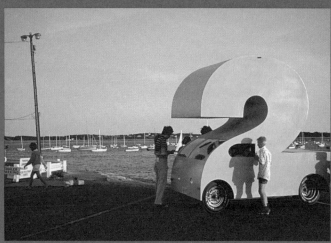

OPPOSITE PAGE
WGBH promotional vehicle
1973–4

RIGHT
WGBH ident applications
1973–4

BELOW
Fundraising '2' toy
1973–4

CHERMAYEFF & GEISMAR (CONCEPT)
AND WGBH IN-HOUSE DESIGN TEAM
(APPLICATION)

The FEAR AND LOATHING *problem*

A creative may think he or she
has come up with the best idea
in the world. But that will not
help the designer who shows the
idea to a junior trying to second-
guess their boss, or to the manager
who refers every critical decision
to his art-student children, or
the simple fact that the economic
circumstances can suddenly change
and render the original brief
completely null and void.

It's not fun but it's part of the game. Every creative has a bottom drawer full of 'the ones that got away', the designs that nearly got to print, or perhaps worse, the ones used briefly and then unceremoniously dumped by a client.

Some of the greatest designers of our time have been subjected to the worst types of client embarrassments and ridicule, but most develop rhino-thick skins to deal with it. Sometimes, the designer might provide the finest of visual solutions, but circumstances change and an idea is left high-and-dry.

Having left the company that he helped create – Apple Computers – Steve Jobs set off with a vision of a new generation of PCs, which he deftly titled NEXT and packaged in black cube-like cases (soon to be emulated by the world), creating a radical interface for the on-screen environment. In keeping with the lofty ideals of the venture, he employed the then-guru of logo design, Paul Rand, for a one-off fee of $100,000 dollars. Jobs himself described the experience of turning the pages of Rand's specially-designed presentation booklet until reaching the final mark: 'I was not quite sure what Paul was doing until I reached the end. And at that moment I knew we had the solution … Rand gave us a jewel, which in retrospect seems so obvious.'[1]

But there was a problem: the logo may have been memorable, simple and effective but the product proved too costly for its cash-strapped target market of educational users. By 1993, NEXT's hardware had been sold and its software sold the following year to Apple, whom Jobs was soon to rejoin. The best logo in the world won't help if no one wants your product.

One of Rand's most famous applications for his long-standing client, IBM, was the rebus he created out of an eye, a bee and the 'M' of the company's symbol. But initially distribution of the poster was prohibited in-house because it was feared it would encourage people to take liberties with the marque.

Alan Fletcher designed one of his finest logos for the Victoria & Albert Museum in London, a clever mixture of a 'V', an 'A' and an ampersand, but the network of colour-coded banners designed to help the visitor navigate an

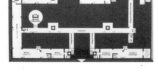

infamously complex space depended somewhat on its map to explain where you were.

Then the client revealed that, for reasons of budgetary difficulties (allegedly some toilets were in need of refurbishing), they were going to re-design the map and print it in-house in two colours.

The museum was left with a beautiful series of banners that now made little navigational sense.[2]

BELOW
NEXT identity presentation booklet
PAUL RAND USA 1986

BELOW MIDDLE
Eye Bee M poster
PAUL RAND USA 1981

BOTTOM LEFT & RIGHT
Victoria & Albert Museum
signage and identity
PENTAGRAM UK 1988–1989

RIGHT
Jubilee Line extension poster
JOHNSON BANKS UK 1999

BELOW
Idi poster campaign
PENTAGRAM UK 1993

BELOW RIGHT
Monotype logotype
JOHNSON BANKS UK 1993

A poster design carefully prepared for the new London Underground extension to the Jubilee Line (which happens to miss out a particularly tangled bit of town and still provide a twenty-minute route across the city) failed to take into account one thing; chronic delays to the opening of the extension meant that London Underground decided not to publicize the opening of the service for fear of negative publicity. The poster lay art-worked but unprinted in a drawer, never to see the light of day.

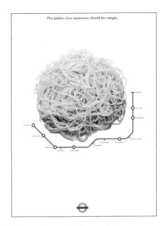

This series of posters produced for the interior design show IDI (Interior Design International) in 1991 rightly made a great impact, employing clever substitutions of the 'd' with all manner of objects from chairs to plugs (see left). The posters were greatly admired and won awards for their design. But the event itself never happened – pulled at the last minute due to lack of exhibitors. A pyrrhic victory, perhaps, for the graphic designer, but not for the event itself.

Sometimes the changing politics within an organization can drastically affect a previously coherent strategy. When the transatlantic type foundry, Monotype, asked for a revised corporate identity in light of the new electronic download and CD ROM marketplace, all the invited parties responded with ideas. The chosen mark went through a careful process of development, tweaking and preparation for all types of print usage. But just as it made it to stationery, and the first CD collection of fonts, the balance of power at Monotype shifted from its English base to that in the States, and the decision was swiftly made to revert to a simpler, type-based form, leaving the new mark high-and-dry having lived for only six months.

Another sad example of short shelf-life is the symbol for Time Warner in 1990. It was universally acknowledged as an instant classic – the graphic designers had managed to

find a way to express the newly-merged corporation as the 'eyes and ears of the world'. But symbol changes of this magnitude need boardroom bulldogs, and as soon as a new set of executives arrived around the table, they lost no time in removing the obvious reminder of a previous decision. The symbol found itself shuttled away to the cable television division, deemed unsuitable after only three years in office, criticized thus: 'the symbol is so strong, it's hard to make it work with the other symbols'[3] (leaving its creators bewildered and exasperated).

Symbols are rarely accused of being 'too strong', but this example shows how, in the upper echelons of identity design, success and failure can become increasingly political and increasingly less to do with the quality of the design.

The new Design **Council believes that words can speak as loud as logos.**

Sometimes the solution to a problem just shows the client that there was a different problem in the first place. A new identity for the British Design Council used simple phrases pointing out the use and value of design, and picked out the words 'design council' within the sentence in red. Ostensibly a simple, neat idea backed-up throughout the stationery and with clever use of gifts and props.

But the problem wasn't solved. Because it is a cash-strapped organization often co-sponsoring events with many other parties (and many other logos), it quickly became apparent to the client that actually what they really wanted, and perhaps should have

Design Council

asked for, was a simpler type of logo. Within a year they found themselves approaching a separate agency to design what they now realized they had needed all along, a simple red box with their name inside it, something that works ten metres or millimetres square.

The dotcom boom of the late 1990s contained many useful lessons for all disciplines, but especially poignant is the story of Boo.com. Pre-hyped for months, with six false launches before the actual one, Boo set up in twelve countries simultaneously and was proclaimed by their founders as the new paradigm for on-line retailing. It was at the vanguard of a whole new way of life; a life to be lived twenty-five hours a day, eight days a week. It also became the classic bubble-bursting story of the internet wave.

When the site finally launched there were immediately problems – it was designed in such a complex way and with such extensive and up-to-date software

that actually using it (even on the fastest computers) was quite problematic. When things finally did load, it was quite cool to view a pair of trainers in 3D rotation (if you were prepared to wait for the pleasure), but deep down we still wanted to go to the shop to check the way the laces did up. Innovations such as the virtual guide (Miss Boo) were nice, but again slowed things down quite a bit.

The ad campaign had hit in a blaze of publicity, featuring strange geeks cycling through Manhattan or skateboarding past hippies. Meanwhile, to return to the title of this chapter, the founders were beginning to be both loathed for their excess and feared by those not wanting to miss out (possibly explaining the limitless funding).

In every respect it was a perfect piece of 'opinion-leader' marketing and design – not really aimed at you and me, but at someone just a little bit cooler than us. Maybe that was the problem? Was it too cool? Or was it that it took an eternity just to download the home page? Or do we secretly still want to go and check the quality of our grey fleece before we actually buy it? Probably all of these things.

After its heady peak, with $100 million (in cash) invested, it was reduced to being sold for its technology alone, for $160,000.[4]

THIS PAGE
Rejected packaging concepts for
Batchelors food (left), Tesco Pizza
(above), Slazenger tennis balls (below)
WILLIAMS MURRAY HAMM UK 1990S

OPPOSITE PAGE
Designs/ads for Paul Smith
ABOUD SODANO UK 1995–2001

A great stumbling block for many great ideas remains the dreaded area, 'research'. All of the packaging ideas here came unstuck when confronted by the focus group of target-market pizza, tennis ball and tinned food buyers. Especially painful for the agency concerned, Williams Murray Hamm, will have been rejection of the concept for Batchelors food which suggested to this everyday, workman-like producer of 'nosh on the go' that they simply accept themselves for what they are and express that on their packs. But because of the design's radical nature and parent company Unilever's innate conservatism, and despite fantastic research results, 'the client eventually lost their nerve'.[5]

Obviously, all of the above make painful (albeit funny) reading. Of course, some of the mistakes could have been avoided, briefs could have been better, clients could have been clearer about what they really wanted. But aside from that, other than good work, to the right brief, that everybody likes, how can creatives ensure that their work is going to be loved, not loathed?

Several designers have discovered that simple chemistry between themselves and a client can be one of the most valuable ingredients in a working relationship. Throughout the 1950s and 1960s, Paul Rand's relationship with Eliot Noyes at IBM led to some of the finest design the world has ever seen, the mutual trust between the two men leading each one to greater and greater things. William Golden at CBS in New York, Frank Pick at London Underground all developed communities of designers and agencies in whom they trusted implicitly.

British design and photography group Aboud Sodano had one important visitor to their degree show in Covent Garden, a certain Mr Paul Smith, on the lookout for a young design company who could help with graphics for his fashion company.

They began with a handful of ads and a catalogue and thus began a relationship now entering its second decade, all the time providing Aboud Sodano with one of the finest design and advertising case studies of modern times.

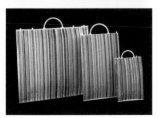

Sometimes fear and loathing drives a creative on to greater heights. Some thrive on a degree of distrust created with their clients – if a creative's job is to challenge conventions then, theoretically, most clients should be fearful and distrustful of their ideas. In ad circles, there is an adage that if the 'suit' leaves the agency happy then the ad isn't edgy enough – ie. if understandable by the mere man in grey flannels, then it isn't an original enough idea.

Of course, an idea outside a client's frame of reference may need some gentle persuasion to get it through – George Lois once threatened to throw himself off a window ledge to persuade the client of the validity of his Matzos ad (apparently screaming 'You make the Matzo, I'll make the ads' whilst hanging onto the open window). A bit extreme, perhaps, but he did sell the ad.

Some, such as photographer Nick Knight, demand complete control of their imagery, and if it is tinkered with reserve the right to withdraw their work. When he and Peter Saville were asked to design the cover of the D&AD annual, they turned the piece into a discussion of the number of creatives who had been killed as a result of commercial advertising worldwide (ouch!) – and for a body celebrating advertising creativity worldwide. But when told their idea was unsuitable they stuck to their guns and simply refused to amend it.

French design agency Grapus built a reputation for social and cultural work and repeatedly challenged their clients' attitudes. Their agit-prop work gained many admirers but their reluctance to

cave in to clients' pressures meant that they found it difficult to develop truly long-term relationships with their commercial clients. But whilst they may not have retired off the proceeds, their extraordinarily angry and aggressive work now stands as some of the most powerful image-making of the century.

Sometimes the problem-solving process takes many twists and turns. Having designed both the logo and the signage for the Musée d'Orsay,

TOP
Goodman's Matzos ad
GEORGE LOIS USA 1950S

ABOVE
Parcs Nationaux de France symbol
GRAPUS FRANCE 1991

LEFT
Rich/Poor poster
GRAPUS FRANCE 1989

designer Bruno Monguzzi declined to enter a poster competition to announce its opening. But all of the entries to the competition were disliked – all that was decided was that any design using photography and art was not acceptable.

Monguzzi was finally asked to produce a design, but struggled until he chanced upon a design using a cropped version of the logo, and a cropped version of a picture by Jacques-Henri Lartigue.

But against all odds – a client who didn't want a photo and The Lartique Foundation forbidding any type of cropping of the master's photos – the poster went ahead. In fact the photographer's widow was moved to write to the president of the museum saying how much her husband would have loved to see his plane flying through the billboards of Paris.

Just occasionally, loathing of an idea becomes love for another client. An idea for an architect which neatly summed up their interest in hospital architecture was rejected and shoved in the bottom drawer. But rather than gathering dust, another client, the Hospital Design Partnership, arrived. In the words of the designer, the new client brought the problem to the solution.

ABOVE
Musée d'Orsay poster
BRUNO MONGUZZI
SWITZERLAND 1986

RIGHT
Hospital Design Partnership logo
MINALE TATTERSFIELD PROVINCIALE
UK 1975

Problem: You've got a fantastic ad but it's pretty controversial.

Solved: Let the authorities decide if it can run or not.

Advertising is littered with ideas that teeter on the edge of acceptability. If an ad or a design is likely to offend, contains swearwords or hints at bodily functions and/or sex, the chances are that it might be banned.

But it's a confusing area – the now infamous ad for Opium perfume, featuring naked supermodel Sophie Dahl lying somewhat suggestively on a velvet background, ran for many months as a magazine ad, almost unnoticed. It was only when transferred onto outdoor poster sites hung above busy roads that it began to receive complaints, eventually leading to its demise.

We're not allowed to tell you anything about Winston cigarettes, so here's a tart leaning on a bar.

LOW TO MIDDLE TAR As defined by H.M. Government
DANGER: Government Health WARNING
CIGARETTES CAN SERIOUSLY DAMAGE YOUR HEALTH

Some advertisers have found ingenious ways to run rings around a potential ban – Winston cigarettes' response to progressively tightened laws for advertising tobacco was to ridicule the rules (see left). Within the same sector the irreverent campaign for Regal cigarettes merely seemed to be playing to its down-to-earth, ordinary image as it featured a fat-looking man called Reg holding his hand over half the pack (the 'al' of 'Regal'), saying 'I smoke 'em because my name's on 'em'. Unfortunately for the agency (and presumably the model playing 'Reg'), the campaign became so popular with children that it turned him into a folk hero in the playground and was promptly ordered to stop.

Religion and politics provide other examples of origination and bans – the fish symbol found on Christian car bumpers worldwide originated from the need for a password in persecuted Roman times. One person would draw an arc with their hand – if the other drew the reverse arc to form the fish they knew they were safe.

The adoption (albeit with a 45-degree twist) of the Indian swastika symbol by the Third Reich and the subsequent tarnishing of the symbol's once positive meanings meant that swastikas are now mostly banned in Germany (as is the SS symbol of the Waffen-SS). Occasionally examples crop up to remind us of the ban (such as this formation of pine trees north-east of Berlin shown opposite, planted by a zealous local merchant in 1937).

ABOVE
Opium press ad
STEPHEN MEISEL USA 2000

ABOVE LEFT
Winston Cigarettes
PAUL FISHLOCK UK 1980S

OPPOSITE TOP
Support for the Nazi regime
GERMANY 1937

OPPOSITE BOTTOM
Regal cigarettes poster
LOWE HOWARD-SPINK UK 1992

PLEASE LORD
LET IT BE TANGO

Meanwhile, ad agencies regularly tussle with the authorities over ads such as the two children looking up into the night sky in an idyllic Christmas scene, accompanied by the strapline, 'Please Lord, let it be Tango'. In this case, though, whilst hundreds complained, the ad was deemed sufficiently humorous not to be banned.[6]

Major corporations often use their legal muscle to try to impose their own type of censure – an anti-McDonald's leaflet cost McDonalds millions in what became known as the 'McLibel' case. They were unable to prove that they had actually been libelled by the leaflet which calls on children to stop visiting the restaurant and features Ronald singing next to a hyperactive lie detector.[7]

But the special prize of this case study goes to Club 18–30 which receives regular bans for their offerings which address the major attraction for their holiday-goers, that is, the promise of copious 'activity' with the opposite sex.

One set managed to be banned between being aired and winning a significant industry award (removing the ability of the organization to actually give the award since it can't give such recognition to banned ads).

Of course the client was probably quite happy with the free publicity (a technique known euphemistically in PR circles as 'ad exploitation').

Another more recent set probably only avoided a ban by only running as posters on the 'rave' island of Ibiza, to be seen once the holiday had been purchased. Great ads but perhaps preaching to the already converted?

AND LET THE POOR CHILDREN HAVE TANGO TOO

What's wrong with McDonald's?

Everything they don't want you to know.

TOP LEFT AND RIGHT
Christmas Tango posters
HHCL UK CIRCA 2000

ABOVE
Anti-McDonalds leaflet
LONDON GREENPEACE
AND MCLIBEL UK 1994

LEFT AND OPPOSITE PAGE
Club 18–30 ads, posters
SAATCHI & SAATCHI
UK 1995–2001

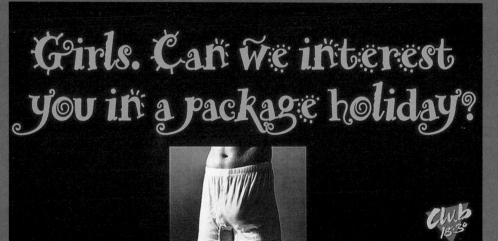

Girls. Can we interest you in a package holiday?

Club
18·30

Spain, Greece, Turkey.
Pack your trunks.

The NOBODY READS ANYMORE *problem*

The theory goes something like this: ours is increasingly a visual culture, no-one's got time to read anymore. So stop writing lots of words in that brochure or ad. Just concentrate on the pictures, that's the important bit. But are they right? Did you actually try to read this book, or were you just looking at the pictures?

Before the advent of eighty-channel television, video games, newspapers with twelve sections rather than just one and more choice in the magazine shop than you ever thought possible, ads did have more words in them. It's true. Pick up an advertising annual from 1982 and it's full of double-page spread ads with 800 words of copy on them.

Look at a current annual and the art of 'copy' seems to be a dwindling one – this may mean that writing within design and advertising should be written off. Perhaps the wordsmiths had a good run and now it's time to hand over. Or was there simply more time to read twenty years ago?

It wasn't always like this; early advertising was based entirely on the word. Advertising folklore likes to put up Ernest Shackleton's ad in turn-of-the-century London newspapers as the beginning of copy ads (even citing the end-line – 'Honour and recognition in case of success'). But the ad was apocryphal, and only ran in people's imaginations.

Real written ads began with classics such as 'They Laughed When I Sat Down At the Piano…', which propelled its writer (John Caples) to advertising superstardom and a lifetime writing compelling books compelling people to write more compelling copy. David Ogilvy reputedly channelled early experiences as a washing-machine salesman into writing 'long-copy' ads for Rolls Royce. Another early classic was a 6,000-word ad from the 1950s for Merrill Lynch, written by its ad manager to help him get stocks and bonds clear in his head.

In England, estate agent Roy Brooks gained a cult following for his newspaper ads which merrily derided his clients' homes (but succeeded all the same).

By the 1960s, advertising was beginning to place more emphasis on how words and pictures intertwined. This famous series of ads for Cadbury's Fruit &

BELOW LEFT
Rolls Royce ticking clock ad
OGILVY & MATHER 1958

BELOW
'They laughed when I sat down
at the piano…'
JOHN CAPLES USA 1925

BELOW RIGHT
Roy Brooks property ad
ROY BROOKS UK 1952–70

They Laughed When I Sat Down At the Piano But When I Started to Play!—

"At 60 miles an hour the loudest noise in this new Rolls-Royce comes from the electric clock"

FASHIONABLE CHELSEA. Untouched by the swinging world of fashion, an early-VIC. lower-middle-class family dwelling, which has sunk to a working-class tenement (2 lousy kits. & 3 sinks). The decaying decor lit by "High Speed Gas." 6 main rms. & revolting appurtenances which cld. be turned into bathrm. & kit. I saw a bare-footed schoolgirl (or student teacher?) sweeping filth from rusty barbed wired playground (it's behind Limerston St.) through holes in the wall into the small back gdn. (sic) of this house – so the first thing to do is to fill in the hole. A few doors away new houses sell for over £18,000 & tarted-up twin houses to this dump can make almost double the modest sum asked for this dump. Lse. 51 yrs. £8,550 and try offers. G.R. £70.

"Hi, nutty"

"Hello, fruit"

"You fond of chocolate?"

"If it's Cadbury's"

"Good. I'll see you in the bar"

Everybody's a Cadbury's fruit & nut case

ABOVE
Ford Cortina ad
COLLETT DICKENSON PEARCE
UK 1967

ABOVE RIGHT
Cadbury's Fruit & Nut Tube card
YOUNG AND RUBICAM
UK 1964

BELOW
Health Education Council ad
CRAMER SAATCHI UK 1969

BELOW RIGHT
Jaffa press ad
SAATCHI & SAATCHI
GARLAND COMPTON UK 1975

This is what happens when a fly lands on your food.

Flies can't eat solid food, so to soften it up they vomit on it.

Then they stamp the vomit in until it's a liquid, usually stamping in a few germs for good measure.

Then when it's good and runny they suck it all back again, probably dropping some excrement at the same time.

And then, when they've finished eating, it's your turn.

Cover food. Cover eating and drinking utensils. Cover dustbins.

Nut mean nothing if you take the words away, they're just simple product shots. The words around the picture give them meaning, humour and the feeling of eavesdropping into a conversation.

At the same time, copywriters on both sides of the Atlantic began experimenting with headlines that became longer and longer until they effectively became the whole ad. Early 'long copy' ads for Ford UK have lasted longer than the cars they are advertising (which might have been the whole idea, of course). Try a little game of replacing the product name at the bottom with a modern car and you'll see just how far modern car advertising hasn't come.

The same team moved on to form what became Saatchi & Saatchi and made an immediate mark with developments of their 1960s formula when asked to produce ads for the Health Education Council. These ads have slipped easily into the annals of the all-time greats, and their content never fails to draw gasps of horror from readers as they make their way down the page of black type to the end-line. And they are already thirty years old. Perhaps judicious choice of timeless type and layout helped, but for a thirty-year-old ad to look as though it could run tomorrow is testament partly to the way it looks, but mainly to the way it reads.

A precedent was set, the world followed, and for twenty years advertising never really looked back. Oranges, cars, museums and political parties all received the long copy treatment.

A word on grapefruit to help you choose the perfect one.

WHAT MAKES THIS SUCH A GOOD ADVERTISEMENT?

In Singapore, an agency eventually began running ads which left the logo off the bottom of the page, so challenging the reader to read the ad in its entirety to find out who the ads were actually for. If the problem was 'no-one reads our ads' then it was definitely solved. Encouraged by his success, the writer then started to challenge the readers further by telling them there was a spelling mistake in the ad, offering a $500 reward to the finder.

The same agency's ads for Chivas Regal played further with this idea, that the words were everything and if the reader had to ask what style was, they didn't have it. Follow-up ads cheekily showed the bottle, but not the front.

LEFT AND BELOW
House ads for The Ball Partnership
THE BALL PARTNERSHIP SINGAPORE
1980S

BOTTOM LEFT, BOTTOM RIGHT
Chivas Regal ads
THE BALL PARTNERSHIP SINGAPORE
1980S

OPPOSITE PAGE
AIGA book cover,
'New York, New York (actual size)',
'The truth behind the overused
publicity photo circa 1985'
PENTAGRAM USA 1989–92

THERE IS A SPELLING MISTAKE IN THIS ADVERTISEMENT
THE FIRST PERSON TO SPOT IT WILL RECIEVE $500.

CHIVAS REGAL IS LIKE STYLE.
IF YOU HAVE TO ASK WHAT IT IS, YOU DON'T HAVE IT.

IF YOU DON'T RECOGNISE IT,
YOU'RE PROBABLY NOT READY FOR IT.

OVERLEAF
Epson long copy ad
COGENT ELLIOTT UK CIRCA 1985

Gary Gray, copywriter
WOODY PIRTLE USA 1985

La Grande Epicerie Paris logotype
LEWIS MOBERLY UK 2001

National Interpreting Service
BROWNS UK 2001

American designer Paula Scher started producing maps and pictures forming images primarily out of words, once describing the use of Helvetica across the US as a wry dig at the then ubiquity of the typeface, once producing a map of New York annotated from her own personal memories, once taking a publicity photograph of herself and writing notes on it concerning what a particular wrinkle cream or haircut meant to her at a particular time of her life.

Computer and printer supplier Epson began running a famous series of incredibly long copy ads – one ad brazenly discusses the old 'They laughed when I sat down at the piano…' ad as it began its Herculean task of demonstrating how many characters their printer could print in sixty seconds (a grand total of 18,000 characters).

At the same time, designers had discovered that clever punning and 'twisting' copy provided the perfect solution to logotypes and corporate identities where a company's product or service could be best summed up typographically.

"We want you to show how much our new £505 printer can produce in 60 seconds," s Epson. "Oh good," we thought, "a short-copy ad." Then they told us their EX800 could print characters a second - and we were as happy as two ducks in a duvet factory. "Half a minute," I sa tapping out SOS messages on a calculator, "if you think we're writing all that, I'm a monk uncle." "Have a banana," they said. Hmph. Such sympathy. We were moved to tears. Anyway, h we are, faced with writing War and Peace Part One and completely on our own into the barg Well, not completely alone - after all, you're still reading, aren't you? Of course you are. You're the sort of namby-pamby who's put off by a bit of eyestrain when there's half a chance of so decent writing, I can tell. You don't need any of those dreadful 'hi-tech' shots with lasers, grids a dry ice wafting all over the shop to grab your attention. The riff-raff might have cleared off alre in search of those ads where big, busty women suggestively stroke some product or other under headline 'Look at the big features on our new model', but have you? No, of course not. Nor are y impressed by any of those corny gimmicks that are just second-rate substitutes for the genu interest that only the printed word can generate. After all, does 'Animal Farm' need a scratch sniff card to make it live? Would 'Lady Chatterley's Lover' be any more interesting as a pop book? (Well, come to think of it …) No, you read to improve yourself, to learn about the wo around you - and even if you don't manage either here, at least there's a chance that you'll lear thing or two about computer printers. This is Epson's ad, after all, so I really should tell you ab the big features on their new mod … oops. What I mean is, the EX800 has a far greater list specifications than any other printer in its price range (which is just as well for us, given amount that we've got to write). As we said earlier, the EX800 costs only £505 (RRP exc. VA which just so happens to remind me of an extremely amusing and interesting fact about mor Now you really are going to learn something about the world! This could even be your big cha to improve yourself. All you have to do is casually drop this into conversation at parties, and pow, instant success! It's far easier than learning how to play the piano, after all. (You m remember the ad I mean - 'They laughed when I sat down at the piano - someone had nicked stool.' Yes, that one. What a load of old rubbish.) Anyway, where was I? Oh yes, this extren amusing and interesting fact. Did you know - and not a lot of people do - that the unit of curre in Vietnam is the dong? It's true, it really is! Look it up if you don't believe me. And just think, for a quirk of geography, it could have been the unit of currency here. Then even our innocent li nursery rhymes would have turned out completely different, e.g. : 'Said Simple Simon to pieman, "Let me taste your wares!" / Said the pieman unto Simon, "Show me first your …"' w you get the idea. We'd better get back to the printer before the Advertising Standards Autho cottons on. The most important feature of the EX800 has to be its speed. It whizzes along at c.p.s. in letter-quality mode, but can manage an astonishing 300 c.p.s. in Elite draft. To give you idea of how quick that is, we'll count up what we've written and then let you know how long EX800 would have taken to get this far. Meanwhile, name that tune. Rumpty tumpty tumpty tu rumpty tumpty tara, rumpty tumpty tumpty tum, piddley piddley pom. No idea? Here's the Rumpty tiddley, tumpty tiddley, rumpty tiddley tum. Rumpty tumpty tumpty tum, rumpty tidc pom. Yep, it's the Archers. And at the third stroke, the EX800 would have been printing for twe seven seconds … beep … beep … beep. Here, hold on a minute. That means we haven't e reached the bottom of the first page. Gordon Bennett, we're going to be here writing all nigh this rate. Still, that's all the more reason to get on with it, I suppose. The new Epson EX80 remarkably easy to use. The new Epson EX800 is remarkably easy to use. (Yes, that was delibe repetition, as this is an important feature - and OK, it does use up a few more characters.) thing is, when you want to change typestyles on an ordinary printer, you have to go through whole rigmarole of making software commands. (Dragsville, Arizona.) The Epson EX800, on other hand, has a 'Selectype' panel on the front. (Freaky City, Florida.) All you have to do to cho

le from the wide - or to use a longer word, extensive - range of print options (N.B. there are
NLQ fonts) is push one or two of the eight backlit switches. Now that's what I call simple. It's
ainly far simpler than, say, balancing a packet of frozen faggots on your head, hopping up and
n on one leg, flapping your arms and shouting, "Yib hoy, snig floy, I am an inter-continental
stic rissole," - and that's a dead cinch. In fact, I just did it right here in the office. There, I did it
n! It's wild! Come on, you have a go. It'll give you a bit of a break - and if you're reading this on
in, it certainly ought to break the ice in your carriage. "But no, enough of all this frivolity," I
you say. "Does this new EX800 have an integral push-feed tractor and short tear-off bar as
dard, with the option of a cut sheet feeder also available?" Wow! What a question. Are you
you're not in the computer printer business yourself? Hmm. You sound pretty clued-up to me.
way, the answer's yes. And before you start asking any more smarty-bottom questions, yes
e is an optional colour unit available. For only an extra £55 (RRP exc. VAT), you, yes you, can
t in seven, yes seven, glorious colours. Get your reports red! Give your accounts a purple
h!! Send blue suggestions to your business associates!!! Well, maybe not. Still, it's about time
had another character-count to see how far we've got. Any requests for music this time?
ething grand and inspirational, perhaps, to lift our hearts and bear us on in triumph to the
essful completion of our epic labour? Something that expresses fundamental optimism in the
ndless potential of the human spirit? You've got it. Here we go, here we go, here we go. Here
o, here we go, here we go-o. Here we go, here we go, here we go. Here we go-o, here we go. All
ther now, verse two - here we go, here we ... oh all right, we'll spare you the rest. The news is,
Epson EX800 would have got here in forty-five seconds. Just fifteen seconds to go! (I was
ys red-hot at maths.) I'd better stick in a couple more product benefits before I finally run out
pace. The Epson EX800 has a very large .. err .. umm .. thingy. I mean whatsit. That is to say, a
dah. Oh very well, a large memory - an 8K buffer to be exact, with the option of an additional
also available. (The point of this is to free your computer for other tasks more quickly - but of
se I'm forgetting again, you probably know that already.) The EX800 is IBM-compatible ...
gh why you aren't using an Epson computer I don't know. I mean, what's the point of us going
about how good Epsons are if people don't take a blind bit of notice?? Oh look, I'm sorry.
aps I wouldn't get so angry at having to mention a rival outfit if they had a name that took up
asonable amount of space, but one that uses an abbreviation? That Is Truly Sickening. The
point to make is that the EX800 boasts the proverbial reliability of all Epson printers. Not that
word 'proverbial' means an awful lot, of course. Have you noticed how many proverbs actually
radict each other? There's 'Look before you leap' and 'He who hesitates is lost'. There's 'Many
ds make light work' and 'Too many cooks spoil the broth'. Weird. It really is time some of these
e brought up to date. How about 'Where there's a will, there's a lawyer'? Or 'A friend in need is
st'? Yes, that's it. He who laughs last has no sense of humour, people who live in glass houses
uldn't take baths, a bird in the hand is better than one overhead, see a pin, pick it up - all day
you'll have a pin ... but I'm wandering again. What I should have said in the first place was
you can count the mistakes the EX800 makes on the fingers of one foot. But look, we're
ost there. The coupon is looming up at last! And the great thing is, we've made it together.
e had our ups and downs, it's true, but you've stuck with us to the bitter end. Terrific. Can't you
feel that bond of comradeship, that deep empathy between us now? Of course you can. And
we've shared so much, we'd do anything for each other, I'm sure. For instance, if we asked you
l in the coupon and send it to Epson, you'd do it for us, wouldn't you? What do you mean, no?
pson (U.K.) Limited, Dorland House, 388 High Road, Wembley, Middlesex HA9 6UH. (Telephone
02 8892) Please send me less information on your EX800 printer - quick.
ne _____ Company/Address _____
_____ Telephone: _____   EPSON

These logotypes for a copywriter, a French epicerie and a translation service rely entirely on clever wordplay to make their point in a purely typographical way; the copywriter Gary Gray was given a symbol which uses the copy-editor's mark for 'transpose' to turn one word into two, whilst the Epicerie cleverly uses the words within the words to make a memorable and simple marque. The interpreting service takes all the foreign keystrokes from a standard font and incorporates them into the logotype itself.

G A R Y

LA GRAN**DE**
EPICERIE **PARIS**

**Nåtiønàl
Intérprētiṅğ
Sërviçê**

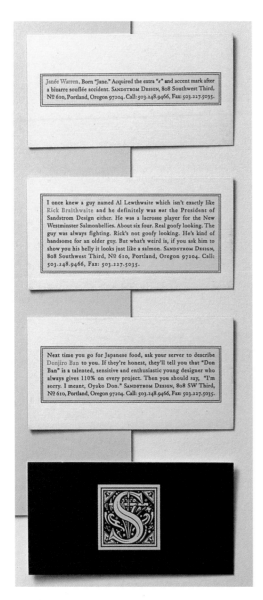

Janée Warren. Born "Jane." Acquired the extra "e" and accent mark after a bizarre soufflé accident. SANDSTROM DESIGN, 808 Southwest Third, № 610, Portland, Oregon 97204. Call: 503.248.9466, Fax: 503.227.5035.

I once knew a guy named Al Lewthwaite which isn't exactly like Rick Braithwaite and he definitely was *not* the President of Sandstrom Design either. He was a lacrosse player for the New Westminster Salmonbellies. About six four. Real goofy looking. The guy was always fighting. Rick's not goofy looking. He's kind of handsome for an older guy. But what's weird is, if you ask him to show you his belly it looks just like a salmon. SANDSTROM DESIGN, 808 Southwest Third, № 610, Portland, Oregon 97204. Call: 503.248.9466, Fax: 503.227.5035.

Next time you go for Japanese food, ask your server to describe Donjiro Ban. If they're honest, they'll tell you that "Don Ban" is a talented, sensitive and enthusiastic young designer who always gives 110% on every project. Then you should say, "I'm sorry. I meant, Oyako Don." SANDSTROM DESIGN, 808 SW Third, № 610, Portland, Oregon 97204. Call: 503.248.9466, Fax: 503.227.5035.

It was inevitable that a company should take the Epson idea of stream-of-consciousness writing and turn it into their own company identity. Seattle-based design company Sandstrom Design feature a densely packed, justified block of type on every piece of corporate 'design' they show to the world, from letterhead to business card, from the exterior of their portfolio case to the front page of their website.

Each paragraph changes, and each is terribly funny. Each different reading leaves you with the feeling that these are smart guys whom you want to ring up and give work to.

All these approaches have one thing in common: they reward the reader for the time spent on reading (sometimes de-coding) the messages within the statements.

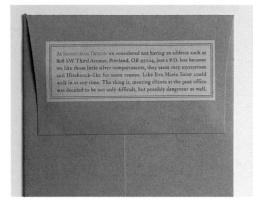

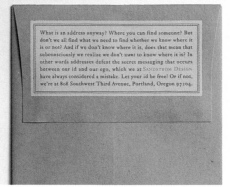

At SANDSTROM DESIGN we considered not having an address such as 808 SW Third Avenue, Portland, OR 97204, just a P.O. box because we like those little silver compartments, they seem very mysterious and Hitchcock-like for some reason. Like Eva Marie Saint could walk in at any time. The thing is, meeting clients at the post office was decided to be not only difficult, but possibly *dangerous* as well.

What is an address anyway? Where you can find someone? But don't we all find what we need to find whether we know where it is or not? And if we don't know where it is, does that mean that subconsciously we realize we don't *want* to know where it is? In other words addresses defeat the secret messaging that occurs between our id and our ego, which we at SANDSTROM DESIGN have always considered a mistake. Let your id be free! Or if not, we're at 808 Southwest Third Avenue, Portland, Oregon 97204.

THIS PAGE
Stationery, portfolio boxes, website
SANDSTROM DESIGN USA 1998–2001

OPPOSITE
XTC 'Go 2' album sleeve
HIPGNOSIS 1978

This is a RECORD COVER. This writing is the DESIGN upon the record cover. The DESIGN is to help SELL the record. We hope to draw your attention to it and encourage you to pick it up. When you have done that maybe you'll be persuaded to listen to the music - in this case XTC's Go 2 album. Then we want you to BUY it. The idea being that the more of you that buy this record the more money Virgin Records, the manager Ian Reid and XTC themselves will make. To the aforementioned this is known as PLEASURE. A good cover DESIGN is one that attracts more buyers and gives more pleasure. This writing is trying to pull you in much like an eye-catching picture. It is designed to get you to READ IT. This is called luring the VICTIM, and you are the VICTIM. But if you have a free mind you should STOP READING NOW! because all we are attempting to do is to get you to read on. Yet this is a DOUBLE BIND because if you indeed stop you'll be doing what we tell you, and if you read on you'll be doing what we've wanted all along. And the more you read on the more you're falling for this simple device of telling you exactly how a good commercial design works. They're TRICKS and this is the worst TRICK of all since it's describing the TRICK whilst trying to TRICK you, and if you've read this far then you're TRICKED but you wouldn't have known this unless you'd read this far. At least we're telling you directly instead of seducing you with a beautiful or haunting visual that may never tell you. We're letting you know that you ought to buy this record because in essence it's a PRODUCT and PRODUCTS are to be consumed and you are a consumer and this is a good PRODUCT. We could have written the band's name in special lettering so that it stood out and you'd see it before you'd read any of this writing and possibly have bought it anyway. What we are really suggesting is that you are FOOLISH to buy or not buy an album merely as a consequence of the design on its cover. This is a con because if you agree then you'll probably like this writing - which is the cover design - and hence the album inside. But we've just warned you against that. The con is a con. A good cover design could be considered as one that gets you to buy the record, but that never actually happens to YOU because YOU know it's just a design for the cover. And this is the RECORD COVER.

But words for words' sake began to reach a point where they were no longer achieving the power they once had. The existential album cover shown above for XTC was ahead of its time in many respects and betrays the writers' true feelings about producing record covers (it was produced by the designers best known for Pink Floyd sleeves and Led Zeppelin composites). But it anticipates the beginning of an age when 'long copy' became an end in itself, and, facing stiff competition from the visual message, it began to look increasingly like some verbose, dictionary-wielding dinosaur.

Advertising increasingly abandoned the word in favour of the picture, and within design, words came out to play only infrequently.

In New York copy only survived as a tool of satire or protest, as in M&CO's clock packaging, which only served to sum up the irreverence of the clocks contained inside; you could choose between one with simply the numeral '5' (for going-home time) or another that featured all the correct numbers, the only problem being that they were completely out-of-focus.

Their ads for long-standing client Restaurant Florent developed their 'clip-art and gag' theme by creating a bizarre little typographic meal for two, complete with typographic crumbs on the floor. This ad happily turned 1980s design on its head as it merrily used terrible typefaces terribly badly (on purpose).

In the early 1990s Drentell Doyle Partners used choice words and gentle layout when producing this flyer protesting against the fatwa against Salman Rushdie. But rather than design some screaming, agitprop piece of type, it was carefully printed onto the thinnest bible paper and then inserted into books, specially designed and placed to creep up on you when you're least expecting it (and to reach the hearts and minds of New York intellectuals in the process).

This set of classroom cards tried to supply frustrated teachers of 'English as a Foreign

ABOVE LEFT
Clock packaging
M&CO USA 1988

ABOVE
Restaurant Florent 'Mirth' ad
M&CO USA 1989

LEFT
Salman Rushdie flyer
DRENTTEL DOYLE PARTNERS USA 1994

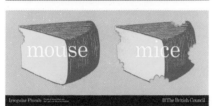

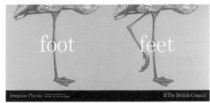

Language' with visual and verbal ammunition in the war against a bored classroom of hormonal teenagers with little interest in comparative superlatives.

But these are rare examples from a time when the world's organizations, increasingly bent on 'globalizing' their images, worked out that pictures crossed cultural boundaries much more cost-effectively than words.

This ad (actually Brazilian in origin) has been produced in a global advertising style, and relies almost entirely on its visual effect to make its point and could have been produced anywhere in the world.

As country restrictions were lifted, more and more ads were made in one place, then dubbed into the world's languages without too much extra expense. This TV ad for a

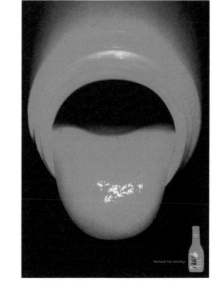

ABOVE
British Council classroom cards
JOHNSON BANKS UK 1996

RIGHT
Parmalat Hot Ketchup ad
DM9 DDB BRAZIL 1999

visual effects, apart from one section carefully shot in many languages to create the 'illusion' of localness. The mechanic directed the pizza delivery boy (nice global food) to the 'fifth floor' in multiple languages on the day of the shoot, but TV viewers would only have seen the version that corresponded to their particular region of the world.

But the global ad, whilst probably now unavoidable, only really succeeds on TV – at least the word can survive, even thrive in a printed form.

The recent ads shown opposite for a British magazine for the homeless (*The Big Issue*) take a leaf out of the history books and simply challenge you to read the wall of type facing you, without taking the easy way out, registering the logo and then turning the page. And the message comes over far more

powerfully than yet another image of a disadvantaged person.

The poster shown left for a conference in London simply left gaping holes in the design for passers-by to fill in their own version, whilst the poster set below promotes the German language in British schools and confronts the country's stereotypes head-on, using words and clichés to draw the viewer into the message about the language.

All of these examples show us the power of words - they force us to notice them and engage.

The famous adage about a picture being as good

as a thousand words was wrong. We can't learn from pictures alone. It's just up to us to think of better ways to use words because, as a communication force, they still can't be bettered.

You're freezing your arse off in some doorway every night, you've got no job, no money, and sod all chance of any of it changing. You haven't got any answers but someone's got heroin. There's always someone who's got heroin. Risks? You haven't got anything to lose, remember. So you get off your face and you feel great. You don't have to think when you're wasted. It's a holiday for your brain. But it's only a short trip. It wears off and your life is still crap. If anything, it seems worse. But at least you've got something to look forward to now. The more you use it, the harder it gets to find the money for it, the more you value it, the more you want it, the harder it is to find the money that you owe for it, the more you need it, the harder it is to think about anything else. Alcohol's kind of the same. Give it up? Oh yeah, right. Why? Just because some dickhead in a duffel coat who's read a couple of Irvine Welsh books is telling you that they understand? Words are cheap. Nothing else is. Selling The Big Issue magazine is a way to earn a bit of cash. No strings. No self-righteousness. No law against it. When the vendors come to collect their magazines each week, they get to know about The Big Issue Foundation, that we offer support to help break addictions. We also offer help with mental illnesses, advice and training for jobs, and, of course, assistance with accommodation. It's there if they want it. But there's absolutely no pressure to take it. And that's why hundreds do, every year. The Foundation exists because we believe that homeless people all have the potential to change their lives. Think about it.

The Big Issue is a social business. The Big Issue Foundation is a charity (No. 1049077) For information call 020 7526 3280

How can you heroin sort your life heroin out when the heroin only thing heroin you heroin can heroin think heroin about heroin is heroin?

Drug addict? Alcoholic? Suicidal?
Apparently, what you need is a nice cup of hot soup.

Cream of tomato, mushroom or even spicy lentil, with or without croutons, is unlikely to have ever satisfied the obsessive cravings of your average crack addict. If mulligatawny is a more effective way of blocking out the abject misery of someone's particular existence than a can or two of super strength lager, then it would probably be illegal by now, or at least a lot more expensive than it is. And if leek and potato really is so comforting that it's ever given a whole new reason to carry on living to the most clinically depressed, then it's news to us. Not that we'd suggest for a moment that anyone should stop giving free soup to homeless people. They're glad of it. Anything is better than nothing. But other people's consciences can be all too easily satisfied by the knowledge that the homeless can always queue up for their nightly broth. They won't starve to death so that's enough is it? We, The Big Issue Foundation don't think so. People become homeless for any number of different reasons. Things go wrong at some point in their lives. Then they remain homeless for the simple reason that they come to accept their predicament, because they don't know how they can change it. Apart, that is, from those who start selling The Big Issue magazine. Earning money starts to rebuild their self-esteem. And when the vendors turn up to collect their magazines, they discover that we offer help with most of the root causes of homelessness: mental illness, various addictions and long-term unemployment. The Big Issue Foundation exists because we believe that every homeless person has the potential to change their life.

The Big Issue is a social business. The Big Issue Foundation is a charity (No. 1049077) For information call 020 7526 3280

Problem: Economics is useful but boring.

Solved: Make it useful and interesting.

It's a deceptively simple idea. As with all long-running and ground-breaking pieces of work, it's almost impossible to remember the ads that ran before.

The Economist may be a dry, intellectual read, but it remains a great way weekly to catch up with the world.

They wanted to pitch themselves ahead as the thinking man or woman's weekly newspaper of choice – formerly based in economics but now much broader in scope. By illustrating *The Economist* as the way to avoid business embarrassment or discover critical facts, the campaign has run for over a decade, and at the time of writing shows no sign of slackening off.

THIS SPREAD AND NEXT *Economist* ads AMV BBDO UK 1989–2001

Apart from the introduction of the odd picture, it's all been done with one typeface and often just one colour – a remarkable exercise in precise writing and the benefits of letting a long-running campaign build on itself over many years, coupled with extreme economy of means in the art direction.

The red Economist box isn't in the corner of the ads because the whole ad is the red box. 'The Economist' isn't even written in the typestyle of the masthead, just in something similar. But it doesn't matter because this is a campaign all about the power of the word, the word as put-down, the word as code that has to be cracked (if you're smart enough).

One of the original ads simply placed the word 'read' in the middle of two lines. The campaign has even shown that it can reflect the times as they change, such as in their send-up of the popular TV game show with the copyline 'You are the strongest link. Hello'.

When a campaign has run for ten years, the temptation is to imagine that it might soon be over, that the client is about to 'pull the plug'. But there seems to be no sign of this, and who would dare finish a campaign that begins its second decade just as strongly as it began its first.

"I never read The Economist."

Management trainee. Aged 42.

In opinion polls, 100% of Economist readers had one.

The Economist

Would you like to sit
next to you at dinner?

The Economist

You can tell an
Economist reader by the
company he owns.

$E = iq^2$

The Economist

On the edge of a
conversation.
One of the loneliest
places on earth.

The Economist

Make the wild guess
an endangered species.

The Economist

Protects against
foot-in-mouth disease.

The Economist

The grapevine.
(First pressing.)

The Economist

Great minds
like a think.

The Economist

Could you handle
people wanting you just
for your mind?

The Economist

If you buy it
just for show, sooner
or later it will.

The Economist

It's lonely at the
top, but at least there's
something to read.

The Economist

Lose the ability
to slip out of meetings
unnoticed.

The Economist

"My husband doesn't
understand me."

Economist subscriber.

No spin.

The Economist

The pregnant pause.
Make sure
you're not the father.

The Economist

"Economist
readers welcome."

Sperm donor clinic.

You are
the strongest link.
Hello.

The Economist

To err is human.
To er, um, ah
is unacceptable.

The Economist

Is your train
of thought subject
to delays?

The Economist

If they did brain
transplants, would you be
a donor or a recipient?

The Economist

"Take me to an
Economist reader."

If more women read The Economist, there'd be fewer jobs for the boys.

Two thirds of the globe is covered by water.

The rest is covered by The Economist.

Rijnsburger Jumbo   Hikari   Bedfordshire Champion   Red Baron   White Spanish   Crossbow

The Economist

If you're already a reader, ask your chauffeur to hoot as you pass this poster.

The Economist

References

INTRODUCTION
1 The quote I'm alluding to was by Alan Fletcher; 'Artists solve their own problems, designers solve other people's'.

The RE-APPPRAISE OR DIE *problem*
1 Between 1985 and 1989 sales of Levi's doubled. Levi's invested $38 million dollars in the 501 jeans advertising campaign, the most ever spent on a single item of clothing.
2 Within three years the percentage of advertising pages in the magazine had reputedly increased by 50 per cent.
3 British Prime Minister John Major said in 1993 '[Britain is a nation of] long shadows on county cricket grounds, warm beer, invincible green suburbs, dog lovers and – as George Orwell said – old maids bicyling to Holy Communion though the morning mist'.

The ASTONISH ME *problem*
1 Marcel Duchamp exhibited a urinal as art in 1917 under the pseudonym 'Richard Mutt', stating that it was simply his presentation of it 'under a new title and point of view' was enough to make it art.

The SOAP POWDER *problem*
1 Emerson was supposed to have written 'Build a better mousetrap, and the world will beat a path to your door,' ie quality will prevail. Incidentally, 400 people still apply for mousetrap patents each year.
2 Smash, made by Cadbury's, was first sold in 1967. The Martian ads were launched in 1973, and Smash became brand leader despite competition from other brands such as Yeoman and Wondermash. At the time of writing it still commands over 50 per cent market share.
3 In June 2002, Virgin's website contained 36 separate companies trading under the Virgin name or prefix.
4 Lee Weinstein, the Nike USA Communications director said of this ad that 'We have a history of pushing the envelope with ads. We know in some cases we're going to generate a reaction, in a lot of cases that's a good thing'. *Advertising Age* called it 'stupid, ill-conceived and repellent'.

5 Nike apologized for the ad saying 'We just feel horrible about this ad. Clearly, disabilties of any form are no laughing matter and that paragraph should not have been included in the ad'. The employee who worked on the ad 'had left the company earlier that year'.
6 If you want to study this more visit www.media.mit.edu/~peretti/nike/
7 According to christian-aid.org.uk, 'A typical pair of sports shoes sells for £50 in Britain. The 40 or so factory workers in the Philippines who made that pair will share just over £1 of that price between all of them. Reebok spends more than £300 million a year on marketing'.
8 The Guardian ran their 'Joy' experiment in July 2001. 1,562 people visited the website or phoned the telephone number. When asked what Joy might actually be, 19 per cent chose 'travel', 12 per cent opted for 'read', 2 per cent opted for 'donate'.

The MESSAGE IS THE PRICE *problem*
1 A recent survey showed that 60 per cent of Americans recognized the line 'the ultimate driving machine', but only 11 per cent were able to identify it as belonging to BMW. (Source: Partners & Shevack, USA, 1999.)

The FUNNY BOO-HOO *problem*
1 Bob Gill, Alan Fletcher and Colin Forbes set up Fletcher Forbes Gill in 1962. It became Pentagram in 1972. Gill left in 1965.
2 The Rossiter/Collins ads for Cinzano began as a spoof on the idyllic lifestyle featured in the then Martini ads. Although hugely popular for their three-year run (and fondly remembered – they were voted eleventh best ads of all time in a turn of the century UK poll) the airing of the commercials always seemed to coincide with a rise in the sales of Martini, not Cinzano.
3 As titled in *Advertising Today*, Warren Berger, Phaidon Press 2001.

The NOTHING SHOCKS ME *problem*
1 Speedy Rice, President of the National Association of Criminal Defence Lawyers, said this about the project: 'We on Death Row is like a prism. Depending on where you stand and the light it will look different to different people. Our goal was to put a human face on some of the people on death row and to provide something of an insight into who that person is.'

2 Beeke said the following in *Eye* 13, 1994, about this poster: 'In the U of Uruguay – a country where most of the Indians have been massacred – I show the mourning colours of those Indians in feathers'. The A of Argentina uses 'dangerous little cactuses', the B of Brazil is symbolic of the Indians' worthless life, the C of Chile represents the 'hair collected by Pinochet's barbers'.
3 Playtex, manufacturer of the Wonderbra, had increased sales by 41 per cent the year of the campaign.

The EVOLVE OR REVOLVE *problem*
1 The GDP of Guadalupe was £3.7 billion in 1995. Source: worldlanguage.com. There are no reliable figures for the value of the world design business, but a 1999 survey found the UK design business alone to be worth £750 million.
2 The first piper scheme was rolled out over a huge set of applications over a two-year period. The implementation budget was £60 million.
3 In July 2000, the chief executive of BP stated publicly that BP stood for 'beyond petroleum'. The group has vehemently denied this ever since.
4 The administrator of NASA said at the time that 'The can-do spirit of the past is alive and well. In honor of this spirit, it seems only fitting that the original NASA insignia be a part of our future'. ID magazine said 'Goldin's cavalier disposal of the NASA system belies the government's disregard of design as an integral organizational process and their commitment to mediocrity' (Sept/Oct 1993)
5 Most commentators seem happy to blame BA's turn-of-the-century business woes on the tailfin designs: 'They give the impression that BA is some well-meaning colonial-era schoolteacher' said Jonathan Glancey in *The Guardian*, June 12, 1999. No one will go on the record about the safety/air traffic control implications of the design but it is a fact that Heathrow's two runways were handling one aircraft every 42 seconds in 1999. The number of flights in the region is expected to double in the next 20 years from 1.3 million to 2.6 million a year.

The CARGO PANTS IN MIDDLE AGE *problem*

1 Coca-Cola even famously re-launched itself once under a new formula, 'New Coke'. It bombed terribly. A commentator called the idea the 'Edsel of the 1980s'.
2 There's a great piece here if you want to read more about OK Soda: www.the baffler.com/glenn.html
3 As quoted by Scottish Telecom managing director Bill Allan at the time.
4 Perhaps not surprisingly, all three are now out of business. There's a moral in this story.
5 As said by then Chief Executive of the Post Office, John Roberts.
6 *The Guardian* of March 25, 2002 reported this: 'Consignia is considering changing its name back to the Post Office after the company's new chairman, Alan Leighton, criticized the £2M rebrand. He admitted he disliked the Consignia brand and would change it back if he could. "It is almost like there is this other company, called Consignia, which is going around attracting derision. Would I like to change the name? Yes I would," he said'. He did, back to The Post Office.

The INFORMATION REJECTION *problem*

1 'Henry C Beck was a 29-year-old engineering draughtsman when he produced his first sketch for the diagram in 1931. At the time he was out of work'. As told by Ken Garland in *Mr Beck's Undergound Map*, Capital Transport, 1994
2 750,000 copies were printed in January 1933, 100,000 more in February.
3 Many observers, whilst appreciating the formal beauty of Vignelli's design, couldn't actually use it. A film once even featured its gangland characters trying to decode the map's instructions (*The Warriors*, 1979).
4 HTML or hyper-text-mark-up language is the coding language most commonly used for the world-wide-web.
5 Yellow Pages UK estimate that the re-designed typeface makes savings that amount to 500 tonnes of paper per edition of 75 books (£500,000).
6 As observed by Jean Widmer, *Eye* 34, 1999
7 Kirk Douglas played Vincent van Gogh in the 1957 film *Lust for Life*.

8 A survey conducted on behalf of the Washington Post showed that Mr Gore had a nearly three-to-one majority among 56,000 Florida voters whose November 7 ballot papers were discounted because they contained more than one punched hole. Source: *The Guardian*, January 29, 2001.

The ETHICAL *problem*

1 Hohlwein, Reifenstahl and Speer are historically positioned as Nazis although their knowledge and involvement are the centre of much debate. Hohlwein of course designed their posters and Reifenstahl was commonly regarded as 'Hitler's favourite film-maker' and possibly his lover, although she has always denied it. Speer is often named the 'good Nazi' – he escaped the death penalty after the war and did much to thwart Hitler's scorched-earth policy, which would have devastated much of Germany. Interested readers should read *Albert Speer: His Battle With Truth* by Gitta Sereny.
2 Roy Carroll wrote the following in *The Guardian* of the whole bizarre spectacle: 'Newspapers and television stations not owned by Mr Berlusconi have gleefully paraded the exposure of what critics call his overweening ambition. A depiction of the former prime minister with a pencil moustache and Sicilian cap, promising "a good contract for all", reminded voters of the corruption allegations he faced'.
3 Most sources back this up: 33 per cent of all cancer deaths are caused by tobacco in the UK, 30 per cent of all cancer deaths are caused by tobacco in the USA.

The CAN'T LEARN, WON'T LEARN *problem*

1 Culture-jamming is the phrase coined by American collective Negativland for protest through cultural and media channels.
2 As documented in the second edition of *Dot Dot Dot* magazine, winter 2000, text by Christopher Wilson.

The OLD CAN BE BETTER *problem*

1 Stafford Cliff once admitted that he had been completely fooled by this pack, believing it to be completely genuine, and not a product of a trendy London design company.

The OVER-DESIGNED *problem*

1 'We're very concerned that most people will not realize that we actually spent a lot of time designing it.' Bill Cahan quoted in *I am almost always hungry* Cahan & Associates, Booth-Clibborn Editions, 1999.

The GROUNDHOG DAY *problem*

1 My Fifth-Avenue deep-throat tells me that Kalman also said 'The perfect state of creative bliss is having power (you are 50) and knowing nothing (you are 9). This assures an interesting and successful outcome'. Kalman also said 'As soon as you learn, move on.'

The FEAR AND LOATHING *problem*

1 As quoted in *Paul Rand*, Steven Heller, Phaidon Press, 1999.
2 This is all according to the memory of Quentin Newark, assistant designer to Alan Fletcher on the project.
3 Taken from a letter written by the vice-president of corporate communications to the symbol's designer, Steff Geissbuhler.
4 The co-owners persuaded some of the world's biggest names, including LVMH and the Benetton family to invest in the sports and designer clothing e-tailer. Some sources put the invested figure higher, at $125 million but it's clear that the real amount invested has been itself subject to a degree of hype. The company's founders attracted fierce criticisms for a lifestyle driven by the 4 c's, caviar, champagne, Concorde plus another I can't mention.
5 These points are drawn from Williams Murray Hamm's supplied captions for these projects.
6 108 people complained about this ad to the Advertising Standards Authority in the UK, but whilst it was in the 'top ten complained about' that year, the ads were not banned. 'The Authority considered that the posters used surreal and light-hearted images that would be seen to be humorous and not trivializing Christmas, the birth of Christ.' The Authority concluded that 'the posters were unlikely to cause serious or widespread offence.'
7 Greenpeace went into battle with McDonalds, accusing them of promoting unhealthy food, exploiting workers, robbing the poor, damaging the environment and murdering animals. Many critics who spoke out were threatened with legal action but Helen Steel and Dave Morris defended themselves in a major UK High Court libel trial.

Selected bibliography

By no means definitive, but if you read all of these you could probably write a book of your own.

A Book about the Classic Avis Advertising Campaigns of the 60s, Henri Holmgren and Peer Eriksson

A History of Graphic Design,
Philip B Meggs,
Van Nostrand Reinhold, 1983

A Smile in the Mind, Beryl McAlhone & David Stuart, Phaidon Press, 1996

Advertising Outdoors, Watch this Space!
David Bernstein, Phaidon Press, 1997

Advertising Today,
Warren Berger, Phaidon Press, 2001

Behind the Seen, Studio Dumbar,
Verlag Hermann Schmidt Mainz, 1996

Beware Wet Paint: Designs by Alan Fletcher, Jeremy Myerson, Phaidon Press, 1996

Brodovitch, Andy Grundberg,
Harry Adams, 1989

Bruno Munari, Air Made Visible,
edited by Claude Lichtenstein
and Alfredo W. Häberli,
Lars Müller Publishers, 2000

Corporate Identity: Making Business Strategy Visible Through Design,
Wally Olins,
Thames and Hudson, 1989

Covering the '60s: George Lois, the Esquire Era, The Monacelli Press, 1996

Design: the Problem Comes First
Jens Bernsen,
The Danish Design Council, 1986

Dutch Posters 1960-1996,
a Selection by Anton Beeke,
BIS Publishers, 1997

Emery Vincent Design,
Gingko Press Inc, 1999

Emigré: Graphic Design into the Digital Realm, Rudy Vanderlans, Zuzana Licko, Mary E Gray, Booth-Clibborn Editions, 1994

Fleckhaus,
Deutschlands Erster Art Director,
Michael Koetzle and Carsten M Wolff,
Klinkhardt & Biermann, 1997

Forget All the Rules You Ever Learned About Graphic Design, Bob Gill,
Watson-Guptill Publications, 1981

Good Enough is not Enough,
Observations on Public Design
Per Møllerup,
Danish Design Centre, 1992

Graphic Agitation, Social and Political Graphics Since the Sixties,
Liz McQuiston, Phaidon Press, 1993

Graphic Design, Mendell & Oberer,
Birkhäuser Verlag, 1987

I am Almost Always Hungry,
Cahan & Associates,
Booth-Clibborn Editions, 1999

Images of an Era: the American Poster 1945-75,
National Collection of Fine Arts,
Smithsonian Institution, 1975

Inside Collett Dickenson Pearce,
B.T. Batsford, 2000

Jazz Blvd. Niklaus Troxler Posters,
Lars Müller Publishers, 1999

Josef Müller-Brockmann,
Pioneer of Swiss Graphic Design,
edited by Lars Müller,
Lars Müller Publishers, 1995

L'Affiche dans le monde, Alain Weil,
Somogy, 1991

Mr Beck's Underground Map
a History by Ken Garland,
Capital Transport, 1994

New Design: Tokyo, Edward M. Gomez and Setsuko Noguchi, Rockport Publishers, 1999

Nine Pioneers in American Graphic,
Design, edited by R Roger Remington and Barbara J Hodik,
The MIT Press, 1989

Obey the Giant, Rick Poynor,
August Birkhäuser, 2001

Paul Rand, Steven Heller,
Phaidon Press, 1999

Powers of Ten Interactive, Eames Demetrios, © 1999 Eames Office/
www.eamesoffice.com, based on the film by Charles and Ray Eames,
CDROM.

Rambow 1960-96, Heinrich Klotz and Alain Weill, Cantz Verlag, 1996

Remember Those Great Volkswagen Ads?'
Booth-Clibborn Editions, 1982

Sagmeister Made You Look, Peter Hall,
Booth-Clibborn Editions, 2001

Saul Steinberg
Harold Rosenberg, Andre Deutsch in association with The Whitney Museum of American Art, 1979

Social Work,
Saatchi & Saatchi's Cause-Related Ideas,
−273 Publishers, 2000

Some People can't Surf,
The Graphic Design of Art Chantry,
Julie Lasky, Chronicle Books, 2001

The 100 Greatest Advertisements,
Julian Lewis Watkins, Coles, 1949

The Art Direction Book, D&AD Mastercraft series, edited by Louise Bishop, Rotovision, 1996

The Art of Advertising
George Lois on Mass Communication,
George Lois and Bill Pitts,
Harry N. Abrams, Inc, 1977

The Art of Looking Sideways,
Alan Fletcher, Phaidon Press, 2001

The Compendium, Pentagram,
edited by David Gibbs,
Phaidon Press, 1993

The Copy Book
D&AD Mastercraft series,
edited by Ian White, Rotovision, 1995

The Films of Charles and Ray Eames,
Volume 1: Powers of Ten, Charles and Ray Eames, 1977, 901: After 45 Years of Working, Eames Demetrios,
1990, www.eamesoffice.com, DVD.

The Graphic Designer and
his Design Problems,
J. Müller-Brockmann,
Arthur Niggli/Hastings House Publishers, 1961/1983

The Power of the Poster, edited by Margaret Timmers, V&A Publications, 1998

Tibor, edited by Peter Hall and Michael Beirut, Booth-Clibborn Editions, 1998

Ways of Seeing, John Berger,
Penguin Books, 1972

Your Private Sky, R.Buckminster Fuller,
The Art of Design Science,
edited by Joachim Krausse and Claude Lichtenstein,
Lars Müller Publishers, 1999

Additional credits

The policy of this book has been to keep the captions short. Some contributors have asked for additional credits, which are reproduced here.

Courtesy of the Academy of Motion Picture Arts and Sciences: 9l, 98bl

AKG London: 183tr

Lorenzo Apicella/Pentagram Design Ltd, London: 197t, 199br

Photos: © Martin Barraud: 19t, 38t, 68t

Lester Beall Collection, Archives and Special Collections, Wallace Library, Rochester Institute of Technology: 194c,b

Michael Bierut/Pentagram Design Inc, N.Y: 37tl, 78, 127br

Pierre Bernard/Grapus: 12tl, 146, 147t, 258c, b

Chris Bleackley, Maggie Mouat/ Brandhouse WTS: 160-163

Photos: © Richard Burbidge: 85 br

Courtesy of Margaret Calvert: 171b

Courtesy of Church Ad Project, Rosemount, Minnesota: 25r

Photo: © Ed Clark: 19br

Photo: © Catherine de Clippel: 148 br

Comme des Garçons Co Ltd: 215cl

Stephanie Couturrier/Arcaid: 199bl

© Jeremy Coysten/Royal College of Art: 176bl

© Richard Davies: 199tl, tr

Design: Mike Dempsey/CDT Design Ltd: 79tl, cl, b/Photo: Michael Hoppen: 79tr/Photo: Andy Seymour, Russell Brownlow: 236r

John de Vries, Peter Force, Marcus Beer: 173tl

© 2002 EAMES OFFICE (www.eamesoffice.com): 196cr

© easyJet Airline Company Ltd: 64l

Photo: Peer Eriksson/Avis: 94b, 95tl

© Stephen Ferry/Liaison, USA: 198tr

Alan Fletcher/Pentagram Design Ltd, London: 109tl, tr, 252bl, br

The Flight Collection @ Quadrant: 167c

Courtesy of The Estate of Abram Games: 173br, 183bl, 194tr

Photos: © Phil Gatward: 227c, b

Photo: Albert Giordan: 67br

© Martin Godwin: 57

© Greg Gorman: 132tr

April Greiman/Made in Space, supplied by Pentagram Design Inc, LA: 100bl

Courtesy of Grey Advertising Inc: 32c

Photo: Frans Grummer: 35tl, tr

Laziz Hamani: 67bl

Kenya Hara, Yukie Inoue, Masayo Takeda: 169tr

Photo: Mr Naoya Hatakeyama: 196bl, br

© Matthias Hermann, Collection Tate Gallery, Gift of Contemporary Art Society, London: 174b

David Hillman/Pentagram Design Ltd, London: 132tl, 253c, bl

'Away from the flock' © Damien Hirst, courtesy of the White Cube Gallery: 19bl

Reportage photos: © Evan Hurd: 68t

Angus Hyland/Pentagram Design Ltd, London: 24c, b

Jewish Museum, Berlin (www.jmberlin.de): 200t

© Michael Kelly/The Flight Collection @ Quadrant: 215 br

Photo: Graham Kirk: 218 c

Alan Kitching/The Typography Workshop/Debut Art: 213bl

JH Lartigue, Rouzat, 1910, detail: 259t

© Arnaud Legrain/Phototheque EPPGHV: 199c

Photo: Nicholas Leong: 112bl

Library of Congress, Washington, DC/The Poster Collection: 182l

Courtesy of the Artist, Maya Lin: 201t

© London Transport: 166tl, tr, 173bl

Photo: © Andrew Olney: 203b

Maiden Outdoor, London: 20tcr

© Adrian Meredith Photography: 143bl, br, 144t, 145l

© 2002 Metropolitan Transportation Authority: 167t

The More Group, London: 39t

Photo: Scott Morgan: 11tr

© Mouron. Cassandre. All rights reserved, 2002: 32tr

© Muji/Ryohin Keikaku Co: 55b

Courtesy of The Estate of Josef Müller-Brockman: 195

Musées de la Ville de Strasbourg: 37tr

Courtesy of the National Park Service: 201l

© New York City Transit Authority 1972: 166br

NSDAP (Courtesy of Kobal): 182br

Olympia Film (Courtesy of Kobal): 182cr

Courtesy of The One Club for Art and Copy, New York: 112tl

Photo: One-Twenty-One Studio: 112tr

PA Photos, London: 64tr, 184cr

© Simon Patterson: 175c

© Simon Patterson: Private Collection, London: 175t

© Simon Patterson and London Regional Transport/Photo John Riddy, London/Courtesy Lisson Gallery: 174t

Photo: Lex van Pieterson: 80tl, r, 168, 197c

Photography © Powerstock Zefa: 9br

Reproduced with kind permission of *Private Eye* Magazine: 158

Rail Images/The Railway Picture Library: 95cl

Remember When/Sunday Times: 128b

Reuters News Picture Service. Photo by Bogdan Cristel: 191bl, r

© Reuters 2000. Reuters News Picture Service. Photo by Marc Serota: 175b

© Reuters 2000. Reuters News Picture Service. Photo by STR: 261t

Photo: © Rex features: 19bc

Courtesy of Siimon Reynolds/ Love Communications: 126tl, 129l

Photos: © David Stewart: 111bl, 203tl, cl

George Stubbs © The National Gallery: 19bl

Photos: © Kevin Summers: 148 bl, 253tr

© Royal Mail: 33tl

John Rushworth/Pentagram Design Ltd, London: 84tl

Stefan Sagmeister and Hjalti Karlsson/Sagmeister Inc: 35cl, bl, cr

Stefan Sagmeister and Veronica Oh/Photo: Tom Schierlitz/Sagmeister Inc: 35br

Design: Stefan Sagmeister/Photo: Tom Schierlitz/Stefan Sagmeister Inc: 130bl, br

Courtesy of Sanctuary Records: 99t

Paula Scher/Pentagram Design Inc, NY: 23, 269

© Seclab/The Flight Collection @ Quadrant: 215bl

Photo: Steve Speller: 101b

Stedelijk Museum, Amsterdam: 213cl

Stiftung Archiv der Akademie der Künste: 183tl

Photo: Seth Taras, Andreas Schmidt and Ross Aldershoff: 198b

TBWA Absolut Country of Sweden Vodka & Logo, Absolut, Absolut Bottle design and Absolut Calligraphy are trademarks owned by V&S Vin & Sprit AB. © 2000 V&S Vin & Sprit AB www.absolut.com Photo: Serge Paulet: 49b;Photo: Andy Glass: 49bl; Photo: Andy Glass – Kim Hrart/Samfoto: 49cr

Photo: Mike Theiler © Reuters 2000: 17tl

thomas.matthews: 13tl

Andrew Tinning: 39cl

O.Toscani (concept); courtesy of United Colours of Benetton and Gregotti Associati: 124br, 125tl

Courtesy of Geoff Turner/Photo: James Cottier: 260l

© Usine-Université-Union: 183br

© Yellgroup plc 171t

Index